# That Undiscover'd Country
## A Traveler's Guide to the Afterlife

# Oberon Zell

Black Moon Publishing
Cincinnati, Ohio

*That Undiscover'd Country: A Traveler's Guide to the Afterlife*
© 2021 by Oberon Zell

*Edited by* Haleigh Isbill

*Design and layout by* Oberon Zell

*Cover design by* Oberon Zell; *Triple Goddess art by* Joanne Barrett. Joanne says: *"The original is 'I Saw Three Ships' from* Baby's Opera *by Walter Crane c. 1900, depicting the three Queens coming to carry the fallen King Arthur to the misty Isle of Avalon. The three faces are all Morning Glory pics from her Facebook photos. I cludged in Photoshop soon after she passed for Lezlie Kinyon memorial."*

All rights reserved.

**Black Moon Manifesto**
*It is the Will and mission of Bate Cabal/Black Moon to effectively manifest unique and insightful occult Works for the esoteric community in a manner that is unfettered by commercial considerations.*

ISBN 10: 1-890399-85-X
ISBN 13: 978-1-890399-85-6

BlackMoonPublishing.com
blackmoonpublishing@gmail.com

United States • United Kingdom • Europe • Australia • India • Japan • Brazil

Black Moon Publishing, LLC
Cincinnati, Ohio USA

# Endorsements of Oberon

Oberon Zell has been near the heart of the NeoPagan/Wiccan/Earth Religions movement for over five decades. His esteem and the respect he commands for his knowledge and wisdom in spiritual counseling and advice is without parallel. He is one of the Last Men Standing, in terms of Craft Elders, and if Paganism were a country, Oberon would be one of its National Treasures. ~ **Judith Hawkins-Tillirson**, Wyrdhoard Books

Oberon Zell is one of the most intelligent and creative people in modern Paganism. He has been doing this longer than anyone else alive, and has been personally involved with many important historic events in the creation of the Earth-based spirituality that is important to so many people today. And he has the unique distinction of being probably the most influential male in the Goddess movement!
~ **John Sulak**, Co-author: *Modern Pagans*

Oberon Zell's work and dedication have always been what he has and will always be known for. There are few others who have put in the time and energy, above all other things, to both protect, teach and lead. His name is recognizable to all those who follow an Earth religion and where Oberon is involved, you know that you are getting the best of both the man and what he stands for. ~ **Nora Blansett**, Owner, Borealis Art

Oberon is extremely knowledgeable in his field. THE worldwide expert would be a more appropriate statement. His humanitarian and ecological efforts are world-recognized. His magnetic personality that is blended with ethical behavior, unwavering honesty, and the highest of moral codes has earned him the respect of religious leaders across the globe.
~ **Jacqueline Zaleski Mackenzie**
PhD Special Education, Bilingual Ed & Sociocultural Studies

Oberon Zell is a pioneer, leader, and visionary among Pagans and within the magickal community. One of the founders of the Church of All Worlds, he also pioneered *Green Egg,* the premier Pagan publication. His work contained therein was always thought-provoking, scholarly, and challenging. ~ **Dana D. Eilers**, Author: *Pagans and the Law*

American NeoPaganism would not be the vital force it is without having benefited from Oberon's creativity and insight. I am, and I think all of us should be, grateful for the services he has rendered to us and to the Gods over many years. ~ **Gus diZerega**, Writer, Futurist

# Books by Oberon Zell

*Grimoire for the Apprentice Wizard,* with the Grey Council (New Page Books, 2004)

*Companion for the Apprentice Wizard,* with the Faculty of the Grey School of Wizardry (New Page Books, 2006)

*Creating Circles & Ceremonies: Rituals for All Seasons & Reasons,* with Morning Glory Zell (New Page, 2006)

*A Wizard's Bestiary,* with Ash DeKirk (New Page, 2007)

*Green Egg Omelette: An Anthology of Art and Articles from the Legendary Pagan Journal* (New Page, 2008)

*Prophecy & the End of the World (as we know it): Apocalypse or Solartopia?* with Harvey Wasserman (TheaGenesis e-book, 2012)

*Barsoom: A New Map of the Mars of Edgar Rice Burroughs' "John Carter of Mars" Novels* (TheaGenesis e-book, 2012)

*The Wizard and the Witch: An Oral History of Oberon Zell & Morning Glory,* by John Sulak with Oberon & Morning Glory Zell (Llewellyn Pubs, 2014)

*Death Rights & Rites* with Judith Fenley (Llewellyn, 2020)

*That Undiscover'd Country: A Traveler's Guide to the Afterlife* (Black Moon Pubs, 2021)

*Song of Gaea,* with Kirsten Johnson & Pratima Sarkar (a children's book, 2021)

# Books in Process from Oberon...

*Goodbye Jesus, I've Gone Home to Mother,* with Haleigh Isbill
*Legendary Journeys: Europe 1987,* with Dona Carter
*History's Mysteries*
*Grimoire for the Journeyman Wizard*
*GaeaGenesis: Conception and Birth of the Living Earth.*
*Walkabout of the Wandering Wizard* (2018-2020)
*A Wizard's Guide to Women.*
*Wizards of the World,* with Nikki "Solaris" Kirby
*Unicorns in Our Garden,* with Morning Glory Zell
*Handbook for My Future Parents*

# Dedication

\*\*\*

The incomparable

## Morning Glory Zell

Beloved Lifemate, Love of my Life
(May 27, 1948 – May 13, 2014)

*She lived a Priestess,*
*She died a Queen,*
*She rose a Goddess!*
(~Susa Morgan Black)

# The Author

**Oberon Zell** earned a bachelor's degree in psychology, sociology and anthropology from Westminster College in Fulton, Missouri, and went on to graduate studies and degrees at Washington University, Harris Teacher's College, and Life Science College. His seminal work on the Gaea Thesis in the early '70s helped foster a global awareness of Earth as living Mother.

A founding father of modern Paganism (and the first to claim that label in 1967), Oberon is one of the most respected Elders in the new movement of "green religion" that emerged in the latter half of the 20th century, helping to bridge the gap between spirituality and science.

Initiated in several mystical traditions, Oberon is an ordained priest of Gaea, and co-founder of the first Pagan Church of All Worlds, incorporated in 1968. He founded the vanguard Pagan journal *Green Egg* and served as its publisher for four decades. His book titles include *Grimoire for the Apprentice Wizard, A Wizard's Bestiary,* and many others.

An international award-winning artist, Oberon has illustrated countless magazines and books since the 1960s. He is best known for his magickal jewelry and altar figurines of Gods, Goddesses, and mythical creatures. His most famous work is his revelatory sculpture of Mother Earth as "The Millennial Gaia."

Oberon is also the founder and Headmaster of the online Grey School of Wizardry, which offers more than 600 classes in 16 departments for students of all ages. After a two-year Walkabout throughout the Western Hemisphere, he is now settled in the state of Washington.

# The Editor

**Haleigh Isbill** holds a bachelor's degree in Sociology. She graduated Dean's List from the University of Nevada, Las Vegas–the same city where she currently resides with her two partners and their three children (plus pets!)

Her editorial achievements include editing and publishing a small local 'zine as well as ghost writing and editing for several local websites. Haleigh was also an editor for her college newspaper. She currently works in the tech industry writing user manuals and surveys.

Haleigh spends her free time on her fiber arts; re-creating ancient methods of spinning yarn and nalbinding, as well as more modern arts like knitting and crocheting. Her pieces are greatly prized among her tribe. She is a yarn witch.

# Prologue

*No one here gets out alive.*
~ Jim Morrison

Y FIRST EXPERIENCE WITH DEATH CAME rather late in my life. I was a month shy of 40 years, and my Lifemate Morning Glory and I were living on Greenfield Ranch – a 5,600 acre Hippie homesteading community of about 100 families in the Misty Mountains of NorCalifa – when our next-door neighbor and friend, and the first modern Pagan Bard, Gwydion Pendderwen, died in a car crash – right at Samhain ("Halloween"), the ancient Celtic Festival of the Dead. He'd just produced his 2$^{nd}$ album, opening with "I'll be Reborn." Ironically, when he'd moved onto the Ranch in 1975, Gwydion had named his 55-acre parcel *Annwfn*, the Welsh Land of the Dead, so it was only fitting that his ashes became interred there. He deeded it to the Church of All Worlds, and it has been CAW's sacred sanctuary ever since. Gwydion's was the first death in our community, and I will never forget the laconic words of one of the founders, Jon Solo: "Those of us who live the longest will bury all our dearest friends."

A few years later, in the spring of 1987, I found myself traveling throughout Europe and the Aegean on an archaeological pilgrimage with my dear Consort, Dona Carter. Here is an excerpt from my Journal:

*1987.3.11— Wed.*
*The Kingdom of the Dead*
*Yesterday we got up talking about various deaths among our families and friends, and we decided to dedicate the day to the dead and visit the famous Catacombs of Paris, not at all sure of what to expect...*

*Down a long spiral staircase, we descended into the bowels of the Earth, then along about half a mile of labyrinthine tunnels without much to see (this used to be a quarry for stone for all the buildings up above, and it was later used for hideouts and secret passages for the Revolutionaries). Just when we were beginning to get bored, we entered a large antechamber from which another passage led out. Over the gateway was the inscription:* Arrete, c'est ici l'empire de la mort! *("Beware, this is the Kingdom of the Dead!").*

*Beyond that portal was a mind-numbing sight: the passage was lined, floor to ceiling on both sides, with countless human bones (remains of more than* six million *people), stacked like cordwood with long bones and skulls arranged in geometric patterns. The passages between these innumerable dead went on and on and on...periodically relieved by white columns inscribed with cheery verses about vanity, dust, mortality, and the like. Much to ponder.*

*Back in our hotel that evening, we got out my Tarot deck and laid out the reading Morning Glory had done for me before I left. Death had been the first card, and Dona revealed that the reading she had received before leaving had also started with Death. We are considering that in fact this may become the key to our pilgrimage – a Fool's Journey through the Underworld – as we visit the various tombs, catacombs, necropoli, crypts, caves, and burial sites of the ancient world... We shall see where the journey leads...*

*Oberon and Dona with dead friends in a Madrid café. 1987*

Gwydion's death in 1982 and my pilgrimage with Dona five years later had a profound effect on the Church of All Worlds, as our ritual observances of the 8-spoked "Wheel of the Year" (Solstices, Equinoxes, and the halfway-betweens) took on a darker, more Chthonic cast. In our ritual dramatizations of the Seasonal Round at Annwfn, we began to focus on the coronation, reign and death of the King of the May, and his descent into the Underworld at Samhain.

Starting in 1990, we also began annual re-enactments of the ancient Mysteries of Eleusis. This involved a journey into the Greek Netherworld of Erebos, to meet its rulers, grim Hades and his vernal Queen, Persephone. As a high school "drama queen," my beloved lifemate, wife, and Priestess Morning Glory was the primary playwright of this sacred theatre – but our entire community participated every year. And so it seems inevitable, in retrospect, that Her own journey beyond the Veil became one-way...

After eight years of bravely battling a relentless cancer of her blood and bones (multiple myeloma), Morning Glory finally succumbed. The doctors told us there was nothing more they could do to reverse the ravages of the fatal disease, so we brought her home from the hospital on May 7, 2014 and set her up with a hospital bed provided by Home Hospice in our Goddess Temple at Raven-Haven, our home for a decade.

Many, many dear friends, family, lovers, Waterkin, priestesses, and priests came by over the final weeks in the hospital and at home – to care for her, lend support, prepare meals, clean house, share stories, and generally take care of everything for everyone.

On May 13 at 5:42 PM, as I held her in my arms, my Beloved released her last breath. One of our people held a stethoscope to her chest, listened to her final heartbeat, and solemnly intoned: "The Queen is dead." I broke down sobbing uncontrollably as everyone in the house responded in one voice, "Long live the Queen!" Her last words to me had been: "Don't let it die!"

Morning Glory's body was laid into the Earth in a green burial, clasping her fencing sabre upon Her chest and with an apple tree planted over her, to rest in the bosom of Mother Gaea until she may return again in new flesh. Her grave on our sacred land of Annwfn overlooks the campfire circle where we have held our rites of Beltane (and Walpurgisnacht) for the past three decades.

I am deeply grateful to Reverend Judith Karen Fenley of Harmonizing Health Center/Choices, who moved mountains and worked miracles at every step of the way, clearing the legal pathways to bring Morning Glory home to die, to return to The Mother.

Arranging all the legalities for Morning Glory's green burial secured Annwfn as an officially recognized cemetery for full body burials – a final gift to the Pagan community from one of our most revered Priestesses. There is a space right next to her reserved for my own eventual internment – many years from now. Several other departed Pagans have since had their green burials at Annwfn. Truly now, in actuality as in name, the Land of the Dead.

## This Book

Out of this profound personal experience emerged a Vision and an Assignment for Judith and me: to create a handbook of Final Passage for Pagans that includes all the information needed to conduct in-home hospice treatment, legal paperwork (wills, death certificates, permits for transportation and burial, etc.), last rites, cleansing and preparation of the body, wakes, home funerals, and green burials on sacred land.

The book would also include illustrated descriptions and visions of the Netherworlds of various cultures, and also of the journey the soul may take after death to arrive at the Blessed Realm – eventually (perhaps) to return in a new incarnation.

Judith and I spent several years working together on this joint book project. But finally, Llewellyn decided that it should really be two separate books. *Death Rights and Rites* was published in Nov. of 2020 – which included mostly Judith's materials, and little of mine. It's a fine book and I recommend it highly. This handbook will meet an essential need for an alternative and truly Pagan approach to that final transition we all must make someday.

Judith's book addresses the concerns of the living in dealing with the final passage of a loved one. Whereas my present book, *That Undiscover'd Country,* addresses the concerns of the dying and what happens afterwards with the journey of the departed soul into the realms beyond – several of which I have here mapped and illustrated.

With the exponential growth in the worldwide Pagan community over the past half-century (now recognized as the 2$^{nd}$-largest and fastest-growing religion in America, with more than 4 million adherents!), the market for such books is enormous. All of us who are alive today will someday face the final passage into "that Undiscover'd Country." Even now, our beloved Founders and Elders are dropping like flies. I know of no one still alive who has been avowedly Pagan longer than I have (52 years at the time of this writing). And the death of my beloved Lifemate after four decades together leaves a great void in my heart and soul.

I feel it is beneficial for all of us mortals to discover how to embrace Death naturally, as has been done for millennia, while supporting those who are involved in processing their own grief and preparing for their own eventual passage. I anticipate this book to be a welcome addition to the many periodicals and books on death, the Afterlife, and how to approach one's inevitable, ultimate journey.

## Addendum

Morning Glory was a Dreamwalker, able to visit people she loved in The Dreaming. This was often confirmed by those She visited. In Her final week, I heard from many that She had shown up to say goodbye, and to assure them that She'd still be around.

After She left this mortal plane and joined the pantheon of Her beloved Goddesses, I began receiving reports from people around the country (and the world…) who had visitations from Her. I have gathered quite a collection of these accounts! Some of them are in the context of rituals where She has been invoked as the "Goddess of Unconditional Love." Some have been of children for whom She appeared as an "invisible Faerie playmate." I've also heard from many of morning glory flowers they never planted mysteriously blooming all over their homes and gardens. And many have reported dream visitations. Our Greek friend Sirius, who lives in Athens, wrote to me about several of these:

> *… she said she is waiting for you and will not move on without you. Of course, I knew that already, but that's another story… She said she will wait for you for as long as it takes. We spoke about 15 minutes flat this time.*

*The last time I saw her was fleetingly, as I awoke up at night, she was by my bed, watching over me it seems. And I told her teasingly "Now you haunt me while I sleep, eh? What am I going to do with you, eh, Melenippe?"*

*And she smiled and said "I will always be with you, my true brother. Family is family, even in death" We smiled at each other, and I slept again like a baby, knowing she is watching over me. That was VERY sweet, I tell you!*

I've had many such visitations in The Dreaming over the 6½ years since Her passing. Each of them seems extremely lucid, and I am fully aware. In them we are usually bustling about preparing for a major Ritual, Sabbat, or Festival, just as we used to do. The first few times, I had to check to make sure, saying, "…but you're dead!" And She would assure me that yes, She was. But She was making a special visit just to remind me that She was still around.

A clear image came out of these visits: Morning Glory is heading up the Welcome Committee on the Other Side for all our (far too many!) Pagan friends who are crossing over. She'll keep doing that until I show up, and then we'll explore the Netherworlds and make arrangements to incarnate together next time, so we won't have to waste so many years trying to find each other again. We want to be reborn in the early 2060s, so we'll be coming of age in the next 60-year cultural renaissance cycle of the 2080s – the Gaiaspora. We want to help colonize Mars together…

~ Oberon
12/21/2020 (Winter Solstice)

*The Wizard and The Witch: Oberon & Morning Glory, 2011*

# Contents

Prologue ............................................................... vii
Contents ............................................................... xiii
Preface: Birthing Death .......................................xiv

## Part I: The Passage of the Body
*"To be or not to be"* – William Shakespeare ....................... 20
Chapter 1 – Rites of Passage: Pagan Funerals & Memorials ..... 21
Chapter 2 – Disposition of the Remains ................................ 51
Chapter 3 – Losing a Loved One: Personal Reflections ............ 67

## Part II: The Passage of the Soul
*"The Garden of Proserpina"* – Algernon Swinburne .......... 81
Chapter 4 – Death Customs & Folklore Around the World ....... 83
Chapter 5 – Postmortem: The Soul's Journey After Life Ends .. 97
Chapter 6 – Netherworlds: Realms of the Dead ....................... 109

## Part III: Intimations of Immortality
*"Thanatopsis"* – William Cullen Bryant ............................. 140
Chapter 7 – Ecos et Thanatos ................................................ 143
Chapter 8 – The Village ....................................................... 163
Chapter 9 – Pilgrim's Progress ............................................. 167

## Appendices
*"Song of the River"* – William Randolph Hearst ................ 173
A. A Dictionary of Cemetery Symbolism .............................. 175
B. Encyclopedia of the Afterlife ........................................... 191
C. Elegies: Pagan Funerary Songs and Poems ...................... 235
D. In Memoriam: What is Remembered, Lives:
   Departed Pagan Pioneers, Founders and Elders ................ 242
E. Movies & TV Shows Depicting Visions of the Afterlife ... 248
F. Resources ........................................................................ 256
G. Bibliography ................................................................... 259
H. Index .............................................................................. 264

# Preface
# Birthing Death
By Marylyn Motherbear Scott

I KNEW THE LAST MINUTE WAS approaching. We'd been at her side for weeks. She was too young to die and had struggled hard against it, going through arduous treatments, just to stay alive. It wasn't her dysfunctional kidneys that were killing her. They were a symptom of all that went before, the general and generative breakdown of bodily organs and functions. It was an aggressive cancer that got her, one she fought for a decade. Sometimes it seemed she was winning. It was the experimental drugs that took her over the top. They were what finally did it. Dialysis was a last-ditch stand.

Her Mississippi-born mom used to say that she loved her daughter *more than anyone but Jesus.* Her Father used to say he loved to fish *like Mama loved Jesus.* They traveled back and forth between socially progressive L.A. and the backwaters of rural Mississippi, giving birth to *her*, whose story I tell, in the late forties, in Southern California.

Drawn to the mysteries of nature and spirit, science and experimentation, history and mystery, her avid interest in the intellectual domain of the renaissance man held her well during her hit-and-miss high school days. College did not compare to the excitement of the cultural and social revolution that was at hand. She got turned on to *higher* education, traveled the folk song trail, explored the mountains and canyons along the way. She married and bore a daughter. Those early experiences settled into her psyche, manifested in an undying relationship to Nature.

She was a quiet epitome of the psychedelic revolution. Transcendent and immanent, she weaved and lived her waking dreams in neo-Pagan splendor. Not only a Priestess, but a collector of stories and statues. Goddesses from the world over. Stories to be told about each one. Hundreds now stood all around. On shelves, under glass. On tapestries. In art. On altars. On tables. In gardens. Their voices seemingly silenced, but for these moments.

Surrounded by her goddesses, she lay struggling against the fate that awaits us all. She was at death's door. In a bed placed in the center of the room, she lay there, herself a living altar, as she silently and relentlessly argued with those who would spirit her away from her substantial being, away from her home, her loved ones, her work, her beloved Earth.

Her preeminence in these matters had brought many living goddesses and gods to breath and body, even in their mundane lives. And so we gathered, in attempts to heal or at least to comfort her as she stood her last stand against that which we know is coming for us each and all, though we do not know the day nor time.

Living goddesses, priestesses and handmaidens, moved in and out, sitting in witness for long hours, offering the medicine of love, of prayer, of song. Her lifemate sat with her throughout the day, slept by her side each night.

In one of her last unspoken directives, she reached for him, painfully turning her head, then her body toward him, lifting her arm, placing her hand on his body, fixing his hand on her breast. Head-to-head, they lovingly lay. Eternal moments.

The beloved friends and family had stayed, gone home, gone out for a break, come back. It went on for a full week. Impatient to let the Fates call the moment, some prayed that her time of passing would come immediately. Distraught yet contained, her daughter said,

*Mom. Let go. I can't do this anymore. I love you. I'm going home to my daughter and husband.* And she left. The die-hard spiritual sisters stayed. And her husband. And some lovers visited from time to time. Weeping. The memories of what she offered them, a polyamorous bouquet, that now transcended time.

I was one of the die-hards. I had been at the bedside of others who had passed—"transitioned' as some prefer. At first, when she was awake, I spent time remembering with her. Stories of the past. Family. Events. Friends. She loved when I sang the songs of spirit. Thanked me. Now, as she drifted into unconsciousness, I began to observe the outward breath, to discern when it would rise up in dusky shades, as it does when life is passing. The release of the soul.

A sign. A purplish mist arose sporadically out of the top of her head, and from her bosom. She had begun to let go, finally. And yet it continued on and off for days. I had never experienced it happening at such a slow rate and in such an irregular manner, as if she was able to grasp it and bring it back into her body. Over days. It was, however, a sign that the end was coming.

Shifts occur. Suddenly, she awoke. She said, *I don't want to die.* She was offered drugs. At first, weeks ago, she said no. Now she said *Yes*. People came in for short visits, laying their grief at the altar of her body in repose. Many spoke words of appreciation for the emotional support, for the wise words of counsel she had at some point given, or for the bodily love she had offered them. Some sang. Some wept.

She wanted quiet. The singing she used to love so much was now too much for her to abide.

*No,* she would murmur.

We stopped singing, stopped speaking, almost stopped breathing. With her. Warned, the visitors would sit silently. Reflective. Praying. Being.

I was in the vortex, journeying, seeking the light. With her. She was in my energetic field. I was holding and protecting her as she fought against inevitability. Another shift. The purple mist poured out of her crown. Her breathing became more difficult. Noisier. Longer pauses. A moment of knowing it. No longer knowing myself. An energy bespoke my body. Eyes closed, my arms raised up, to each side, over my head. The goddess blessing. Time spun and lifted itself into the Eternal.

A younger priestess had quietly entered the room. She saw, felt the energy, raised her arms along with me. We stood. Held the space. Just the two of us and her. No one entered the room. It was the last minute. I knew. I indicated, *Call her husband into the room.* I moved closer to her, uttering words as they came to me. Suddenly. In a rush.

*Do you remember when we were new moms? Remember how we breathed our babies into birth? ... It's time now ... Birth yourself a new body. I'm going to breathe with you. I'm going to breathe you over.* During the hardest moments, I panted. She panted. *Now, a long cleansing breath.* I breathed long and deep. She breathed with me, long and deep. *A cleansing breath. Just like when we gave birth.* Together, we breathed. A long cleansing breath. The last one. Long. Then silence. No more breath.

I leaned over her, staring into the eyes that saw no more. I sent out my thoughts to her as hard as I could,

*Where are you now? What is it like?*

I held very still and listened inward and I heard her voice say to me, a light silvery laugh making it seem like a song, *Don't be in too much of a hurry, you'll find out everything soon enough.*

The collapse into grief takes more than a last minute. A lifetime had passed. A vastness of space in its place. Mundane matters ensue. The time of death noted. The host of friends and family entered the room. Hugging. Weeping. Sighing. Singing. We sang all the songs she loved. All the songs we loved.

Into the night we sang. We washed her body. Prepared her for green burial. Dressed her in a beautiful dress. Laid her sword upon her body, hilt in her hands. She lay, a warrior priestess, having fought her last battle. Chakra stones were ritually placed at the energetic points. She laid in grace for three days.

When her body was transported to the remote and sacred burial place; she lingered in the air outside her home, floating close above my vehicle, wanting to be seen. Her diaphanous gown of mauve and lavender billowed as she cavorted in the air, smiling. Nothing to say. Nothing to do. I turned the key in the ignition and drove on down the road, up the highway, into the hills.

She floated forward above my vehicle, all the way up the highway. Out of one county into another. Through a vineyard and up a rugged one-lane dirt road. A code was needed to open the gate. She disappeared amongst the canopy of trees. Down the dirt road, across a creek, and up a winding, steep road to the place where Pagans worshipped. She had vanished into thin air.

Our vehicles could go no further. It was a walk, over the dam of a pond, into a circle. The corners of the circle were laid out with altars, beautifully built with rock and precious stones, wing-bones and feathers, trinkets and talisman, embroidered clothes of silk and cotton. A devotion to the four cardinal directions. The circle spread out sparingly in the small meadow surrounded by hills that leaped up protectively on one side; and, on the other side, rolled down through groves of trees all leaning into an abyss of seemingly endless, wandering realms, shadowed and uncertain. We had stepped into Annwfn, the Otherworld.

Within one circle, another. Men, women and children stood, speaking to one another. At times, laughter sweetened the atmosphere by remembrance of a time past in which she stood, strong and tall, leading the circle in ritual. A fire, not yet ignited, was laid in the center.

A coffin, hand-made out of redwood, sat to the west. Its closed floor was lined with dirt and flowers. It had open, slatted sides. No lid. And now, the somber heartbeat of a drum resounded. Men carried a cardboard box that held her body. They were dressed in various garb, neo-Pagan ritual wear — fierce, Nordic-looking men with sword and axes hung on their belt or over their shoulder, kilted Celts, cloaked Welsh, women in long skirts and boots, circlets upon their head, flowers in their hair. An amazing assemblage, the lore of tales, faerie and folk. Not everyone dressed up; some wore ordinary on-the-land clothes. During the morning hours, they had been digging a deep hole on the almost level ground, below the hillside. Six feet deep.

Quiet except for the drumbeat and the sounds of nature. She was set down near in the west, near the coffin, then lifted, somehow, gracefully, out of the cardboard box and into the coffin. We smoothed her dress and fussed with her hair. Flowers were strewn copiously upon her. The singing began.

*We all come from the Goddess*
*And to Her we shall return,*
*Like a drop of rain*
*Flowing to the ocean...*

Rhythms, notes, words, sounds added by those who now raised their voices. Spirits were raised as well. The flask got lifted and passed.

I had been asked to lead the circle.

*I cast a circle all around*
*From the far-reaching heavens to this sacred ground...*

Circle cast and quarters called, the remembrances were voiced. Small children clung to parents, parents that had been kids themselves during her mom-hood days. They had been raised in these same Pagan circles where the Sabbats were honored, each in their Season.— the cardinal points, Solstices and Equinoxes; the cross-quarters, Imbolc, Beltane, Lughnasadh, Samhain. They each had a story to tell, a story of the deep Earth, the high heavens. Stories of seeds and plantings, games and craftings, Maypole dancing, the late-night fires, the bardic circles. Poems, stories and music.

The fire was ignited, the cardboard box, painted and decorated for her journey, was burned. The flames rose high. Remembrances were told and sung, the last goodbyes uttered. It was time again. The casket was lifted up, majestically carried by strong men and women, to the gravesite. Ropes had been laid upon the ground nearby, and the casket put upon them. Lifted up in an amazing display of grace and balance, three strong on either side, it was lowered down, into the grave.

It was not easy to cover her with dirt. She was still whole and beautiful. A Priestess. A Goddess. Human. Woman. Wife. Mother. Grandmother. Colleague. Friend. Lover. I was the first to take a handful of dirt, casting it down upon her.

*What is remembered lives.*

The flask was passed to me. And so it went, handful of dirt after handful of dirt. And flowers. Sip after sip. Songs. Incantations. Invocations. Handfuls of dirt. And more flowers.

When each had taken all the turns they wanted, the shoveling began. Shovel after shovel. A show of strength. Even though an elder, I lifted and threw down several shovelfuls. Thrice is the charm. All who wanted to, did so. The strongest of the strong finished the work of filling in the hole, building up a mound. The edges were shaped and sculpted. A tree was planted at the head. The last songs were song. The last sip, tippled.

The fire blazed, then fell into ashes and embers. Those who could stay, shared supper. Done, as done can be. Each in their own time, made their way down the hill, over the single lane dirt roads, through the gate that closed behind each vehicle, down through the vineyard, through the neighborhood surrounding the land and those who live there, onto the highway to a home that, for many of us, never looked the same.

I had entered a tunnel and approached the light at its end. A tunnel of myth and legend. I held hands with a radiant goddess passed into shade. Eyes that see, ears that hear, hands that touch, hearts that feel, might nevermore experience their feet firm upon this holy ground, nor walk surely, in this life, upon the Earth, but in a Mystery that cannot be truly told.

# Part I:
# The Passage of the Body

## To be, or not to be

By William Shakespeare (1564-1616)

*To be, or not to be: that is the question:*
*Whether 'tis nobler in the mind to suffer*
*The slings and arrows of outrageous fortune,*
*Or to take arms against a sea of troubles,*
*And by opposing end them? To die: to sleep;*
*No more; and by a sleep to say we end*
*The heart-ache and the thousand natural shocks*
*That flesh is heir to, 'tis a consummation*
*Devoutly to be wish'd. To die, to sleep;*
*To sleep: perchance to dream: ay, there's the rub;*
*For in that sleep of death what dreams may come*
*When we have shuffled off this mortal coil,*
*Must give us pause: there's the respect*
*That makes calamity of so long life;*
*For who would bear the whips and scorns of time,*
*Th' oppressor's wrong, the proud man's contumely,*
*The pangs of despised love, the law's delay,*
*The insolence of office, and the spurns*
*That patient merit of th' unworthy takes,*
*When he himself might his quietus make*
*With a bare bodkin? Who would fardels bear,*
*To grunt and sweat under a weary life,*
*But that the dread of something after death,*
*That undiscover'd country from whose bourn*
*No traveler returns, puzzles the will*
*And makes us rather bear those ills we have*
*Than fly to others that we know not of?*

(~Hamlet, Act 3, scene 1. 57-78)

# Chapter 1
# Rites of Passage:
## Pagan Funerals & Memorials

*Carve your name on hearts, not tombstones. A legacy is etched into the minds of others and the stories they share about you.*
~~Shannon L. Alder

*I don't want my life to be defined by what is etched on a tombstone. I want it to be defined by what is etched in the lives and hearts of those I've touched.*
~~Steve Maraboli, *Life, the Truth, and Being Free*

AST RITES ARE GENERALLY CONDUCTED for someone on their deathbed, to prepare them for their final journey from this life into the next one. This is all very well if the person is dying predictably, as at the end of a long illness, and there is time to make all the necessary arrangements. But very often people die unexpectedly, and there will have been no opportunity to prepare them, or their family and friends. Even so, it is appropriate to conduct a final Rite of Passing to facilitate their transition to that "undiscover'd country." Many departed spirits seem bewildered, not realizing that they have actually died. Rather than moving on, their ghosts hover about the places and people they knew in life. They are held as much by the emotional anguish, love, grief, and guilt of those left behind as by their own unfinished business. So a magickal sense of closure is needed when someone dies—to liberate their spirit, as well as the spirits of all who loved them.

Rites of Passing include laying-out of the body—bathing them, brushing their hair, making them up, and dressing them in their funerary finest (for Pagans, usually their ritual regalia). These proceedings have traditionally been conducted by women. Fresh flowers may be arranged around the body—even covering it like a blanket. And as they lay in grace and honor, friends may come to pay last respects. Their favorite songs should be sung or played—especially those they may have said they'd have liked played at their funeral.

There are many funerary customs in different cultures for disposal of the body. Simple burial has been the most common from the dawn of time, often involving little more than laying them into a hole and filling it in, with a marker of some sort upon the grave. The body may be placed in a coffin, and grave gifts interred as offerings. Important figures—such as royalty—were generally entombed in crypts or mausoleums, which could be astonishingly elaborate. Think of King Tut's tomb! Mummification was an important practice in many cultures in an attempt to, as embalming remains today, preserve the semblance of life. Parsis, Incas, and some North American tribes exposed their dead in high places, to be consumed by scavenger birds—perhaps returning later to collect the bones. And cremation is today becoming increasingly popular, leaving ashes that may later be kept in an urn, scattered in some favorite place, or even shot into space!

Any of these customs and practices are to be conducted in a ritual manner. My personal favorite—which I would choose for my own disposition—is the old Celtic custom of "green burial;" burying the dead within 3-4 days of discorporation, without embalming or coffin, and not too deep. They would be dressed in their finest clothes, accompanied by a few favorite items as grave goods. A winding sheet would enshroud the body.

And then a sapling fruit tree (generally apple) would be planted upon the grave. As the tree grows, its questing roots will draw substance from the decaying corpse, recycling what was once human into a thriving memorial tree. And one day that tree will put forth its fruit, to nourish the people, and the cycle of life will come full circle. (Hear the song by Oscar Brown, Jr: "The Tree and Me.")

An extension of this custom involved a couple desiring a child making love on the fresh grave over the following nights, ritually inviting the spirit of the beloved dead to incarnate into the new life being conceived. The child would be given the name of the departed, and their afterbirth would be planted beneath the grave-tree, which would become their own sacred totem tree. Apple trees normally live about as long as humans, so the fate of the child and his or her tree would be intertwined. [1]

In addition to rites and practices involving the disposition of the body, there are two other very important ceremonies of passing that are as much for the living as the dead. These are Wakes and Funerals.

Wakes are best held as soon after the death as possible. All those who knew the deceased are invited to a big party in their honor. In former times, the corpse would also be present on a bier. Whiskey and other intoxicants would be passed liberally around the circle, as people took turns telling increasingly outrageous stories of their departed friend, laughing, singing songs, and generally having enough fun and making enough noise to "wake the dead." Conducted ritually, a Wake is very similar to a Bardic.

Funerals are generally more formal affairs. These days, they are usually held in churches or funeral parlors, which are set up with the coffin or urn on a platform or altar at the front of the room, and seating arranged as if for a lecture presentation. There will likely be a prescribed Order of Service, starting with a eulogy ("good word") presented by the deceased's closest kin.

One at a time, selected people may be invited forward to tell their stories, as in the Wake. And according to the deceased's spiritual beliefs, selected inspirational hymns of passage to the Afterlife will be sung, of which my personal favorite is "Into the West," sung by Annie Lennox at the end of the movie, "Return of the King."

And finally, an Ancestor Altar should be established in the West side of the family's temple room, with images and mementos—including ashes or other relics—of the deceased.

\*\*\*

---

[1] An apple tree can live up to 80 years, and have a productive life of 30-40 years. Much like people.

# Last Rites

By Richard Ely (CAW Priest) and
Marilee (Starwhite) Lewis (CAW Priestess)

ML: _____, you lie resting and waiting between the worlds. We two, Richard and Starwhite of the Church of All Worlds, have come to celebrate with you, at this significant time. Thank you for asking us to come. We are told that you have venerated and served the Lady, the Goddess, and that you are ready to rejoin Her. Soon you will travel to that place of bright light and beloved faces. The Great Mother has promised, "I await you, at the end of all desire."

RE: _____, we believe you have also known the Lord, the God who was known to ancient people, in ages long ago. He it was who was born, young and vital and green in the spring. He was lover to the May Queen, and when the corn and fruits were harvested at Lammas, He lay down and gave up his life to feed His people. He was born to die, and He died so that He, and all His people, might live again—anew.

ML: It is time to make a circle, a safe and sacred space within a boundary of energy to keep the mundane world out. We will do this in an Irish Celtic manner, but will try to include elements of Native American practices as well. What we call a magickal circle is also a medicine circle. We will also salute the four directions. We greet and honor the Native spirits of this place. We offer a little corn, tobacco, and white sage to show our respect for your traditions. We ask your patience and forbearance while we do this work. "To all my relations."

*BOTH: "We are a circle, within a circle..." (descant "Corn and grain..." (softly, 3 times)*

ML: Life comes out of the void and into AIR. The newborn child gasps a first breath and cries out to the world, "I am!"

RE: Life comes into its own, and burns as FIRE. Energy, passion, and the will to do things—all smolder and flame—and lend purpose, power, and savor to life.

ML: Life is created from, and is kept alive with, WATER. The rhythms of the oceans course through our veins, and our feelings are transmuted with raindrops and brooks, rivers and seas. At life's end, we sail westward to Avalon and the Misty Isles.

RE: Life is also created from, and is at last laid to rest in, the EARTH. Our Mother, the Earth, provides the matter for our bodies. She sends forth Her love from deep down in Her bones, the stones, down deep below our feet. She provides green shade and green plants, flowering, fruiting and ripening. Thus She nurtures all the animals dear to Her: furred, feathered, scaled and skinned. When our body can no longer be used by our life force, she takes it back inside Herself to sleep the everlasting sleep.

ML: Here is a small branch of evergreen, symbol of life everlasting. It comes from a big Coast Redwood tree. I am going to place it in your hand, if that is alright with you.

RE: We in California have all seen where lightning has blasted and burned a mighty redwood tree; but in the decomposing body of the mother tree, seedlings sprout up from the roots and form a kind of Fairy circle. New life is reborn out of the old.

ML: _____, your granddaughter _____ is also here with us. So is/are [names of others, if any]. She has [or, These people have] inherited from you some of your genetic patterns. Part of you will live on in them, and in their children and their children's children, encoded in the double helix of DNA that twines and spirals in every cell of their bodies. This double helix is, in another sense, the serpent of ancient legends, the Goddess symbol of birth and death and rebirth in many places around the world. The snake had many names; in northern Europe, one name was Ouroboros, the world serpent under the ground.

RE: A mythic snake lives in each of our bodies, and connects our vital energy centers. It is called Kundalini, and it spirals upward from the lower end of our spine, where it is red-orange, moving upward through the solar plexus, where it is gold, and reaches the heart, where it radiates green light energy. Then it moves through the throat, place of sound and blue-green color, and up to the third eye, a blue spot.

ML: If you approve, I would like to anoint your third eye with a few drops of water. This water comes from Ireland, from a sacred Brigid's well in Kildare. The Irish Gaelic name for that well is

"Tobar Bride." I will draw a pentacle, to wash and clear your third-eye vision, the better to see the world beyond this world. Blessed Be, and joyous may your journey to the other world be.

RE: When the Kundalini serpent reaches the crown of your head, the color there is purple. Your crown also gives off rays of white light, and this is the center of your spiritual energy. If you can feel this purple-and-white energy, smile for us. You can radiate even more of this energy, and be more easily seen and recognized, by the Blessed Beings who wait to greet you. Shining even brighter, you will move easily and gladly to join them. This is the triumph of your life! You are coming to a place of no pain, no fatigue, no grief—a place where you will find peace, fulfillment and ecstasy.

*[ADD whatever seems right here—a chant; recorded music while we recite (voice-over) poetry, etc. If she is open to it, a short guided visualization (if ML is so inspired?) could be added, to enhance the positive energy.]*

ML: It is almost time for us to leave you now. Is there anything you wish to tell us or convey to us? Is there anything more you would like us to do? Do you remember a favorite song we might know? Do you have a special Deity you want us to address on your behalf? Would you like to smell some meadow herbs from Ireland? Would you care to hear any descriptions of the places I saw last summer, on a tour of the sacred sites of Ireland?

RE: Are you experiencing any troublesome feelings of fear, or sorrow, aloneness or leave-taking? Is there something we might do to comfort you?

ML: Does anything feel unfinished, or would you like anything more said? We want you to feel that we have provided you with a suitable "going away party" for a very special lady.

BOTH: *Devoke any Native spirits, deities, or other spirits, if or as appropriate.*

RE: *Dismiss Earth, then (after Water) Fire.*

ML: *Dismiss Water, then (after Fire) Air.*

RE: The misty curtains part, and the energy we put up to keep the mundane world at bay must now go to ground. Let it soak into the floor, into the ground below, and down into the bedrock far beneath us.

ML: The circle is open, but the love, the caring, and blessings we have worked to generate will remain with you. We will continue to think of you, and send you our hopes and wishes for an easy departure from this life. May the Goddess bless and watch over you. Farewell, _____.

RE: May the God bless and watch over you, as well. Peace be with you. Farewell, _____.

\*\*\*

# Rite of Passing for a Deceased Pagan
Compiled by Larry Cornett and designed
with members of VisionWeavers Coven

### Items Needed (In Addition to Usual Ritual Items)
- Soil from dead person's home in clay dish.
- Chalice, bowl or libation cup for (or preferably owned by) deceased and placed at West quarter of Circle, along with Magical cord and tools owned by deceased.
- Gold and silver candles, anointed with oil favored by the deceased.
- Silk to wrap gold and silver candles.
- Mead and Shortbread (or other ritual drink and food favored by deceased).
- Appropriate incense favored by the deceased.
- Small pine tree.

**Dumb-Supper** (silent meal with a place for the dead)

**Establish Sacred Space and Call Powers**

**Procession and chant**: "Blood of the Ancients" by *Ellen Klaver*

**Earth, Air, Fire, Water space clearing** in which everyone intones:

> Earth and Air and Fire and Water,
> Surround us with protective light.
> Earth and Air and Fire and Water,
> Guard us with your magic might.

*Come Watchers come and balance our circle.*
*Come Watchers come and balance our group.*
*Come Watchers come and strengthen our auras.*
*Come Watchers come and strengthen our work.*
(—Selena Fox)

**Salt water purification** (as in Starhawk's *Spiral Dance*)

**Guided Tree Meditation**, with connections to Underworld and Upperworld.

**Name Attunement** (intone your name and everyone intone it back sending good energy to person, repeat for person to the left, etc. — when get to west, intone the name of the dead one).

**Cast Circle.** Say *"Hand to hand, we cast the Circle"* and clasp hand to your left, next person does the same, until Circle is complete.

**Call Quarters** with Winds (Light Candle, Make Invoking Pentagram, Invoke powers of direction, then everyone intone wind name (Eurus at East for air, Notus at South for fire, Zephyrus at West for water, and Boreas at North for Earth)

**Call Cerridwen and Cernunnos** (Chant *"Come to us now, O Cerridwen!"* four times while feeling Elemental winds form a tornado of Akashic power, then invoke Cerridwen on this energy field. Do same to invoke Cernunnos) <Different Goddesses and Gods can be invoked instead, depending on pantheon participants and the deceased's work with as gatekeepers related to the Realm of Dead>

**Speak thoughts on life, death, rebirth, etc. related to the deceased**: *Friends, let us remember that...*

- *Consciousness is an aspect of the interconnection of everything in the universe. Normal, mundane, waking individual consciousness has been shown by science to be a manifestation of that interconnectedness, resonating holistically in the brain of an individual.*
- *Let us also remember those non-mundane, magickal states of consciousness, when we are not limited to the body, when we experience unity with our surroundings, when we transcend the limits of time and space, and when our magick makes things*

- *happen. Many of us have shared such consciousness in circle with <name of deceased>.*
- *While <name of deceased>'s old, physical, brain no longer resonates, his non-localized interconnections continue in the web of consciousness that we all share.*
- *Since <he/she> left <his/her> old physical body, several of us have had contact with <name of deceased>—in dreams, through scrying, and in other ways. <He/She> also lives on in our memories.*
- *Many of us have also experienced past lives and telepathy, when our awareness resonated in other times and other bodies. Reincarnation is a manifestation of the consciousness that brings such awareness, and thru it we may again meet our old friends on the physical plane;*
- *And so, in this space between space and this time between time, we call out on the web of consciousness and invite <name of deceased> to once again join us in our circle.*

**Light Gold and Silver Candles** and place the lit candles for Dead Person's Spirit in the center of the circle, and

**Shamanic journey to connect with the deceased**: Call *"Come to us now, O Spirit"* x 4 (one for each direction while feeling and experiencing the elemental wind), then:
- Intone OM while the elemental winds combine to form an Akashic field (spirit power)
- Invite Dead Person to join in the circle
- Guided meditation in which participants travel through roots with Cernunnos opening the gate and Cerridwen connecting us strongly with <his/her> spirit (if it is right), silent meditation, and return inviting deceased person to join us, if <he/she> desires. Start with slow drumming and then:

**Tree meditation:** then travel through roots and through veil into underworld:

**Cerridwen** *(Queen of the Underworld, bring those it is right to be with into contact with us)*

**Cernunnos** *(Lord of the Dead, Gatekeeper, Guide, help us make the needed contact)*

**Silent journey** into Otherworld

Before leaving, ask that messages be left in our consciousness as we return and that <name of deceased>. join us, if <he/she> desires.

**Message** to begin to return, thanking Spirits, Goddess and God on return.

**Say something about the tree** that will be planted in memory of the deceased at another time, with his/her cords and other selected magickal items at the roots, soil from his/her home, and some of his/her ashes (if applicable).

**Take out the mead and shortbread, and invite deceased person to partake** and join in our circle, and bless with: *"From the Earth, She brings forth bounty. He ferments it with His fire. Through us it dances in the dance of life, and then returns again to the Earth. Earth Mother, Sky Father, Spirit of the Departed, join us in this feast of love"*

**Consecration** *("As the chalice is to the female, so the athamé is to the male, and conjoined they are one in love.")*

**Pass the chalice**, pouring a libation for deceased when it would be his turn (also pass shortbread)
- First time silently passing chalice
- Second passing, CAW-style Water Sharing using beverage favored by deceased. Say *"Never thirst"* to person while passing them the chalice, and person receiving says *"Thou Art God/dess"* to person handing you the chalice [with special wording at dead person's libation cup, about having a special experience of being God/Goddess now that your body is no longer your anchor]
- Third passing, say something about Dead Person
- Additional passing, remembrances, thankfulness, etc.

**Empowerment of the Spirit of the Deceased**

*"As we end this circle, we invite you to take advantage of the portals that the quarters provide and to exercise your own free will in choosing what direction or directions you go in."*
- *Behold the portal of East, the realm of air, the realm of thought and logos, and the opportunity to fly free, to visit other places in this world, to visit other worlds, the possibilities are endless.*

- *Behold the portal of the South, the realm of fire, the power of life, death, the entry portal leading to rest and rebirth.*
- *Behold the portal to the West, the realm of water, the Summerland, the place of rest, renewal and of interconnectedness.*
- *Behold the portal of the North, the realm of Earth, the realm of manifestation, of reincarnation, and of imprinting one's presence in the physical world.*
- *Behold Cerridwen, behold Cernunnos, they can be your guides, friends, helpers, and advisors in whatever paths you choose.*
- *"As we end this rite, we offer you power to ride upon should you so choose."*
- Drumming and chanting: *"Horned one, lover, (son/daughter), leaper in the corn, deep within the Mother, die (fly, be high, etc.) and be reborn."*
- Intone OM and blow out deceased's candle when power peaks.

**Thank Cerridwen and Cernunnos**

**Thank and dismiss Quarters**

**Open Circle**

Wrap and keep Gold and Silver candles for remembrance ritual in which candles should burn for a while and then record dreams. Dedicate small pine tree and plant at power spot special to the deceased in Spring.

\*\*\*

# A Druid Memorial Service
## By Ian Corrigan, ADF

Simple shrine – small Fire, Well & Tree, big censer for incense offerings, if Fire can't be kept going.

### 1. Welcome (ending with: )

In Pagan paths, we are taught that death is a part of the cycle of existence. No form can be eternal—all arise from the matrix of the world, and vanish again in their time—but essence can endure. Many wise people have believed that a soul, a spirit, remains alive after death, that death is just the leaving of one form for another, while our eternal essence carries on. We hope that this is so. Yet, as long as human memory does not fail, we can be sure of another sort of endurance—we endure in our deeds, in the memories of those whose lives we have touched. The dead live in us, of that we can be certain, even as we look outward into the unknown adventure that may await us all.

So, we are joined here by our memory, by our lives with [DECEASED], by our affection, and by our sorrow. Let us spend a few moments preparing our hearts...

## 2. Attunement/ simple Two Powers
- Take a few moments to settle your body... and take a deep breath... let it out and take another... and another...
- In our work, we remember the impersonal divine as Fire and as Water...
- Just as every tree is rooted in the deep, sustaining water that flows in the land, so each of us is rooted deep in the rich, fertile power of the divine.
- Just as all life derives its energy from the shining sun, as all are guided by the moon and stars, so are we illuminated and guided by the shining fire of the divine.
- Take a deep breathand feel the deep in you, the light in you.

## 3. The Gate To Home
- It is by this flow, and shining, that each of us is connected with one another, with the holy world in which we live, and even with the Gods.
- So we will open our Gate. The Gate Between is our Fire... is our Well... it might be a shining mist... a spiraling light... a deep opening... an oaken door...
- When we open the Gate, we open ourselves to the divine... in ourselves, in the world, and in the realms of dream and story that we call spirit...
- Today we make this Gate for ourselves—to make our connection to [DECEASED]... to his story, to our memory of him, and to his spirit.
- We also make this Gate for [DECEASED]—that this fire be a beacon to his spirit, that he see us and hear us, that he see clearly his way forward in his next great adventure...
- Let the Gate be open...

## 4. The Invitations

> Now to the Sacred Fire I call
> The Threefold Kindreds, spirits all
> Mighty and beloved dead
> Be welcome at the Fire
> Wild Ones, Spirits of the Land
> Be welcome at the Fire
> Eldest, wisest, Shining Gods
> Be welcome at the Fire

- Come to our Fire, spirits, join us in this remembering, in this blessing, of [DECEASED], his life and his legacy.
- So open your hearts, and fill your memory with [DECEASED]... Let him be present in your heart... call to him with the joy you felt in his life...
- [DECEASED], we speak to you from this world you knew, though we know not where you are. We keep this fire, for a time, to guide you to us. We kindle a fire in ourselves in your memory.
- We set this table for you... (drink) and (bread), in the old way, that you might be certain of your welcome
- In the Mother's Love be welcome
  In the Joys of Life be welcome
  Be welcome here among those who remember you with love.
  So be it!

## 5. The Eulogies

*Each comes forward in turn to speak of [DECEASED], or make an offering of incense or drink his memory.*

## 6. The Death Song

> You go home this night to your home of winter,
> To your home of fall, of spring, of summer
> You go home this night to the Turning House,
> To your pleasant rest in the House of Joy.
>
> > Rest you, rest, and away with sorrow
> > Rest this night in the Mother's breast
> > Rest you, rest, and away with sorrow
> > Rest, O beloved, with the Mother's kiss
>
> In the Many-colored land
> In the Land of the Dead,

In the Plain of Joy
In the Land Beneath the Wave
In the Land of Youth,
In the Land of the Living
In the Revolving Castle, the House of Donn

> Rest in seven lights beloved
> Rest in seven joys beloved
> Rest in seven sleeps, beloved
> In the Grove of the Cauldron, Morrigan's Shrine

The shade of death is on your face, beloved
But the Cauldron of Rebirth awaits you
The Threefold turning of your fate
When your rest has given you your peace

> So rest in the calm of all calms
> Rest in the wisdom of all wisdoms
> Rest in the love of all loves
> Rest in the Lord of Life and Death
> Rest in the Lady of Life and Death

'Til the Season of Turning
'Til the Time of the Returning
'Til the Mystery of the Cauldron

## 7. Thanks & Goodbye
- Before we end this formal remembrance, it is proper for us to give thanks to all who have aided us.
- First, we thank you, [DECEASED], for being here with us. We will hold you in our hearts as we go from here, but we do not hold you to your life. Let the Gate and the Fire guide you, let the waters of the Well sustain you, as you go on your way. We thank you!
- Remember again the Gate, our connection with the divine… While we never truly banish that connection, we must now turn our hearts away from the past, and toward the future.
- So, let us close what we have opened, the oaken door be shut, the connection loosened for now…

Let the Gates be closed.

> We offer our thanks to the Mother of All.

We offer our thanks to the Gods, Dead, and Spirits.
May the Three Sacred Kins
Bring joy to all beings, and renew the ancient wisdom.
To the Fire, Well and Tree
We offer our thanks.
May Wisdom, Love and Power
Kindle in all beings and renew the ancient wisdom.
To the Earth, Sea, and Sky
We offer our thanks.
May the ancient wisdom be renewed,
And may all things know peace, joy and happiness
In all the worlds.
So be it.

And so, our work is ended. Let us remain, for a time, joined in fellowship.

\*\*\*

# Crossing Over Ceremony for a Child

From Dagonet Dewr, Membership Director,
International Pagan Pride Project,
Clan Chief, Thalia Clan, Neo-Pagan Mystery Tradition.

*(This is the service we did for the child of one of our coveners. Name and eulogy removed. It was a compromise ceremony for Wiccan parents and Lutheran and Roman Catholic in-laws.)*

We gather here today to honor this child, CHILD, who in such a short time touched many of us here deeply. We gather together to give what comfort we can to the families of this child, for while we understand that he has gone ahead to the ever-verdant meadows of peace and rest, we still remain here without him. Our grief and pain, even our anger, is natural. We allow ourselves to feel it, to express it, so that we may in turn move past it, along the road to acceptance and to peace.

Because a circle has no beginning and no ending, it is a symbol of eternal life of which, though absent from us, CHILD still partakes. So I would like to ask everyone to join hands in a circle, to begin this ceremony in honor of CHILD's crossing from this life to the next. We recognize that in joining together, we make this a space sacred, "set apart," by our shared love for this child, in the unity of The Eternal.

**Let us pray:**

Great Spirit, Eternal Source, You who are Mother and Father/Parent to us all, as we know that when we gather in Your name You are in our midst, so we know that You are with us tonight as we join with this mother and father/these parents to cherish the memory of their child.

Though we who gather may come from many different religious traditions, it is to You that we all turn in times of sorrow.

As we remember this child, help us have the faith of a child. Though now we grieve, let us remember that You still bring joy. Though now we hurt, let us remember that You bring end to suffering. Though now we face death, let us remember that You bring us the promise of eternal life. As You hold us now, let us remember that You also hold CHILD in Your light, and in Your love.

Amen.

**Addressing the parents:**

MOTHER & FATHER: Out of your cells came the mortal body in which CHILD's eternal spirit lived. Out of your love for each other came the love for him that you showed so strongly, even through the difficulties and fears of his surgery and the continued problems with his heart. You loved him, and he knew it, and we who know you saw it. Do not let your fears rob you of the knowledge that you gave this child a home where he was cherished! The memory of that love is the blessing that will carry you through these difficult days, and through the days that follow, when you will once again welcome a child into your lives and your hearts.

**I speak now to the families:**

No man is an island. Each of us is but a thread in the tapestries woven by our family before us. And you, his family, bequeathed to CHILD the tapestries in which his thread was woven. You welcomed him with such joy and gladness! Both of your families were delighted that he was the thread that joined you. Now that thread is gone, returned to the Weaver. But the bond he forged between you, woven of love, strengthened by adversity, is not gone. It remains, and though this separation causes such grief, the bond is still there, and will be there as you welcome the new child, and begin again the cycle of love and life.

**I now address the friends and coworkers of MOTHER, FATHER, and their family:**

Though we who are their friends are not MOTHER and FATHER's family by blood, we are family of their hearts. We waited with MOTHER through her pregnancy. We gleefully passed along news of CHILD's birth. We held our breaths and said our prayers when we learned that he would need surgery. Our love helped sustain his brief life, and helped sustain his parents. In the end, it may seem we ran out of miracles. But CHILD taught us about miracles. He taught us how to care, how to come together, how to hope and dream and feel, and even now that he is gone he brings us together, not in sorrow for his absence, but in celebration of his life and in an unbroken circle around his family. I think I can speak for all of us when we say that our lives would have been lessened, had we not known CHILD. And so it is fitting that we be here, at the end of his life, when he is taken from our cradling arms into the cradling arms of The Eternal.

**I say this to the children among us:**

We know you loved Baby CHILD. And we know it's hard to understand that he has died. You may think that only old people die, and not understand how your playmate did, when he was still so young. But remember, he had a problem with his heart, and even though the doctors tried to fix it, they weren't able to. Death can happen to anyone. And many times we are sad when people die, and miss the people because they're not here with us anymore. But we try not to be afraid of death, because we know that while our bodies might die, our spirits live on. And we know that whatever happens, God loves us, even after we die. So we know, we're not ever alone.

**And to NAME himself:**

CHILD, your tiny light illuminated our hearts. We had eleven short months with you. And we miss you, and will continue to miss you, for the rest of our lives. We know your spirit now travels to the happy lands beyond death, where the Eternal light shines. We offer you our blessings on your journey. And we thank you for the blessings you gave us:

The bright blessing of your laugh.

The divine spark in you which shone so brightly.
The depth of emotion you evoked in all of us who feared for your life.
And the proof your life gave us, that love is eternal, and that it does transcend death.

**Eulogy:**

**Song:** "We are all one with the infinite sun"

**Prayer:** "Do not stand at my grave and weep" by Mary Frye

We know that as long as we remember CHILD—as long as we see him in the winds, the sunlight, the rain, the grain—he will live forever, in our hearts. And as we close this service, we leave you with this ancient blessing:

May the road rise up to meet you,
May the wind be always at your back,
May the sun shine warm upon your face,
And the rains fall soft upon your fields.
And, until we meet again,
May God hold you in the palm of His hand.
Our rite is ended: go in peace.

*\*\*\**

# Crossing the Veil Ritual
### By Moose Dixon

*("Crossing the Veil" is a full ritual that involves setting up an inner and outer circle. Participants entering the inner circle may do grief work with their unquiet dead. Jack-o-Lanterns are used to good effect here.)*

**Ritual Team**: Aspergers, Quarter Callers, High Priest and High Priestess of Life, High Priest and High Priestess of Death, Fire Tender, Dedicated Grounders. Aspergers and Quarter Callers may be the same. Fire Tender and HP/HPS of Death may be the same. Grounders and HP/HPS of Life may be the same. A ritual team of this number presupposes a large number of participants.

**Ritual Prep**: Earlier in the day, participants have carved Jack-o-Lanterns from pumpkins they have personally grown/harvested or brought with them (or been provided). Set Jack-o-Lanterns in a circle around a fire pit, facing outwards, leaving approximately 10

feet of walk space between the fire's edge and the pumpkins. There should be a space in the circle to be used as a gate.

Participants are briefed on the flow of ritual. Make sure each participant understands that this is a full crossing the veil ritual, and that grounders will be available at all points during the ritual.

**Cleanse Ritual Area**: Cleanse the ritual area in a manner appropriate to the tradition of the participants. Light candles set in the Jack-o-Lanterns at this time.

**Asperge Participants**

**Cast Outer Circle of Life**: HP and HPS of Life triple cast a strong circle which will contain the entire ritual. A circle guardian may be used if appropriate to the group's tradition. The HP/HPS of Life will anchor all the energy and keep participants grounded.

**Call Quarters**

**Cast Inner Circle of Death**: The HP and HPS of Death will cast a circle delineated by the pumpkins. Inside this circle lies the other side of the veil. The HP/HPS will take on the aspect of the keepers of the land of the dead, and speak to the ritual participants as such. Their purpose is to maintain the inner circle while allowing ritual participants to enter and work through grief with the unquiet dead.

The number of participants inside the inner circle at any time should be relatively small, just enough to comfortably fill the fire's edge. If the total number of participants is large, the HP/HPS of Death may choose to use a dedicated Fire Tender.

**Crossing the Veil**: Each participant may approach the gate and be passed from the HP/HPS of Life to the HP/HPS of Death. They are led from the gate to the fire's edge where they may sit and communicate with those who have recently passed. Crying and screaming are not uncommon reactions, and the HP/HPS of Death must be emotionally strong enough to both comfort the participants and allow them to work through their communications. Supplies of tissues at the fire's edge may be useful.

When each participant is finished, the HP/HPS of Death leads them to the gate and passes them to the HP/HPS of Life. Immediate grounding of the participant is appropriate, using a small bit of sweet fruit juice and a bread product with a bit of salt. Chocolate covered cherries also work well. The HP/HPS of Life may choose to hand participants to dedicated grounders if needed or the total number of participants is large.

Those participants who remain in the outer circle, before and/or after they have done their work in the inner circle, should respect the sanctity of the work being done. There should be no idle chatter while their fellow participants are working through their grief. The HP/HPS of Death should also be sensitive to the number of participants waiting their chance to cross the veil and not allow those at the fire's edge to dwell there unduly.

**Devoke Inner Circle of Death**: After all participants are finished and have exited the inner circle, the HP/HPS of Death bring down the circle in a manner usual for their tradition. They may themselves need a brief grounding after the inner circle is devoked.

**Cakes and Ale**: All members of the ritual should be grounded through food and drink. If there is community business (induction of new members, announcements, etc.), this is the time to do such.

**Devoke Quarters**

**Devoke Outer Circle of Life**

***

## Memorial Ceremony
### By Morning Glory Zell

**Altar arrangement:** *A large portrait of DECEASED should be central. Other smaller items—such as significant jewelry, stones, etc. should be arranged artistically. Flower arrangements may be placed behind these, and/or on the floor.*

**Opening music**: *The Incredible String Band* "My Name Is Death"

**Introduction and Greeting:** The general content here should be to introduce yourself and mention your connection to DECEASED, greet people and welcome them to this Memorial. Let them know that we are all here as friends and relations of DECEASED and will do the best we can to honor her wishes and her memory.

**Creating the Circle:** (Priestess) I would like to create a Circle here and honor the four directions: East, South, West and North; and the four elements: Air, Fire, Water, and Earth that are such a part of so many people's spiritual journey. Everyone please join hands and form a Circle.

*She walks clockwise around inside the Circle and gives little rosewater spritzes to cool and refresh everyone as she speaks:* Circles are a part of our Ancient human traditions. They are still alive in many people's spiritual practices and in the games of children everywhere in the world. Today we meet together in a Circle of Community. We are a Circle of friends and family; we are a Circle of heartbeats and breaths and conjoined senses. Let us all hold hands for a moment as we join together in a Circle of memory, a Circle of love and compassion, a Circle of tears and truth. We invite DECEASED's spirit to commune with us here in this Circle that we create together in her honor.

**Circle Casting:**
I cast this Circle of ancient lore;
Waves upon a timeless shore.
With no beginning, nor an end;
Always knowing foe from friend.
Ouroboros, of legends old;
Rings of power forged of gold,
Wheel of the year, circle of stones,
Cycle of life from birth to bones.
A ring around the silv'ry moon,
I cast you now, O ancient rune!

**Invoke the Goddess** (Priestess): I call upon the Lady as Crone. We know Her by a hundred names. She is the One Who harvests all that lives. Who has taken DECEASED by the hand and led her into the Summerland, there to rest, reflect, and to dance with joyful abandon "the company of the Goddess and the God, 'til it be time for her to be reborn again to the Circle of Life. For the Lady is also the Mother of all things and the Lady of rebirth, She shall surely grant DECEASED the gift of life again when the Wheel has turned.

**Invoke the God** (Priest): I call upon the Lord of the Dance of Death and Resurrection. He Who guides us safely through the perils of the underworld, to receive the sun's warmth upon our faces once again. We are gathered here to celebrate the life of our friend, DECEASED, and to say farewell until we meet again in the Summerland or in another life.

**Poem:** "Metempsychosis" *by Gwydion Pendderwen*

**Song** (recorded): **"Breaths"** *by Sweet Honey in the Rock*

**Statement of Purpose:** This portion begins the actual Memorial or Wake portion of the Ceremony, the earlier portion is sort of a framing for the Ceremony. This would be a great place to talk about how though we all loved DECEASED she was somewhat of a Mystery Woman in some ways and most of us only knew parts of her.

**Eulogy:** Tell what you know about DECEASED's life first and then tell a story about her from the time of your friendship. When you are finished then you can take the "talking stick," explain about that process and kick off the first memory sharing.

**Elegy:** "Do not stand at my grave and weep" by *Mary E. Frye.*

**Group Sharing of Memories:** We invite each one here to share your favorite memories of DECEASED. Tell us how you first met her, or any anecdote that stands out and you wish to share. When you are done, "I will remember DECEASED. And what is remembered, lives." And everyone else, please respond with "What is remembered, lives."

*After everyone who wishes has shared their stories of DECEASED, everyone sing:* "We All Come From the Goddess" *by Z Budapest*

**Closing Song** (recorded): "Into the West" *(by Fran Walsh, Howard Shore, & Annie Lennox)*

**Conclusion and Benediction:** Say some final words that wrap up the experience; perhaps something along the lines of how we have learned more today about DECEASED than we ever knew before and perhaps the complexity of a life can only be comprehended at all once it has ceased the constant state of change that is called being alive.

**Closing:** Everyone please take hold of each other's hands once more to affirm the connection of the Circle that we have created here today in honor of our dear DECEASED. For everything there is a time and a season: a time of joy and a time of grief, a time to mourn and a time to dance. Our time here is now complete and it is time to return to our lives but always in the knowledge that love has the power to transcend even death. We will never forget DE-

CEASED and we will take these stories and memories out into the world to share with all the others who could not be here with us today and as we share them again and again her story will continue, because: what is remembered; lives on!

**Song:** "Return to the Land of Your Soul" *by Rafael Simka-Kahn & Schlomo Carlebach*

**Dismissal:** "All from Air, into Air" *by Gwydion Pendderwen*

**Closing Song** (recorded): "Song or Suicide" *by HIM*

\*\*\*

# Another Druid Funeral Service
*(Irish Pantheon)*
by Rev. Kirk Thomas, ADF

**The Welcome:** *Priest rings a bell three times three, says:*
Children of the Earth, we are here to celebrate the life of _____
While this is a time of grief, it I also a time of joy!

**The Precedent:** *Priest says:* In days of old, Classical writers wrote about the Celts. Diodorus Siculus wrote, "For they do not fear death, but subscribe to the doctrine ... that the human spirit is immortal and will enter a new body after a fixed number of years."

Pomponius Mela also wrote, "Thus they burn or bury articles useful in life with the dead. For this reason, in past times, they would defer business and payment of debts to the next life."

**Uniting the Three Worlds:** *Priest says*: Children of the Earth, let us call the powers of Earth and Sky to join within us here.

**Prayer:**
    O Waters of the Earth, deep and dark,
    Arise, primeval powers, fill us now
    With all your wondrous possibilities,
    That through the Earth, our Mother
    We may ground and join as one.

    O Fires of the Sky, O blinding light!
    Descend and crystallize within us all
    That spark of order on which life depends,
    That through the Sky our Father
    We may shine and share as one.

You powers dark and light, you liquid fire,
Conjoin and blend this mixture volatile
That powers great will join within ourselves,
Connecting all the Worlds
So that the circle is complete.

**Dissolving the Barriers:** *All present say:*
 O Donn, son of Mil!
 Manannán, son of Lir!
 O Lords of the isles where the newly dead go,
 We pray to You now – hear our call!

Your magics are great, Your powers intense,
We ask that you join Yours with ours.
Let the barriers standing 'tween this world and Yours
Dissolve in our hearts – hear our call!

With love and with joy, we humbly pray
For our dear friend to join us here now.
As our newest Ancestor to cross the divide
We welcome you home – hear our call!

**Remembrance and Offerings:** *Priest says:*
Newest Ancestor, ___*name*___, we welcome you here!
And though we will miss you here in the Midworld,
We take comfort in knowing that you are quite near,
Just beyond the veil of the Worlds.

When the Veils are thin and the Gates open wide,
We will welcome you here once again!
Just as one day we hope that you'll welcome us, too.

*Priest:* Children of the Earth, this is also the time of the living!
We now call on those who have cared for ___*name*___ and
who miss *her/him*.
To come forward and speak, sharing a memory of happy times.
And in days of old, offerings were made to the newly dead
To accompany them on their way.
We invite you to bring up your Grave Goods, that you
May make offering to our new Ancestor.

*The People come up one at a time, and leave an offering (such as silver or beer or other food) on the altar for later burial or disposal, or put it in the shaft or the Well or pour it on the ground.*

*After an offering is made, the person may speak for a time about the deceased. When each person is finished speaking, the Priest will say:* Bíodh sé amhlaidh! (BEE-uh SHAY Ow-LEE) So be it!

**Intercession:** *When everyone who wishes to speak has spoken of the dead, the Priest says:* Donn, son of Mil, keeper of *Tech Duinn*, Assembly Hall of the Dead, we make offering to You!

*Priest offers silver and whiskey.*

We ask that you welcome _____*name*_____ into Your Hall,
And prepare him/her for the further journey.
Offerings are made for the Sacred Well of *Tech Duinn*! Needle's Eye is crossed!
Eagle's Nest is mounted! Grant that _____*name*_____ may reach Your holy Hall.
Mighty Donn, accept our offering!

*All say:* Mighty Donn, accept our offering!

*Priest says:* Manannán mac Lir! Rider of the waves and Lord of *Emain Ablach,* We make offering to You!

*Priest offers silver and whiskey. Priest says:*
We ask that You meet _____*name*_____ at the Assembly and carry him/her
Across the Western Seas, that *he/she* may be reborn in *Tir na nOg*!
Offerings are made where the sea meets the land! The sacred cloak is shaken! The golden Cup of Truth is whole again! Grant that _____*name*_____ may reach the sacred isles.
Great Manannán, accept our offering!

*All say:* Great Manannán, accept our offering!

**The Closing:** *Priest says:*
    Children of the Earth, now is the time to let go.
    Great Manannán and Mighty Donn, we thank you for your aid.
    Departed Friend, our love and thanks go with you on your way.
    And Mother Earth, we sing to you of thanks and loving praise.

Now look we deep within our hearts
And closing Gates discern.
We know that death is but a door
And loved ones will return!

*Priest rings bell three times three. Priest says:*
Walk with wisdom, Children of the Earth, this rite has ended.

*Song:* "We're Ancestors Now"
From out of Her bosom we come to this life,
In joy and in sorrow we live all our days.
The Good Earth sustains us, in union or strife,
For She is the Mother, we sing to Her praise!

And when the day comes that we leave this green Earth
To take that great journey beyond the endless seas,
Our bodies return to this womb of our birth,
And we are reborn in a land of great ease.

Our lives you may celebrate, so do not despair!
For death in this world is a birth in the new,
No sorrows or troubles shall weigh upon us there,
We're Ancestors now and we'll watch over you!

\*\*\*

# Excerpted from: A Rite of Passage For Richard Joel Ravish (Magister Azaradel)

*(Salem, Massachusetts, September 19, 2012 e.v.)*
Performed by HPs. Rev. Gypsy Ravish & Friends

From the source of all for the good of all we turn to the East, South, West and North, the realms of the elements of Air, Fire, Water and Earth, and Great Spirit to bless and empower this sacred temple and all within. Sacred Pair who were before the dawn of time and shall be until the dusk, Great Mother and Father of the Universe, Goddess and God, in your name and in your honor, we begin this rite of passage. So mote it be.

Let this be a rite of release out into the Universe, the ultimate destination we all share, for Richard's Soul and Spirit. Let there be no fear of death. Death and Life are but two sides to one coin. No one is ever really alone and this is the time to draw in the light and send out the energy of perfect healing and energy that Richard needs for his journey homewards.

And just as the Sun sets in the West only to rise again in the East reborn in the light of a new day, so the wise have always trusted in the soul and the soul's journey.

The time will come when all of us must leave behind all that we were, all that we think we are now, leaving behind us all possessions, all passions, all attachments that bind us, to prepare and move forward to the life to come. That time has come for Richard.

We call upon the Angels Michael, Raphael, Gabriel, Uriel, Cassiel to assist in Richard's great initiation. We ask Richard's own Holy Guardian Angel to open the Way. We call upon the peace that is Yeheshuah to go with Richard on his pathway home.

There are no easy answers about the death of a loved one for those of us left behind in this land of the living. So that's where our inner knowing, our belief in God, the God and the Goddess, the Gods, our cosmic connection with the Universe, and the Source of Sources comes in to guide us. The energy and consciousness, the spirit and soul and body of light, that we knew as Richard Joel Ravish now moves effortlessly through the planes in the realms of Angels.

The Witches' Wheel is a Circle without beginning or end. At the end of each life is a doorway to the next. We believe there is a place between the worlds where souls return and abide with the Great Spirits between lives. This is the Summerland and Richard will be there to rest, enjoying perfect health, enjoying perfect peace, at one with the Gods, comforted and renewed in the embrace of the Great Goddess, as he continues the journey onwards.

Let Richard's mind be untroubled and clear. Richard, we are here to help you. Do not be afraid. May your compassion be as limitless as space. Become aware of the clear radiance of the White Light of your true nature. May your liberation be instantaneous! The four elements of your body, earth, air, fire, water released till only Spirit is left behind, your Buddha nature unveiled. You are not alone in this world and you will be able to comfort your loved ones when they follow in their own time. Your hopes and fears have lost all meaning. Though this world seems stable and solid, nothing here is permanent. Like water and snow and ice, life here is always changing and shifting form.

It is time now Richard to quit the place of sorrow and change. Embrace the White Light. You were Richard Joel Ravish, but now you are so much more! Now there is no darkness, no separation, no directions, no shape, only brilliant light free from bondage of any kind. It is the brilliant radiance of the Enlightened Ones, the Angels and the Ascended Masters. Recognize your real nature. You can see us, your family, your friends, your relatives. We call out to you. You are not alone in leaving this world. Richard, listen to us carefully:

Do not cling to the past. Go forward!

We draw upon these words drawn from and inspired by the Egyptian Book of the Dead, Coming Forth by Day:

*Richard's heart is righteous. It comes forth victorious from the Balance. It hath not sinned against any god or any goddess. Thoth hath weighed it according to the decree coming forth from the Company of the Gods and it has been found most true and righteous. Grant thou that cakes and beer be given unto him and may he be welcomed into the presence of Isis, Osiris and the Gods as a true son of Horus. May his soul lift itself up having been found pure when on Earth. May he come into the presence of the Gods and arrive at the Nome of Maati.*

May Richard rise up on his seat like a god endowed with life and give forth light like the Company of the Gods who dwell in Heaven. Anpu-Khent-Amenta give thee for repast thy thousands of loafs of bread, Thy thousands of jars of beer, thou thousands of vases of oils, thou thousands of oxen, thou thousands of changes of clothes, thou thousands of oxen. So mote it be.

Let us see Richard climbing the Rainbow Ladder to the Summerland. The Goddess and God and the Great Spirits are with him now, just as they are always with us. No one is ever really alone and this is the time to draw in the light and send out the energy of perfect healing and energy that Richard needs for his journey homewards. Healing and comfort for Richard; healing and peace for those he must leave behind. We promise to keep sacred his memory. Goddess of Life, Goddess of Death, grant us peace.

He is free now, from stress, from worry, free from pain, free from sorrow, one with the light. In this temple of light, in the sight of All that is Holy, we give our love and blessings to Richard and bid farewell knowing that we will meet and know and love again. So mote it be.

*From the East, South, West and North*
*Powers of Magick we call thee forth!*
*From the North, South, East and West*
*That our offering be truly blessed!*
*In perfect love and perfect trust*
*For Richard's greatest good*
*For our greatest good*
*And for the Good of All*
*So Mote it be.*

\*\*\*

# Ceremonial Burial of Ashes
### By Bran th'Blessed (Samm Dickens)

*Here is the ceremony I have proposed for our burial.*

1. Dig a hole about 12-18 inches deep and maybe one to three feet wide. Circle the walls of this pit with nine stones, each about the size of a skull or so.
2. Pour our ashes into the grave and cover them with at least one to three inches or so of soil.
3. Build a fire in and above the grave pit.
4. A ceremony may be performed as the fire burns. Sprinkle incense upon the fire during the ceremony. Perhaps singing the old chant, "We all come from the Goddess, and to her we shall return…" In our case, a Biblical verse might also be read, since Becky was a liberal Christian and a Christo-Pagan. (Or just sit and watch the fire and talk together.)
5. When the ceremony is done and the fire has subsided mostly to embers, water should be poured upon the fire site, not only to douse the flame but also to complete the ritual cycle.
   - Placing the soil upon the ashes is the element of EARTH.
   - Burning the pyre above the soil is the element of FIRE.
   - The smoke from the fire and incense is the element of AIR.
   - And finally, the fire is doused with the element of WATER.
   - The fire returns our spirits to the heavens, the Sky, while the water returns our bodies to the ground, the Earth.

6. Now remove the nine skull stones (carefully) and fill the pit with the remaining soil that was removed from it. Press it down firmly, and place a stake squarely in the center of the grave site. Attach a cord measured to 15 inches to the stake; then use that cord to inscribe a three-foot diameter circle around the grave. One may place small flags or stakes to mark the perimeter, one every foot or so. This three-foot circle defines the grave site.

7. Now mark the grave site with the nine skull-sized stones as follows. Around the perimeter, place one stone precisely at due North (use a compass), and moving deosil (clockwise) place another stone at Northeast, East, Southeast, South, Southwest, West, and Northwest. Then replace the center stake with the ninth stone. Once the stones are firmly in place, all other markers for the perimeter may be removed. The grave circle is finished.

8. When the time is right for planting such trees, a tree should be planted at the center of the grave, moving that stone just to the north to shelter the sapling. The trees roots will burrow into our ashes, and they will become part of new life, symbolizing that life never ends. Flower beds may be planted around the perimeter circle, or any other such desired decorations and memoriams as the family or friends may choose, but the simple tree encircled by stones is enough. The eight stones at the circle perimeter are symbolic of the eight Sabbats that celebrate the Cycle of Life and the afterlife we experience.

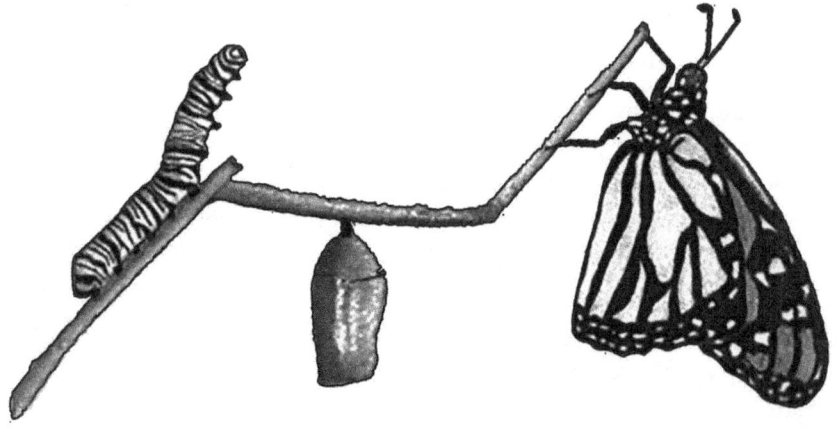

# Chapter 2
# Disposition of the Remains Options & Alternatives

*Life should not be a journey to the grave with the intention of arriving safely in a pretty and well-preserved body, but rather to skid in broadside, in a cloud of smoke, thoroughly used up, totally worn out, and loudly proclaiming, "Wow! What a Ride!"*
~~Hunter S. Thompson

## Death is a Two-Edged Sword
by Morning Glory Zell

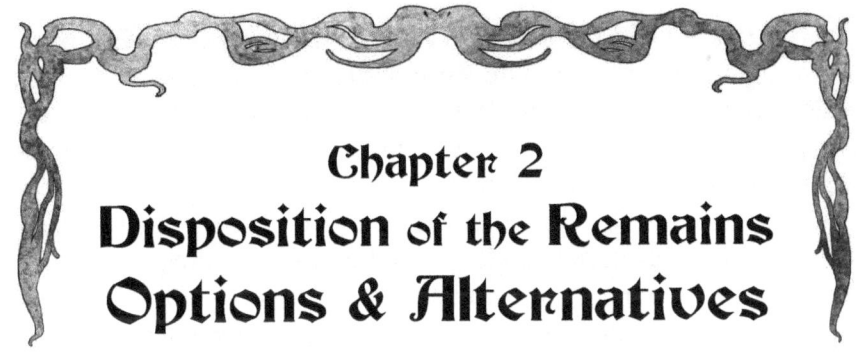

DEATH IS A TWO-EDGED SWORD THAT affects not only the person who passes on, but also the loved ones who are left behind. It is for those loved ones, their grief and their needs, that I write these words.

Beyond religious creed or blood ties, beyond age or gender or lifestyle, often we find that it is our pain that brings us together in unity. Suffering has the power to transform and strengthen us, whether it is our own suffering or that of those we love. It moves us like a windstorm, like an earthquake; it shakes us loose from our old comfortable patterns and forces us to look at life with new and childlike eyes. Pain instructs us, tramples our defenses, and brings us to our senses when it brings us to our knees.

When we walk into the darkness of pain and grief, we undergo a kind of test. That dark night of our soul is our Initiation. What do we find and bring forth out of that darkness? When we face the unknown fear and doubts, we often discover that we are not alone in our pain. We find that out of the darkness grows the seeds of hope that we have sown. Those seeds can empower us to go on with the business of living our lives as if each day mattered.

But if we dread the darkness and reject the experience of pain, if we try to cover it up with false smiles and sugar-coated platitudes, we miss the opportunity for spiritual growth that comes with the pain. Darkness is a womb as well as a tomb, and it is no accident that these two words rhyme.

The name of the game is Life, Death, and Rebirth — and that's the secret of all Nature and all spiritual faiths, regardless of the differences in metaphor or semantics. *"Everything lost is found again, in a new form, in a new way. Everything hurt is healed again, in a new life, in a new day."* — Starhawk. The Mystery of Rebirth is the heartbeat of Mother Nature; Death is part of life and part of that Mystery. Without death there is only stagnation — there can be no birth, no growth, no soil, no seed, no promise of renewal. Death is the great giveaway that releases energy to nourish life.

The four Elements: Earth, Water, Fire, and Air live together in our bodies, but they go their own way at the moment of death. What happens after death? The whole human race argues that one... Some say you go to Heaven, others that you become a ghost. Some say you get close to God or that you just die and you are dead and that is all. The Hindus insist that you are a bit of sky reflected in a jar fated to shatter. Perhaps you end where you begin, a reflection arising from water, mixing with water, and finally becoming one with the water.

For those of us who survive the test and go on living in the joy of our newly-awakened awareness of the preciousness of life, let us live it fully each day, trusting in the power of the unquenchable spirit that fires us and shines out of the darkness of our pain like a candle in the night.

# Disposition of the Remains According to the Elements
### by Oberon Zell & She' d'Montford

It's truly remarkable how many creative means have been devised over time to dispose of the bodies of the dead, once the spirit has departed and the physical vessel is no longer needed. There are four types of disposal of the remains, according to the Elements:

# Earth

By far the most common form of disposal of the dead is burial or entombment in the ground, which has been practiced for at least 100,000 years (Neanderthals were the first people we know to have buried their dead, as discovered in the Skhul cave at Qafzeh in Nazareth, Israel). The simplest and most natural kind of funeral monuments, and therefore the most ancient and universal, are a mound of earth *(tumulus)*, or a heap of stones *(cairn)*, raised over the body or ashes of the departed; mention is made of such monuments in the *Book of Joshua* as well as in *Homer* and *Virgil*.

The primitive Greeks were originally buried in their own houses, but they later established burial grounds on desert islands and outside the walls of towns, thus avoiding infection from those who had died of contagious diseases. In ancient Rome, families originally also buried deceased relatives in their own homes, according to the Roman practice of ancestor worship. The Twelve Tables enacted in 449 BCE forbade this practice, so the later Romans buried their dead in *necropoli*.

Necropoli – "cities of the dead" – were great cemeteries of many ancient civilizations, such as Giza and Saqqara in Egypt, Knossos in Crete, and Cerveteri in Etruscan Italy. The famous Catacombs beneath ancient Rome where early Christians met in secret were lined with niches where bodies were arrayed, and similar subterranean realms of the dead may still be seen today under the streets of Paris and London, as well as in Egypt, Malta, Spain, Finland, Mexico, Peru, and Italy. Cathedrals throughout medieval Europe had *crypts* beneath their floors lined with sarcophagi. In places such as New Orleans and Venice, Italy, where the water table is too high to permit underground burials, above-ground tombs or *mausoleums* are common.

A *mausoleum* is a free-standing building constructed as a monument enclosing the interment space or burial chamber of a deceased person or people. A monument without the interment is a *cenotaph*. A mausoleum may be considered a type of tomb, or the tomb may be considered to be within the mausoleum. A Christian mausoleum sometimes includes a chapel. The word derives from the Mausoleum at Halicarnassus (near modern-day Bodrum in Turkey), the grave of King Mausolus (377-353 BCE), the Persian satrap of Caria, whose elaborate tomb was one of the Seven Wonders of the Ancient World.

An *ossuary* – "place of bones" – is a chest or other repository for human skeletal remains. A body is first buried in a temporary grave, then after some years the bones are dug up and removed to an ossuary. The greatly reduced space taken up by an ossuary allows the remains of many more people to be kept in a single tomb. Persian Zoroastrians and Mycenaean Greeks used deep wells as ossuaries 3,000 years ago. During the time of the Second Temple, between 516 BCE and 70 CE, Jewish burial customs in Jerusalem included primary burials in burial caves, followed by secondary burials in limestone ossuaries placed in smaller niches of these catacombs. The Roman Catholic Douaumont Ossuary in France contains the remains of more than 130,000 French and German soldiers who fell at the Battle of Verdun during World War I.

Ossuaries are also a longstanding tradition in the Eastern and Greek Orthodox Churches. In Orthodox monasteries, when one of the brethren dies, his remains are buried for one to three years, and then disinterred, cleaned and gathered into the monastery's *charnel house* (a vault or building where human skeletal remains are stored). If there is reason to believe that the departed is a saint, the remains may be decorated and placed in a *reliquary;* otherwise the bones are usually mingled together (skulls in one place, long bones in another, etc.). The *Capela dos Ossos* ("Chapel of Bones"), at the entrance of the Church of St. Francis, is one of the best-known monuments in Évora, Portugal. The interior walls and pillars are covered and decorated with skulls and other bones from hundreds of individuals, held together by cement.

Several ancient cultures—most famously the Egyptians, Peruvians, and Chinese—practiced mummification: removing the internal organs, stuffing the cavities, and treating the body with sophisticated concoctions of embalming fluids before wrapping it in linen windings and sealing the linen with tar. Deceased rulers and nobles would be placed in a beautiful coffin with their portrait carved and painted on the lid, and that would be placed within a massive stone sarcophagus in a secret tomb for all eternity (at least, that was the plan). However, some Pharaohs were entombed within gigantic pyramids, so everyone knew just where to find them. Since the Egyptians, Mesopotamians, Mycenaeans, Chinese, Inca, Vikings, and other great Bronze-Age civilizations commonly entombed their dead rulers with the entire national treasury, there was considerable incentive for tomb-robbing by their successors and pragmatic opportunists, so few such tombs escaped plunder.

Jewish religious laws such as *halakha* and Islamic religious law, *sharia,* call for immediate burial of the body after a basic ritual of bathing and shrouding the body, accompanied by prayers and readings from the scriptures. Both religions forbid embalming, and the corpse is never displayed for viewing. In many Jewish communities, the deceased is positioned in the grave with the feet towards the Temple Mount in Jerusalem (in anticipation that that the deceased will be facing the reconstructed Third Temple when the Messiah arrives and resurrects the dead). Muslims position the body in the grave so that it is facing towards Mecca on the right side. Cremation is prohibited in Islam and Orthodox Judaism, but allowed in Reform Judaism.

These days rural cemeteries have become economically popular. Green burials emphasize recycling. The body is not embalmed, and is buried in a shallow (3-foot-deep) grave, wrapped in a shroud and/or a casket made of recyclable materials. It is a common practice to plant a tree on the grave – traditionally an apple tree – so that the eventual fruit will return the elements of the beloved deceased back into the community.

Italian designers *Anna Citelli and Raoul Bretzel* have created a concept they call the *Capsula Mundi*. [2] This is an egg-shaped starch plastic container in which the dead body is placed in a fetal position. A seedling tree is then planted atop the biodegradable pod, to be nourished by the decomposing body beneath it. The tree is chosen when the person is alive; relatives and friends care for it after the burial. A cemetery will thus become a sacred forest. However, this is rather expensive, and I cannot see how it is an improvement over simply planting a tree upon the grave of a green burial, as we did with Morning Glory.

## Fire

In modern cremations, bodies must be burnt in an oven of a licensed crematorium at super high temperatures (1,400°-1,800° F), to render the ashes sterile; you can then keep or dispose of the ashes *(cremains)* however you like. In many ancient cultures, bodies

---

[2] Capsula Mundi, http://www.capsulamundi.it/ accessed 1/15/18

were placed on a carefully-constructed funeral pyre and set alight at dusk with great ceremony, to burn throughout the night as people sat vigil. At dawn, any bone remnants would be retrieved from the ashes to be buried appropriately.

Hindus believe that the burning of a dead body facilitates the release of the spirit and that the flames represent Brahma, the creator. About 12 hours after cremation, family men collect the ashes and small pieces of white bone called "flowers." In crematoriums these are ground to dust, and arrangements must be made to preserve them. Ashes are carried or sent to India for deposition in the sacred Ganges river, or the ocean, along with garlands and flowers. However, many poor people in India cannot afford the cost of cremation, which at a minimum of about $40 is far above a poor person's monthly wage. It is also Indian custom to not cremate unwed girls.

Buddhists prefer cremation – but if firewood is in short supply then Air, Earth, or Water burials are acceptable. After a cremation, small bone fragments are passed among the relatives with chopsticks.

In Sikhism, as in Buddhism, cremation is the preferred method of disposal; although if this is not possible then other methods such as burial or submergence at sea are acceptable. On the day of the cremation, the body is washed and dressed and then taken to the home where hymns from the Scriptures are recited by the congregation. After the cremation, the ashes are deposited in the five sacred rivers of Punjab in India).

The famous "Viking Funeral" involved placing the deceased warrior in a boat with his weapons, personal effects, grave goods, and kindling. The boat would be set adrift at dusk, and ignited from shore by flaming arrows.

Most ancient Romans were cremated, with the ashes collected in an urn and placed within a niche in a collective tomb called a *columbarium* (literally, "dovecote"). Rome prohibited cremation or inhumation within the boundary of the city, owing to both sacred and civil considerations that the priests might not be contaminated by touching a dead body, and that houses would not be endangered by funeral fires.

## Water

Burial at Sea. As with cremations, there are strict laws associated with this type of burial. You must obtain a permit to perform a sea burial, and then you must charter a suitable vessel, crew, and sea captain that will transport the body and the funeral party to the permitted destination. The body must be correctly weighted down and dropped over the continental shelf, at least 600 feet deep and no closer than three nautical miles from shore. This can be a quite expensive undertaking.

A simpler and less expensive compromise is to scatter cremated ashes at sea. This may be done from a boat or plane, from a clifftop, or from a bridge over a waterway. Scattering of ashes is not offensive or damaging to the environment; it is sanitized dust and disburses harmlessly.

While it is illegal in India today to dispose of the dead in rivers, poverty often drives poor people to conduct water burials to avoid the cost of cremation. And some practicing Hindus believe that giving an unwed girl a water burial in the Ganges or other sacred river will ensure that she will be reincarnated back into the family.

Unlike land burials, a burial at sea or the scattering of cremated ashes at sea cannot be reversed; nor can the body be relocated or exhumed for an autopsy. It also means a memorial cannot be erected at the burial location. Because of this, you may wish to consider a permanent memorial at another site so that in the future others have somewhere to visit to gain a sense of the person who has passed away.

## Air

Sky burial is a funeral practice in which a human corpse is placed on a high place such as a mountaintop to decompose through exposure to the elements, or to be eaten by scavenging animals — especially birds of prey. Sky burial is traditionally practiced by Vajrayana Buddhists in Tibet, Mongolia, and in the Chinese provinces of Qinghai, Sichuan and Inner Mongolia, where the ground is too hard and rocky to dig a grave and there the is a scarcity of fuel above the treeline that make fire burials impractical. Sky burials in those mountainous regions were more practical than the traditional Buddhist practice of cremation. Sky burial is also practiced by Parsi Zoroastrians in the Middle East, as well as some indigenous peoples in North America and Peru. The body may be placed on a large flat rock, atop a "Temple of Death" or "Tower of Silence," or on some other high platform. This is considered the way to facilitate the fastest reincarnation and be carried closest to the heavens, but it is illegal in most Western countries.

A Tower of Silence, or *Dakhmeh*, is a cylindrical structure built on the top of a hill, consisting of concentric slabs surrounding a central pit. Bodies were arranged into three concentric rings: men outermost, then women, with children innermost. Although the birds of prey needed less than an hour to leave nothing but bones, the skeletal remains were left to bleach in the sun for no less than a year before the *nasellars* (pallbearers) could come and push the bones into the underlying ossuary pit. Running through sand and coal filters, the disintegrated bones were eventually carried away by the sea.

One primitive tribe in Bali lays the corpse on a wooden platform atop a cliff to be consumed by the birds and beasts. Anything left after three days is simply tipped over the cliff edge.

### Tibetan "Chod" Practice
by She' D'Montford

The practice of "Chod" was established by the 17th century, when Buddhism began its secular rule of Tibet. Though the encroaching Indo-Buddhism opposed the power of the native Tibetan mystics and the indigenous Bon religion, certain aspects were absorbed by Tibetan Buddhism. One of these is the "Sky Burial," sometimes just called *Chod,* meaning "to chop."

In Tibet, corpses are not usually burned or buried; they are chopped into pieces at a dismembering ground and left for carrion birds. This was a practical and spiritual practice, as the frozen ground made it impossible to dig graves and lack of timber above the tree-line made Indian-style cremations nonviable.

The new form of Buddhism in Tibet readily assimilated the native sky burial rite, changing it into a ritual expressing a Buddha-like non-attachment to the physical body and a releasing of the fear of death, leading to their cycle of rebirth.

Original indigenous Tibetan Chod ritual had a dual spiritual function:

Firstly, it enabled the departed to have great freedom and influence by being assimilated quickly into other living beings, thus continuing their existence on Earth.

Secondly, it prevented the return of the departed's spirit from the *Bardo*—a realm between death and life. If the newly departed is confused by his/her change of state, and is drawn back to the familiarity of its body or home, it is painful for both the living relatives and the departed, resulting in confusion and distress. If the body had gone in many directions with the eagles, vultures, and other birds, the departed's focus is spread much wider. In that expanded state of consciousness the departed can then choose either another incarnation or total re-absorption into Prana/Nirvana.

## Cryogenic Suspension
### from the Cryonics Institute website [3]

*Cryonics* is a technique intended to hopefully save lives and greatly extend lifespan. It involves cooling legally-dead people to liquid nitrogen temperature where physical decay essentially stops, in the hope that future scientific procedures will someday be able to revive them and restore them to youth and good health.

In 1962, a physics lecturer at Wayne State University named Robert C. Ettinger founded the cryonics movement with the publication of his book *The Prospect of Immortality* and introduced the world to a groundbreaking concept he termed "Cryonics." Ettinger was placed in cryostasis July 28, 2011 at the Cryonics Institute facility in Michigan at the age of 92.

The Cryonics Institute provides suspension at cryogenic temperatures, also known as cryonics. They provide long-term storage and security for members at their cryonics facility in Clinton Township, MI. They specialize in full-body cryo-preservation of humans and pets, DNA & tissue storage as well as cryonics outreach and public education about the cutting-edge science they are engaged in. Members are afforded the opportunity to be preserved at cryogenic temperatures in hopes that future medical technology may be able to someday revive and restore them to full health.

---

[3] http://www.cryonics.org/ accessed 12/12/17

While suspended patients cannot be revived with current technology, cryonics proponents believe that scientific advances may well make possible the future revival of patients from cryonic suspension.

## Mushroom Ingestion

One innovative concept for disposal of the remains is mushroom ingestion as a catalyst for rapid decomposition. A company named *Coeio* (Latin, "assemble, or come together") has created the "Infinity Burial Suit"—a handcrafted biodegradable garment to be worn by the deceased. The suit was co-created with zero waste fashion designer Daniel Silverstein.

The Infinity Burial Suit and the Infinity Burial Shroud for open-casket viewing are both made from organic cotton and infused with a biomix made up of mushroom fungi and other microorganisms that together aid in decomposition and neutralize toxins found in the body. The end result is that bodies are transformed into vital nutrients that enrich the earth and foster new life.

Because the mushrooms in the suit do not consume live flesh, the suit can even be modeled prior to death. In a living person, the immune system deters the mushroom's activation; when a person dies, lack of an immune system permits the corpse to become food for the microorganisms.

The suit or shroud may be incorporated into an eco-friendly burial container; or merely laid directly in the ground. As long as they are kept in a cool, dark storage location, all Infinity Burial Products will last indefinitely. This eco-option is legal and should be of interest to anyone planning a green burial. More information (and videos) can be found on Coeio's website. [4]

## Alkaline Hydrolysis

Also called *biocremation, resomation, flameless cremation or* water cremation, alkaline hydrolysis combines a water and alkali-based solution to accelerate the natural process the body goes

---

[4] Coeio, http://coeio.com/ accessed 2/16/21

through at the end of life. The body is placed in a biodegradable shroud or coffin and carefully positioned in a pressure vessel that is then filled with a mixture of water and lye, and heated to around 320°F, with enough pressure to prevent boiling. The body is effectively broken down into its chemical constituents, which takes on average 3-4 hours.

The end result is a quantity of green-brown liquid and soft, porous bone fragments that are easily crushed into a white dust, which can be returned to the next of kin in an urn as with flame cremation. The liquid may be disposed of through the sewer system, or used to irrigate a garden.

Originally developed and patented in 1888 by Amos Herbert Hobson as a method to process animal carcasses into plant food, alkaline hydrolysis s is currently used in the agricultural industry to sterilize animal carcasses that might contain pathogens. Several companies in North America now offer the procedure for pets.

The term *Resomation* (Greek/Latin, "rebirth of the body") was coined for resolving the body back to the basic organic components and its rapid and beneficial recycling into the ecosystem. Resomation Ltd was formed by Sandy Sullivan in Scotland in 2007 to promote high pressure alkaline hydrolysis as an alternative to burial and flame cremation.[5]

## Memorial Reef

Another option is for cremains to be mixed with natural concrete and incorporated into an artificial undersea reef that enhances habitat and increases marine life populations. *Eternal Reefs* [6] and *Neptune Memorial Reef* [7] – provide this service off the Florida coast.

Eternal Reefs' spherical reef balls are made of environmentally-safe cast concrete designed to replicate the natural marine environment that supports coral and microorganism development.

Located 3.25 miles east of Key Biscayne in Miami FL, Neptune Memorial Reef™ is the largest man-made reef ever conceived, transforming over 16 acres of barren ocean floor.

---

[5] Resomation, http://resomation.com/about/need-for-change/ accessed 2/16/21
[6] Eternal Reefs, http://www.eternalreefs.com/ accessed 1/16/21
[7] Neptune Memorial Reef, http://www.nmreef.com/ accessed 2/16/21

Neptune Reef is an artistic representation of the Lost City of Atlantis, 40 feet under the sea. These structures have produced a marine habitat to promote coral and marine organism's growth while creating the ultimate 'Green Burial' opportunity. A marine study conducted by the Department of Environmental Resource Management concluded that marine life around the Reef has gone from zero to thousands in the first two years.

## Other options

Other cutting-edge approaches include *space burial*, offered by Celestis Memorial Spaceflights; [8] *mummification,* offered by a religious organization called Summum; and *freeze-drying*.

*Promession* is an environmentally friendly way to dispose of human remains by way of freeze-drying. The concept of promession was developed by Swedish marine biologist Susanne Wiigh-Mäsak, who derived the name from the Italian word for "promise" (*promessa*). She founded Promessa Organic AB[9] in 1997 to commercially pursue her procedure of immersing a body in liquid nitrogen, making it brittle, evaporating the liquid and shaking the body apart with vibrations; and then putting the remains in a shallow grave, where they decompose quickly and turn into compost.

If you like the idea of shooting your ashes into space, Celestis is the only company to have successfully conducted Memorial Spaceflight missions, the only company to have been selected by NASA to honor one of its scientists, and for more than two decades an iconic pioneer and global leader of the commercial space age. Missions may go into Earth orbit, to other planetary bodies, or into deep space. The cremains are not actually scattered in space, but remain sealed inside the spacecraft until the craft either burns up on re-entry (Earth orbit missions); reaches its final extraterrestrial destination (e.g. the Moon); or leaves the solar system (deep space missions).

Summum first introduced the public to Modern Mummification in 1975. Since that time, Summum has continued to research, develop, and refine this exoteric and esoteric art and science. Today,

---

[8] Celestis, https://www.celestis.com/ accessed 12/12/17
[9] Promessa, http://www.promessa.se/ accessed 12/13/17

Summum is the only organization in the world to offer this distinguished tradition of preservation, dating back to ancient Egypt. [10]

# Body Donation

Donating your body to science after death is a way to eliminate the funeral and burial costs and continue your contributions to society. Donate to a medical school and you could end up practiced on by medical students, a resident on the Body Farm (*University of Tennessee's Forensic Anthropology Center*), or a crash test cadaver (*Wayne State University School of Medicine*). Donate to a museum and you could end up a skeleton (*Maxwell Museum of Anthropology*) studied by anthropological researchers, on display to be studied by physicians brushing up on their skills (*Mütter Museum*), or plastinated in a traveling exhibit (*Body Worlds*). Donate to a body broker and they will distribute parts or your whole body to organizations that will use your body for scientific purposes.

## Forensic Anthropology Center at Texas State (FACTS) [11]
from the FACTS website

The gift of one's body is an invaluable contribution to the education of forensic anthropologists, and ultimately the advancement of science. The Forensic Anthropology Center at Texas State (FACTS) accepts body donations for scientific research purposes under the Universal Anatomical Gift Act. Your full body donation makes cutting edge research in forensic sciences and biological anthropology possible. Your gift supports scientific research, training, and professional education. The areas of research conducted with donated bodies include:
- Reconstructing the postmortem interval to determine time since death and related studies in human decomposition,

---

[10] Summum, http://www.summum.org/ accessed 12/13/17
[11] Forensic Anthropology Center at Texas State, http://www.txstate.edu/anthropology/facts/donations.html accessed 12/13/17

- Osteological research that advances knowledge in developing a biological profile (for example, age, sex, ancestry, and stature) and assisting in the identification process, and,
- Advanced forensic analyses including human skeletal variation, trauma interpretation, and histological and chemical analyses of bone.

The overall aim of this type of research is to assist law enforcement agents and the medicolegal community in their investigations as well as advance scientific knowledge in human decomposition, human skeletal variation, and osteological methods.

If you would like to will your body or the body of a deceased family member to the Forensic Anthropology Center at Texas State, go to their website and download and complete the appropriate form. Discuss the form and your wishes with your family, and contact them with any questions you might have. If you would like more information about the program before you make a commitment to body donation, do not hesitate to contact them.

## Maxwell Museum of Anthropology [12]
(from their website)

Biological Anthropology at the Maxwell Museum of Anthropology emphasizes Human Osteology and Forensic Anthropology. The large holdings of archaeological and forensic materials are being continually augmented by an active body donation program and collectively comprise one of the pre-eminent comparative collections of human osteological material.

The Museum's Laboratory of Human Osteology is the location for a variety of projects on human skeletal pathology and group morphology, the study of modern human populations and the practice of forensic science. These programs actively involve researchers from around the world along with numerous university undergraduate and graduate students.

The forensic anthropology program operates in partnership with the New Mexico State Office of the Medical Investigator, located in the UNM School of Medicine, with this collaboration representing a rich research resource.

---

[12] Maxwell Museum of Anthropology, http://www.unm.edu/~maxwell/ 12/13/17

Recent and ongoing projects include studies on the biomechanics of modern humans, microevolution of modern human populations, and projects relating to facilitating the identification of unknown individuals.

## MedCure [13]
(from the MedCure website)

Throughout history, human cadavers have provided the best model for medical education and research. Body donation is also important for teaching and learning anatomy, studying the pathology of diseases as well as development and practice of new innovative, minimally invasive surgical procedures.

MedCure is the leading non-transplant tissue bank devoted to compassionate, ethical services that connect whole-body donors to medical research and education while providing innovation and opportunity for scientific medical advancements. MedCure is fully accredited through the American Association of Tissue Banks (AATB), the only U.S. national tissue banking organization. MedCure assists donors and their families in making body donation arrangements and matching the body donation with current medical research and educational studies.

MedCure was founded in 2005 and the main office is located in Portland, OR. Additional locations are in Orlando, FL; New England; Henderson, NV; and St. Louis, MO. The Nevada, New England, and Oregon locations are also Surgical Training Centers.

## Organ Donation

Many people die in good health, such as from accidents. In such cases, previously arranging to donate healthy organs to replace failing organs in other persons can be a meaningful form of life-extension. In other cases, organs may be given by healthy living donors to save a loved one who is experiencing organ failure. Donating organs can save one or many lives, depending on which organs are recovered and transplanted.

---

[13] MedCure, http://medcure.org/ accessed 12/13/17

There are no costs to the donor in any case; all expenses will be covered by the insurance and medical agencies responsible for recovering and transplanting the organs. To register as an organ donor, just say "yes" to organ donation when you get your driver's license at the Department of Motor Vehicles (DMV), or apply to the official U.S. Government Organ Donor Registry.

In the case of post-mortem donations, the organs are recovered as soon as possible after brain death of the donor in a hospital environment. Donation after brain death allows for many different organs to be transplanted, including heart, kidneys, lungs, liver, pancreas, corneas, and small intestines.

Kidney transplants are by far the most common form of organ donation from living donors, as the human body can function normally with only one healthy kidney. The ideal kidney donors are close relatives who will have a strong genetic match with the recipient, thus providing the best chance for acceptance and longevity of the transplanted kidney.

**Post-Mortem Club with Past Member**

8/3/1934- The Post-Mortem club, an organization of naprapaths, held its annual breakfast with all chapter members present although the president, J.M. McAdou, founder, had died during the past year. One of the rules of the club is that each member will his skeleton to it, for attendance to club meetings despite death. The banquet photo shows presiding president Oakley Smith, members and the skeleton of Mr. McAdou. *Naprapathy* is a blend of chiropractic and osteopathic hands-on healing.

# Chapter 3
# Losing a Loved One: Personal Reflections

*The only truly dead are those who have been forgotten.*
*~~Jewish saying*

*What is remembered, lives.*
*~~Pagan saying*

IN RECENT YEARS THERE HAVE BEEN FAR too many deaths in the Family as the Pagan community ages and cancer seems to be spreading epidemically. And now, of course, we have the COVID pandemic. How does one cope with the death of a Beloved? A husband, wife, soulmate, life-partner? A child? A parent? I asked this question of a few Pagan friends who've lost someone dear to them. Here are some responses, beginning with a tribute to my own departed Lifemate:

## Morning Glory
By Susa Morgan Black 2014
*(Tune: Amazing Grace)*

The stars are gathering in the skies
To form a Circle round.
Within the hill, our Goddess lies
Where healing can be found.

Between Her hands a fountain flows
And myriad forms take shape.
By Her skill, new life now grows
As She lifts Her floral cape.

Ancient Ones from far and near
Themselves see in Her art.
By Her hand, Goddesses appear
A gift from M.G.'s heart.

The Fey are standing, hand in hand
Singing their praise of Her.
Throughout the sacred Fairyland
Her magic does occur.

Animals of every breed
Cry in a single voice:
Goddesses, whose call we heed
Your presence, we rejoice.

Our Guardians of sacred Space
Whose passions all enrich,
We are all within the grace
Of the Wizard and the Witch.

In Summerland, where keeps the Grail
On the bright and distant shore.
Don't weep for those beyond the veil;
They will greet us at the door.

Time itself is standing still
For love of Morning Glory
As She climbs that sacred hill
To begin anew Her story.

\*\*\*

# On Dealing with Death
*by Bill Genzoli*

My father, Ronald Genzoli, studied alongside Morning Glory and Oberon. My brother and I were subsequently raised among the two of them as an extended family. There were more than a few of us that would fall into this category over the years. I remember the early days of living on a mountaintop with no access to any of the things we grew up expecting; but we had our Mother — along with some guitars, drums, and each other — which was enough to get us by. In later years, I find myself remembering those times as the best in my life.

My brother Daniel was going through a very tough time in his life. I had no idea exactly how tough it was as our talks, though almost every day, never dwelled on the negatives each of us was going through. We were the positive in each other's lives. Though we were over a thousand miles apart, we maintained a closeness that would help each other over the years.

My brother checked himself into a local hotel room in a rather bad part of Southern California one day when his depression and anxiety were at an all-time high as he and his wife struggled with family issues. Two days after, he put together a shopping list of items that would be used to take his own life later on that evening. I cannot describe to you the impact suicide has on those who become labeled as Suicide Survivors, as they are left behind in the wake of this person's decision. Simply put, it shattered me to my core. The tattered pieces of myself I find I am still picking up to this day.

Earlier, I had found that Morning Glory had passed away. My heart yearned to be there at Annwfn for the service, but I could not. Annwfn was another home we stayed at while Gwydion Pendderwen was still with us. Gwydion had acted as yet a third father for my brother and I as we grew up. The death of Morning Glory and the struggles of Oberon would later provide me with a means of understanding and coping with what I would come to when my brother passed away.

These past few years have been...transformational. I am simply not the person I was three years ago before any of this happened. I saw this man, twice my age, dealing with a loss so profound that even he, with his internal strength, was having difficulty grasping how he would continue his work. It made me question my own self. When Daniel passed away, my friends came together, and with Oberon's blessing, they paid all of the expenses there were to scatter my brother, my father, and my two fur babies among the remains of Morning Glory. Oberon allowed me the honor of scattering them in the only place I really knew as 'Home.'

I simply do not have words for the feeling I have for that man for this gesture...

This past year I saw Oberon challenged yet again, saw him have this incredible weight put again on his shoulders when their son passed away. Their son was not much older than I am. But, yet again, this man rose out of these ashes and continued on down the path. This year I have questioned my own sanity and have been in such a dark place that I tried to take my own life. It was not until I recalled every single thing people like Oberon have gone through, that give me a glimmer of hope that I might very well be able to get through this myself.

I struggle with my own 'demons' daily; however, it is in these times that I remember that it is OK not to be OK. And also, that there are people who are struggling like I am but are making the choice of moving past instead of giving in. While I did not allow myself the luxury of feeling depression (or worse) the crushing anxiety that now is a part of my daily life I do own.

What this has done for me spiritually is that it has gotten me in closer contact with Oberon. So much so that I have enrolled in his online school. Now the highlights of my day are filled with the knowledge of him, his works, and the works of others — providing an inner calm that medication, group therapy, and counseling simply did not provide. If I am anything, let me be proof that none of us suffers alone — even though at times the tunnel seems long, dark, and crushing — there is light at the end of it. One step, however small, is still a step. That is how I get through my day and I owe it to the reminder of one man whom I hold dearest to my soul.

\*\*\*

# On Death, Dying, and the Rituals of Passing
By Bran th'Blessed (Samm Dickens)

I lost my dear wife, Rebecca Ann Dickens, in 2013. She died on July the 5$^{th}$ at the age of 60, some 24 days before her next birthday, but that was not when I lost her — that was when we finally brought her peace and surcease of pain. She had entered the hospital on May the 16$^{th}$, two days after our 21$^{st}$ wedding anniversary, due to a sudden and undetermined illness. The time between her hospitalization and her death was an ordeal for her that I will not detail. But death came gentle and was welcomed as a saviour. My Becky couldn't talk, but she smiled when we told her that we were taking her off life support on doctor's recommendation.

At the time of her illness, we had already discussed the possibilities of our deaths (singly or together) many times. We had agreed that neither of us wanted to be kept alive if our mental acuity was severely damaged. We had discussed how we wanted our bodies disposed of — both of us choosing cremation. And we had discussed our will along with the disposition of our meagre properties and our animals. I had planned to be buried but Becky preferred cremation and, in our discussions, we decided both to be cremated, have our ashes blended together and thus buried. We even decided to have our little dog's ashes added to our own, symbolically to combine our lives and destinies together hereafter. When each of us dies, there is to be no funeral service — only a Wake to be held in our memory, a festive and upbeat affair with a minimum of sorrow and tears. We did this for Becky on her birthday at our daughter's home.

These wakes must be times of celebration, times to realize the life we shared with our loved one, both the good times we enjoyed and the hard times we endured together. We do not believe the spirit/soul dies. It returns to our Mother Earth, from whom it has come, and experiences an afterlife in the spirit world. Then, rejuvenated and purified, it is incarnated into yet another life in an unending cycle of rebirths. We do not grieve at the end of lives; we only grieve the loss of dearly beloved friends from our own lives. We celebrate their legacy and cheer them on their way, confidant that we will meet again and forever along the cosmic paths we follow. This is the attitude and atmosphere of our wakes. Joyful celebrations of our loved ones.

I know that Becky has communicated with me somehow across that veil between the spirit world and the physical world. There is no division, you see. We are in both worlds while incarnate, and in the spirit world alone between incarnations. Our lives are mortal and apart, but our spirit is one and forever. I have come to understand this most clearly since my Becky's death. She has told me what the spirit world, our Summerlands, is like. I understand now what intuition truly is: the voice of the spirit. This voice whispers from the heart and guides us through our lives. It is our conscience, our character, our potential, our motivation, and our creative spark. All of this is spirit speaking to us through intuition.

And I am learning more from that voice all the time. My imagination and insight have blossomed since my darling's death. The bond of love cannot be broken and she whispers to me intuitively in some silent language that one feels rather than hears. Nor am I alone in experiencing this marvellous phenomenon. Many others will relay similar messages. The veil is sheer and it is only our moribund physicality that blurs our vision and prevents us from seeing through it. Jesus told his disciples that the Kingdom of Heaven was not someplace far away, but was all around them. If he were talking about the spirit world, as is likely, I know precisely what he meant.

It is my understanding that we live all of our lives in three realms; the physical universe that we share with other conscious beings (which we may call the realm of the world) is only the most obvious of these realms. Here our bodies exist as objects in space and our actions are the agents of change.

The second realm is another place, a place beyond places, where the mind has its home — we cannot touch it or see it because it is not located in space, but we know its every activity, its thoughts and emotions, imagination and dreams, memories and intuitions, hopes and fears. This we call the realm of the mind, the realm of time, the realm in which consciousness itself has its seat.

And finally, there is the realm of spirit — the foundational realm, the realm of existence and potential that is beyond both place and time, the ground of all being, the seed from which both the roots (mind) and trunk (body) of the tree arise. The DNA of our bodies is a physical expression of our spirit; our character and values are mental expressions of our spirit. But spirit itself is deeply hidden within the unmoving center. Spirit speaks to us through the heart and thus, the heart is master of us all.

Her loss has taken from me more than her presence in my life. She never wanted to lose our home — it meant the world to her. Her loss was also the loss of our home, although I'm glad we had it until she died.

I had to abandon our home of 21 years, the home in which we lived our married lives and raised our kids. I also had to abandon most of its contents, most of the library of books and tapes and CDs and DVDs. So much lost, so much of her life and work gone, and I swear she was an amazing human being! I underwent a huge change in my life.

But the vacuum of that chaos has been filled by new circumstances that are better, new friends around me, new opportunities. In my life at least, good has almost always come from bad. My wife and I knew many desperate days, but we worked through them; what else could we do? And we were brought to better days. The same is true for me now. I am happy. But I have come to accept that I can no longer do what I once could, that I can no longer be what I once was, that I am an old man, with illnesses that seem content to bide their time in killing me. I live in pain and will find Death as kind a stranger as my wife found her when at last she comes to free me from this dwindling and weary incarnation. Oh, I still have something to contribute in my words and my wisdom, but I cannot choose who will listen and who will turn away. I am an old man waiting for Death to come to me and take me, at long last, home again; I hope she is not offended that I will not walk to greet her.

\*\*\*

# On the Death of an Infant
*by Raven Kelso*

Many years ago, almost 27 now, my six-week-old daughter died at home from sudden infant death syndrome. At the time I was a working paramedic and was just looking at going back to work from maternity leave. My husband and I had two older daughters — one was just about to turn five years old and the other was not quite three. We had discussed the possibility of having another child, but had not actually decided we wanted one, when surprise! I was found to be pregnant. She was born five and a half weeks early, but in good health with no ill effects from being born early. In fact, she was the largest of all of my kids.

Due to the trauma of finding my baby no longer living I really cannot tell you what her services where like nor how they were done, as my family took care of the arrangements. What I can tell you is how her death affected me, and how I found my way through it. I can also tell you how I continued to live on.

First, I would like to tell you how I managed to get past her death. For around the first six to seven months I pretty much stayed in a fog and just went about day-to-day life because of the two older children. What brought me out of the fog was finding out that I was pregnant again just short of the first anniversary of her birth. Once this was confirmed I can tell you that I was scared. Not wanting to risk the same thing happening again, but with the help of my husband I slowly came to terms with this.

As that pregnancy progressed I came to realize that the baby I was carrying had a purpose that only the Goddess could know. She had to be born and that would not have happened if her sister had not come to us when she did and then went Home to be with the Goddess when she did. She gave us the desire to have one more child, but she was not the child that needed to be born to us. Once the idea of having three instead of two children was firmly fixed in both mine and my husband's minds, her purpose was served and the Goddess called her Home so she could continue on learning what she needed. While I am still not sure what the Goddess has in mind for my youngest daughter, I firmly believe that either her or one of her offspring are destined to do great things.

Each day I look at my daughter or one of her sons I thank my daughter who brought her to us. It will always be if not for Amanda, then there would be no Molly or Roanin or Murphy. I have used what I learned from her to help others who have lost infants or children. I firmly believe what a friend said when his young daughter died. He didn't need outside counseling because he knew he could survive this because I survived it and that is the best counseling you can get. I help others by example and by simply living each day.

\*\*\*

# The Passing of a Son
### *by Oberon Zell*

Today is Wednesday, October 19, 2016, and I'm in Califia. Yesterday, my son Bryan was visited in the Florida hospice by a wonderful local Pagan Priestess named Doreen Lavista. She knew Morning Glory and me, and she gave Bryan his Last Rites. After that he seemed relaxed and peaceful as he hadn't been in months.

Last night, we watched a very magickal movie called *Interstate 60*. At one point in the film, the moon was seen in the sky, and I noticed that it was exactly the same phase as the actual moon was that night. Then later in the movie, a significant calendar date was shown: "Tuesday, Oct. 18." Which of course was yesterday. And October 18 only falls on a Tuesday once every 7 or 8 years, to say nothing of the correspondence of moon phase! Two such synchronicities called for paying attention — and looking for the next one.

After the movie, as we headed off to our respective beds, I noticed that the consecrated blue "Dreamwalker" candle we had burning for Bryan on the ancestor altar had gone out. I tried to relight it, but the wick would not ignite. I said to Anne, "I can't seem to relight it."

She replied, "Perhaps you don't need to." And we knew. I immediately called the hospice, told them I was Bryan's father, and that I had an intuit that he had just passed. It was 10:55pm my time (PST), and thus 1:55am in Florida. The duty nurse said she would go check on him, and put me on hold. I waited, but she never returned to pick up the phone, and soon it went dead.

Shortly thereafter I got the call from Bryan's best friend Dana Hall, who told me that Bryan had passed peacefully at the very time I called, and that an enormous owl had simultaneously appeared at Bryan's window. According to Dana:

"Hospice said they never before had any family call at the same exact time a loved one had just passed. They also said they never before saw any owl at this Hospice House and again, this owl was huge."

Morning Glory, as a devotee of Hecate, particularly related to owls as Hecate's bird. Indeed, during our long involvement with Wildlife Rescue, we had a male Great Horned Owl named Archimedes living with us for eight years. To be as huge as Dana reported, this one would have had to have been a female (the females are much larger than the males, and they are a worldwide species). So, I believe that was a visit from Morning Glory herself, come to escort her beloved stepson over the Rainbow Bridge.

The next day, when Morning Glory's granddaughter Alessa returned from school, her mother (Morning Glory's daughter) told Alessa that her beloved Uncle Bryan had left his body the night before, and that a huge owl had appeared at his hospital window at the moment of his passing. Alessa spontaneously responded, "That was Grandma coming to take him home!"

Let these memories lessen grief. What is remembered, lives.

\*\*\*

## Death of a Mother
*by Valerie D. Dillon*

I feel the need to preface this with the fact that my Mother, Dee, had been very sick off and on for several years and in and out of the hospital. She was also bedbound (wheelchair).

It was about mid-June (give or take) of 2013, when she was getting kind of bad and I could not do anything more for her. Finally, one day when I was cleaning her and trying to change her linens, I discovered she was literally stuck to the mattress...she had developed bed sores overnight. She screamed in pain, it was almost her whole back...so red and torn. It killed me to see her in so much pain...I had to get over the "this is my Mommy" and force myself into "this is my patient" mode... When the ambulance got there it took some time and maneuvering to get her off her bed and onto a stretcher with as little pain as we could manage.

In the ER, she was treated with all kinds of fluids, catheter, etc. All the usual we always dealt with. I had kept talking to her about fighting and staying with me, I couldn't live without her...she was my Mother, Friend, and Soul Mate.

Fast forward to July 24th... I was there for my daily visit. Mom was not really aware of anything since being admitted. She was intubated. They knew she had a major infection, but had been able to find the origin, it was basically everywhere. So all they could do so far was keep her breathing, her kidneys had started to shut down, so she was on dialysis 24/7.

When I got there on the 24th, I combed her hair. it had gotten tangled being so long in bed, held her hand and talked. I got up for water and by the time I turned around, alarms started to go off. A lot of people rushed in and I was guided out. As I stood outside her door, I saw someone get on top of her to start CPR. That is when I started to hyperventilate and someone took me away to the nurses break room a few doors down. I sort of remember a nurse staying with me, trying to get my breathing under control. It seems like it was hours, but I am guessing only minutes. A doc came and told me that they got her heart started again, but it was really hard. They had maxed out the blood pressure meds they could give her and told me my options.

Finally, I made the decision that the next time her heart stopped they needed to let her go.

Teresa went to the room with me once I was able to go back. That's when I told Mama that it was OK for her to go, to let go and be where she needed to be. That I would see her over the Bridge when my time came, we *would* be together again and that I would be OK in this life...she needed to not worry about me anymore.

The nurse said they would call me with any news...it was just a matter of time before her poor heart gave up. I left around 4:40-5 pm to go home. I still have no idea how I made it home, I was so numb... retreating inside myself like I used to...

At 7:03 pm, I got the call...she passed at exactly 7pm on July 24, 2013. I sobbed...that's all I remember of that night and a few days... I do remember waking up the next day and upset that the world just went on, it seemed like nothing had changed but it all had...at least for me.

It gets a bit dark from there...but I did come out of it...it still hurts horribly and will always, but I survived.

**Arrangements:** Mom had never wanted anything big, just wanted to be cremated. Since it was just me and her, there was no viewing or funeral. She was simply cremated in a card board box and her ashes placed in a simple wooden box, kept out at home with her amethyst Buddha on it, until I find the perfect urn for her. I did place an obituary in the paper, so anyone reading the paper (estranged family, friends, etc.) would see it, if they wanted.

**Coping/Surviving/Living:** The first several months were very hard, dealing with arrangements, estate crap, and stuff I had never had to deal with before. But each day I just let the knowledge sink into me, kept telling myself I could do it, that she was with me and always would be. I know that, I can feel that. I did use my pendulum to talk to her at times, other times (and I still do this) I just talk to her anyway. If I really need an answer, I wait for a signal or feeling of some kind, I have always been a little empathic. Sometimes are harder — her birthday, death day, certain songs, etc... will make me cry and dwell, but each day, each month, and each year gets little easier to live. I know she would not want me to do anything stupid like feel guilty. We talked a lot about it before she passed. I also have my own very informal rituals, like talking to her, lighting candles, energy pulling, self-healing, crystals, and affirmations/mini spells that keep her close to my heart, make me feel she is here when I need her.

Awhile after she passed, I sat myself down and did a personal inventory of what I wanted. I felt I was ready for love to return to my life, whatever form it took, though I mainly concentrated on romantic love. I was ready to accept into my life what I wanted, needed, and deserved.

Soon after that I met my current boyfriend. October this year will be our 3-year anniversary. I am also a step mom to his seven year old son who lives with us...so I keep busy and have gone back into the caretaker mode I am so used to and so good at, even if it is frustrating at times. Men/boys are SO messy!! They help me live, help me stay in the moment. And my boyfriend's family has taken me in as their daughter and sister.

**Spiritual Path:** I feel my belief system has somehow solidified more with her passing, kind of like becoming an orphan (how it felt) and becoming an adult at the same time, even though I was in my late 30's when she passed. Believe me some days I really HATE being an adult, but here I am, 41 and coming into who I was always meant to be.

**What was taken from me:** My heart — it will never fully heal, and my best friend — Mom had always been my best friend and I could talk to her about anything. I have always had a hard time getting close to and opening up fully to anyone. She is (was) the only person who knew me the most, totally (with very few exceptions). I am pretty open with my boyfriend but it's not the same. I feel still like part of my soul is missing.

**Lessons Learned:** That I am capable of taking care of myself, that I can go on, it does get better, that I am in control of how my life can go, but also that there is a "Fate" — a meant to be. I have believed for a long time that no one passes "too soon" and we all go exactly when we are supposed to in order to further our learning in this life and our loved ones in the next life.

***

# Suicide of a Father
*by James "Raven" Stefanowicz*

It was in the spring of 2015 that my father committed suicide. His life had never been easy, and seemingly unbeatable battles constantly raged within him. After finding out that he was expecting two twin boys in the fall, he fell into old habits that eventually led to the entrapment of reason. He took his life with a hunting rifle and remained on life support until my family and I had to make the decision to disconnect him. Considering I had lost two of my friends to suicide prior to this, I had some understanding of what to expect in terms of the aftermath.

The relationship between my father and I had never been one of fluidity. There were many years in which his drug abuse led to voluntary estrangement, and there were many things that I simply could not bring myself to offer him forgiveness for. But throughout even these things, a reciprocation of love remained ever present.

He was always my father, and I his son. As my family and I held vigil at the trauma center, awaiting the doctors to eventually unplug his life support, I realized that the Gods had gifted me with a rare gift: a chance at resolution. It was then that I had everyone leave the room so that I could have a moment alone with my father. I stood at his bedside and cried over him, I kissed him, and then I did what seemed at the time to be the easiest thing I've ever done. I forgave him.

To satisfy the dictations of his religious customs and those of my paternal grandparents, a Catholic Mass was held to honor his passing. The ceremony was beautiful—bound together by a web of shared memories, warm embraces, fond farewells, and beautiful music. But while the majority of those around me accepted the service as the "last goodbye," to me it was just the beginning of what would be a much longer and much less solemn journey.

As a Pagan, my beliefs about death greatly differ from those shared by my predominantly Christian family. Throughout the duration of the bereavement process, the attempted words of solace most often spoken were ones allocating his spirit to "Heaven." And while it brought me great joy knowing that this concept aided in the emotional healing of so many of my friends and family, I had already found peace in my own spirituality. It is my belief that when we die our human bonds are loosed, allowing our spirits to become a part of the communion of energy that permeates all things. I also believe that the part of the spirit containing the human consciousness breaks away, embarking on the journey of whatever afterlife is applicable.

The night of my father's death I performed a solitary ritual of transcendence in commemoration of his life. I reminisced on memories we had made, called on my ancestors to welcome him, raised many glasses to honor him, and held candlelit vigil with his picture in hand. At the heart of the ritual, was the veneration of the Gods. Throughout my entire life thus far, the Gods have always been there for me. This situation was no different. They came to me in one of the darkest moments of my life, and comforted me so that I could comfort others. Quite honestly had it not been for them as well as the convictions of my faith, I do not think I would have gotten through any of it.

When asked how I manage to go on living without him, my answer is really very simple. When he died, he did not just evaporate up into a kingdom of clouds. He became all, and all became him. I feel his love in the sunrise, his kiss on the spring breeze, his voice in the crashing waves and his spirit in all that is beautiful. He never really left me; he became an even bigger part of me. And my relationship with him now is stronger than it was while he was alive. As a Pagan, I honor him (along with my other ancestors) regularly, and communicate with him freely. Now, there are no "ins and outs." He is with me always, and he lives in me. Love is stronger than death.

***

## Loss of a loved one...
### by Gypsy Ravish

That's a hard road. Very personal. Grief, mind numbing, gut wrenching grief. Some people believe in seven stages, I have not found that to be the way it was for me, but, as I said, each person's journey through the waters of sorrow and grief is personal. There is no right way to mourn, though many cultures have well-worn paths of custom and expected behaviors. There is no wrong way to mourn, though sometimes friends have confided in me that they are full of regret for how they are reacting to the loss of their loved ones. We know there is no death. The soul is eternal. We are in our mortal forms for time, then, out through the key hole. Doesn't mean we don't miss them though. We miss our good friends, our family, our lovers, our husbands, our wives, our children, our sweet pets. I have found that in addition to missing some one, what I miss most is "us."

# Part II
# The Passage of the Soul

## The Garden of Proserpina
By Charles Algernon Swinburne (1837-1909)

*Here, where the world is quiet;*
*Here, where all trouble seems*
*Dead winds' and spent waves' riot*
*In doubtful dreams of dreams;*
*I watch the green field growing*
*For reaping folk and sowing,*
*For harvest-time and mowing,*
*A sleepy world of streams.*

*I am tired of tears and laughter,*
*And men that laugh and weep;*
*Of what may come hereafter*
*For men that sow to reap:*
*I am weary of days and hours,*
*Blown buds of barren flowers,*
*Desires and dreams and powers*
*And everything but sleep*

*Here life has death for neighbour,*
*And far from eye or ear*
*Wan waves and wet winds labour,*
*Weak ships and spirits steer;*
*They drive adrift, and whither*
*They wot not who make thither;*
*But no such winds blow hither,*
*And no such things grow here.*

*No growth of moor or coppice,*
*No heather-flower or vine,*
*But bloomless buds of poppies,*
*Green grapes of Proserpine,*
*Pale beds of blowing rushes*
*Where no leaf blooms or blushes*
*Save this whereout she crushes*
*For dead men deadly wine.*

Pale, without name or number,
In fruitless fields of corn,
They bow themselves and
    slumber
All night till light is born;
And like a soul belated,
In hell and heaven unmated,
By cloud and mist abated
Comes out of darkness morn.

Though one were strong as seven,
He too with death shall dwell,
Nor wake with wings in heaven,
Nor weep for pains in hell;
Though one were fair as roses,
His beauty clouds and closes;
And well though love reposes,
In the end it is not well.

Pale, beyond porch and portal,
Crowned with calm leaves, she
    stands
Who gathers all things mortal
With cold immortal hands;
Her languid lips are sweeter
Than love's who fears to greet her
To men that mix and meet her
From many times and lands.

She waits for each and other,
She waits for all men born;
Forgets the Earth her mother,
The life of fruits and corn;
And spring and seed and
    swallow
Take wing for her and follow
Where summer song rings
    hollow
And flowers are put to scorn.

There go the loves that wither,
The old loves with wearier wings;
And all dead years draw thither,
And all disastrous things;
Dead dreams of days forsaken,
Blind buds that snows have
    shaken,
Wild leaves that winds have
    taken,
Red strays of ruined springs.

We are not sure of sorrow,
And joy was never sure;
To-day will die to-morrow;
Time stoops to no man's lure;
And love, grown faint and fretful,
With lips but half regretful
Sighs, and with eyes forgetful
Weeps that no loves endure.

From too much love of living,
From hope and fear set free,
We thank with brief thanksgiving
Whatever gods may be
That no life lives forever;
That dead men rise up never;
That even the weariest river
Winds somewhere safe to sea.

Then star nor sun shall waken,
Nor any change of light:
Nor sound of waters shaken,
Nor any sound or sight:
Nor wintry leaves nor vernal,
Nor days nor things diurnal;
Only the sleep eternal
In an eternal night

# Chapter 4
# Death Customs & Folklore around the World

*It's the Blood of the Ancients that flows through our veins,
And the forms pass, but the Circle of Life remains.*
~~Ellen Klaver

OMENS OF DEATH ARE EXTREMELY common across cultures and time, and many of these involve animals. Dogs in particular are thought to have a peculiar sense of approaching death, and it is thought that in cases of sickness, they know the outcome ahead of time. If a dog howls persistently under your window, it foreshadows a death in the house.

## Birds and Bees; Beasts and Trees

In Romanian villages, harbingers of impending death in a household include a rooster suddenly starting to cluck like a hen, a dog howling in the yard, or an owl hooting in a tree close to the house.

In Germany, if a black cat sits on the bed of a sick person, it is a sign that they will die. The meowing of a black cat at midnight is a sure sign of coming death. And if a black cat crosses in front of a funeral procession, someone in the family of the deceased will die in three days.

If a bird flies into your house, there will soon be a death in the family. One of the surer omens of death is a bird entering the bedroom of a sick person and landing on the bedpost.

A white bird or a black crow flying against a window at night foretells of a death in the house within a year. A pigeon flying against the window is a sign of death.

Seeing six crows is a sign of impending death. (Seeing two crows is witnessing an attempted murder...) Some believe that a whippoorwill singing near the house is an omen of death, while others believe it just means trouble will come.

If you walk under a tree in the evening and an owl hoots right above your head, it means a relative or friend of yours will die within a year. If an owl hoots while perched on your rooftop, death will pay a visit. Some parts of the world say that an owl simply hooting in the neighborhood is foreshadowing death nearby.

If bees swarm a rotten tree, there will be a death in the family owning or living on the property within a year. Likewise, bees swarming a house are a sign of coming doom.

A white rabbit crossing your path is an omen of death and seeing two white rabbits together at night means a death in the family.

If a cedar tree that you have planted dies in your yard, a member of your family will die. Also, death will come to the man who moves a cedar tree, once the lower limbs grow to the length of the coffin.

## Black Butterflies

The meaning and symbolism of black butterflies changes from one culture to another, but they are usually seen as a sign of impending doom and death, especially in places such as Brazil, Colombia, Central America, as well as China. Spotting a black butterfly in the house supposedly means that a member of that household will die, although on rare occasions black butterflies may appear in the house after a family member has already died.

Butterflies represent the souls of the dead among the ancient Greeks, Etruscans, Romans, and Celts. When deceased persons fail to find their place in the afterlife, they turn into black butterflies and return to the places they used to live.

In Mexico, the Black Witch moth is known as the "butterfly of death." It is believed that when the butterfly of death enters a sick person's house, that person will die. In southern Texas, however, it is believed that a death occurs only if the butterfly visits all four corners of the house. In Hawaii, a black butterfly is considered an embodiment of a loved one who has come to say goodbye. [14]

---

[14] 10 Eerie Omens of Death, http://listverse.com/2016/05/10/10-eerie-omens-of-death/ accessed 10/13/17

## At Death's Door

There are many superstitions surrounding the removal of a body from the home. The deceased was always taken out feet first in the coffin so that the dead could not look back at its home and the spirit remain inside the house. Many houses of the mid-to-late Victorian period had a special niche called a "coffin corner" cut into the stairwell so that the coffin could make the turn in the flight of stairs by fitting the head of the coffin into this little niche shelf. Some old homes also have a showcase window in the front of the house, a sort of bay window where the deceased could lie in honor for people to pass by on the street and pay their respects.

The expression "at death's door" is applied to someone so ill as to be at the very brink of death. In ancient tombs and modern funeral statuary in cemeteries, a door is often used as the symbol for passing through the portal from Life to another state. Arches, windows, and portals carry the same meaning.

Sometimes in remote rural homes, a door was used to lay the body upon when carrying it downstairs (as most died in upstairs bedrooms). Boards made of wide planks of wood or caned surfaces were used as "cooling boards" to lay out the body during autopsy or embalming before placing the deceased in a casket or coffin. [15]

## Food

Food has always been an important element of funeral customs around the world. We would think that food would be of no interest to the dead, but in fact food was often put into the grave; presumably so that the dead would not starve during their long journey to the Afterlife. Tombs were often stocked with imperishable "food" made of stone or clay; it wouldn't go bad, and the dead would not know the difference.

Roma mourners place food and drink into the casket as it is lowered, and spill beer into the grave before it is filled in. There are as many traditions as there are tribes, but one of the largest

---

[15] Friends of Oak Grove Cemetery, https://friendsofoakgrovecemetery.org/category/victorian-funeral-symbolism/ accessed 10/13/17

Roma tribes is the Kalderash tribe. Within the Kalderash, the close family of the deceased are only allowed water, coffee, and brandy until the grave—and its body—receive food first. This is so the *mulo,* or spirit, of the deceased is not jealous of its living family. This can cause the mulo to become stuck on the physical side of the veil. Only after the deceased has "eaten" does the family eat, and a big feast is held. This feast is called a *Pomana.* It occurs on the day of the funeral, six weeks after, six months after, and again on the one-year anniversary of their beloved's passing. This last feast is when the family officially stops mourning.

Etruscan tombs had elaborate scenes of feasting painted on the inside walls featuring banquet tables laden with fine foods and pitchers of wine. Some of the paintings even depicted the deceased having rowdy sex! A table and chairs would also be set up, so that the families could visit and feast with their dearly departed. And many cultures actually hold the funerary feast at the graveside.

Some cultures even went so far as to place a tube into the mouth of the corpse leading up from the grave to the surface so that they could continue to receive nourishment as long as someone continued pouring food (or drink) down the tube!

Feasting has been a universal staple after funerals, as one of the best ways to know you are alive is by your enjoyment of food (along with sex, of course!). Lisa Rogak's delightful book, *Death Warmed Over,* is a compilation of funeral recipes and customs from 75 different cultures.

In Poland it is customary during the 13 days from Christmas eve through Epiphany to set out meals for the dead at the place where they sat in life at the family table.

Bretons set out a dish of butter when a person dies from cancer, so that the illness will go into the butter rather than into another member of the household. The butter is then buried outside.

Speaking of butter, in northern India, the Moslem Badaga sect forces the dying person to eat. If he cannot swallow, they will dip a coin into butter and place it in his mouth. This is called the rite of coin butter, or *hana benne,* believed to be necessary not only to buy food and drink in the afterlife, but also to pay the toll on the journey (as with the coins for the ferryman in Greece). The butter is to give him strength for the trip. If he chokes on the coin, it just speeds things along.

And one of the more obscure omens of death comes from early settlers of Pennsylvania, who believed that if the clock struck 12 during lunch, and fresh bread was being served, it meant impending death. [16]

## Grave Goods

As with food, grave goods have been buried with the dead in every culture since the earliest recorded burials. These are most commonly jewelry, eating utensils, and other personal items that belonged to the deceased in life. In modern Italian villages, everything from candy and cigarettes to jars of antipasto may go into the casket with the deceased. But more elaborate burials in ancient times have contained tools, furniture, chariots, and treasure. Among the ruling classes, even pets, horses, widows and slaves would be sacrificed and buried—presumably to continue their service in the Afterlife.

Indeed, it seems to have been the custom in many ancient civilizations—from Egyptians to Chinese to Vikings—to bury the entire national treasury along with the deceased ruler! Consider the treasures of King Tut's tomb. This meant that such treasures needed to be amassed during the lifetime of the ruler by constant raids and warfare—and the next chief, king, emperor, or pharaoh would begin their reign in poverty (along with the nation), and would have to embark upon their own lifelong campaigns of conquest and looting. Thus, tomb robbing became a lucrative and essential profession—made easier, I'm sure, by the spectacular monuments erected over the tombs to show the robbers where to dig.

One widespread funeral custom is for the bereaved to cut a long braided lock of their hair and place it into the casket.

## Earth laid upon a Corpse

An old funeral rite from the Scottish Highlands is to bury the deceased with a wooden plate resting on his chest. In the plate were placed a small amount of earth and salt, to represent the future of

---

[16] Superstition Dictionary, http://superstitiondictionary.com/omens-of-death-folklore-and-superstition/ accessed 10/13/17

the deceased. The earth hinted that the body would decay and become one with the earth, while the salt represented the soul, which does not decay. This rite was known as "earth laid upon a corpse." This practice was also carried out in Ireland, as well as in parts of England, particularly in Leicestershire, although in England the salt was intended to prevent air from distending the corpse.

## Saved by the Bell

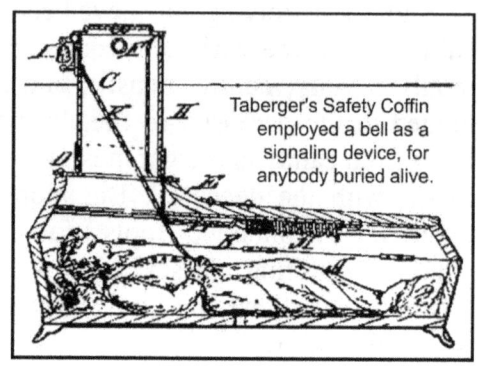

Taberger's Safety Coffin employed a bell as a signaling device, for anybody buried alive.

It is popularly believed that the expression "saved by the bell" originally related to people being buried alive. The idea was that, if someone were comatose and mistakenly pronounced dead and interred, they could, if they later revived, ring a bell that was attached to the coffin and be saved. The idea is certainly plausible as *Taphophobia*, the fear of being buried alive, was and is real.

Just as real were the devices themselves, several of which were patented in Victorian England and the USA. Known as "safety coffins," several designs were registered in the 19th century and up to as late as 1955. However, there is no evidence that anyone was ever saved by these coffins or even that they were ever put to use.

In fact, the expression "saved by the bell" is boxing slang from the late 19th century. A boxer in danger of losing a bout can be saved from defeat by the bell that marks the end of a round. [17]

# Ghosts

Among the Kaingang tribe of Brazil, it is believed that the ghost of the deceased will hang around after death to claim a helpmate —

---

[17] The Phrase Finder, https://www.phrases.org.uk/meanings/saved-by-the-bell.html accessed 11/2/17

usually the widow or widower. To prevent this, the surviving spouse is cast out of the village for a time, then purified before returning so that the ghost will not recognize him or her, prompting the spirit to wander off, never to return. During their exile, the spouse may not eat cooked food, but must subsist on raw veggies and honey. They must kill an animal and smear its blood over their body to confuse the ghost.

In Iceland, if a persistent ghost continued to annoy the family, they would open the grave, decapitate the corpse, and place its head under its buttocks. That way the ghost couldn't tell its head from its ass, and could not figure how go out haunting.

In Eastern Europe, when funerals were conducted at home, the body would always be positioned with their feet towards the door (preferably the western door), and would be carried out feet-first. When the dying person came close to drawing their final breath, the windows would be opened to let the soul escape. In Hungary, however, all the closet doors would be shut after death to prevent the ghost from hiding in them. Perhaps failure to do so is why so many children are afraid of a ghost in their bedroom closet!

If a ghost or spirit becomes depressed and eventually dies this loss of joy takes the personality down. Getting joy back or "en-joyment" allows the entity to rise up to be born back into the ghost realm and eventually into the physical.

If a person perishes whilst manically depressed or commits suicide, it can pass quickly through the ghost realm to the shade and shadow realm. This is where we get our myths of Purgatory or Tartarus. It is a dark realm in that it there is not much light. The individual consciousness blocks out the light of hope. The individual can dwell here a long time lost in the isolation of its sadness. It is a lonely and lost place. Lighting a candle for such ones and sending them your love can help to light their way home.

### Hungry Ghosts

The Hungry Ghost Festival, *Yulan* or simply *Bon* (Spirit) is a traditional festival held in Asian countries. The Ghost Festival is held on the 15$^{th}$ night (Ghost Day) of the seventh month (Ghost Month) in the Chinese lunar calendar. On this day spirits are allowed to wander the living realm. Everywhere the smell of sandalwood incense fills the air. In every street, large feasts are held for the dead to show respect and to propitiate them. The living show that they are still concerned for those on the other side and are willing to take care of their desires by burning joss paper, or paper-mâché models of material items such as clothes, gold and houses.

It is believed that malcontented spirits long for the pleasures of this world. What is most missed is the ability to enjoy eating. Great elaborate feasts are placed in the streets in front of businesses and larger private homes, with empty seats for the deceased. At the family meal for the night, the deceased are treated as if they are still living. Paper effigies of beautiful homes are set up near these feasts for the spirit to inhabit. An enormous amount of paper replica money, called 'Ghost Money,' is burned to add to the deceased's spiritual bank account. Other festivities include releasing miniature paper lotus lanterns on water, giving directions to the lost ghosts and spirits of the ancestors and other deities to flow on with joy. (— She' D'Montford)

## The Ghost Bride

The most curious and ultimate act of concern is the tradition of the "Ghost Bride." In Chinese tradition, a ghost marriage (*mínghūn;* literally: "spirit marriage") is a marriage in which one or both parties are deceased. Forms of ghost marriage are practiced worldwide, from the Sudan to France.

Chinese ghost marriages are set up by the family of the deceased and performed for a number of reasons, including the marriage of a couple that were engaged before one member's death. Then the potential groom could make sure that his potential bride had no disadvantages, in this world or the next. Or a ghost marriage may simply be arranged to ensure that the elder brother marries first, especially if the younger brother is soon to be married.

If a son dies before marriage, his parents may arrange a ghost marriage to provide him with progeny to continue the lineage and give him his own descendants. Often the family will pay someone an ongoing annuity to assume the wifely roles of bereavement after death. There is a marriage ceremony and then she mourns him like a widow and is obligated to take care of him, his grave, his memory, and his reputation forever after — even if she remarries. The family is then also obligated to take care of her and her family.

**Citipati** is a protector deity or *Dharmapala* in Tibetan Buddhism and Vajrayana Buddhism of the Himalayas. It is formed of two skeletons, one male and the other female, both dancing wildly with their limbs intertwined inside a halo of flames representing change. They symbolize both the eternal dance of death as well as perfect awareness. The Citipati is a protector of graveyards and is known as Lord of the Cemetery. They are invoked as wrathful deities; benevolent protectors of fierce appearance. The dance of the Citipati is commemorated twice annually in Tibet.

## Festivals honoring the Beloved Dead

**Samhain** (Nov. 1-7): Among the ancient Celts, *Samhain*—the festival of "Summer's End"—was held for seven days to commemorate the death of Belenos, the Sun-God, and prepare for his journey to *Tir-fo-Thonn*, the land under the sea, where he would then reign as Lord of the Dead through the winter season.

Celtic wakes were held for seven days and seven nights. The body would be washed with sea water for the journey to Tir-fo-Thonn.

Samhain is the opposite hinge of the year from Beltane, and is the Celtic New Year, marking the beginning of the Winter half of the year. Bonfires were lit and blazing straw from the fire was carried through the villages and over the fields to drive away any remnants of the old year.

The central rite of Samhain is the "dumb supper," eaten in silence, and shared with the beloved dead whose names are called in invitation and memory. An empty place is set at the table, and living relatives honor the departed as though they were at dinner with them. One plate of food is prepared for the dead, and afterwards taken outside — ideally left on a grave. Many Samhain traditions are popularly retained in Hallowe'en customs.

**Hallowe'en** (Oct. 31): (also **All Hallows' Eve** or **All Saints' Eve**), is Christianized version of the old Gaelic *Samhain*. This is the time when the veil between the worlds is thinnest and old graves are tidied and candles are lit to brighten the dreary existence of the deceased. Activities include trick-or-treating, costume parties, carving pumpkins into jack-o-lanterns, bonfires, apple bobbing, divination games, playing pranks, visiting haunted attractions, telling scary stories, and watching horror films.

**All Saints' Day** (Nov. 1): A Christian festival in honor of all the saints, known and unknown. It is a national holiday in many Catholic countries, giving God solemn thanks for the lives and deaths of his saints, famous or obscure, including individuals who have personally led one to faith in Jesus, such as one's grandmother or friend.

**Dia de los Muertos** (Oct. 31-Nov. 1): The "Day of the Dead" in Mexico and other Latin American countries and cultures is colorful and comforting for both the physical and the ghostly realms. The two-day holiday focuses on gatherings of family and friends to remember and pray for relatives and loved ones who have died, and help support their spiritual journey. Ubiquitous shrines and altars (called *ofrendas*) feature little dioramas of skeletons in lifelike poses, along with sugar skulls, food offerings, and photos of the dear departed. Candles are lit in every room and food and drink are put out for the visiting souls. Marigold blossoms are everywhere, decorating graves and altars.

**Genesia** was celebrated in Ancient Greece in honor of the deceased. The ancestral hero *Epops* was honored at sundown, and libations of wine, milk and honey were poured onto the Earth, holder of the departed.

A festival called **Nemeseia** (by some identified with the **Genesia**) was held at Athens. Its object was to avert the nemesis of the dead, who had the power of punishing the living if their cult had been in any way neglected

**Parentalia** (or *dies parentales,* Latin, "ancestral days") (Feb. 13-21) A nine-day festival held in ancient Rome in honor of family ancestors. Sacred offerings of flower-garlands, wheat, salt, wine-soaked bread, and violets were made to the *Manes* (shades of the dead) at family tombs, located outside Rome's sacred boundary. These observances were meant to strengthen the mutual obligations and protective ties between the living and the dead, and were a lawful duty of the *paterfamilias* (head of the family). Parentalia concluded Feb. 21 in the midnight rites of *Feralia.*

**Feralia** (Feb. 21) was a placation and exorcism culminating the *Parentalia,* when the paterfamilias addressed the malevolent, destructive aspects of his *Manes*. It functioned as a cleansing ritual for *Caristia* on the following day, when the family held an informal banquet to celebrate the amity between themselves and their benevolent ancestral dead (*Lares*).

The **Hungry Ghost Festivals** in Asian countries where food, drink, candles, and other offerings are provided for the spirits of the dead (see above).

**Commemoration of the Dead** is a Russian Pagan holiday to honor dead relatives, held on the second Tuesday after Easter (originally Spring Equinox). The memory of the departed ancestors is honored with foods of grain brought to the memorial mass, and afterwards placed on the ancestral graves: porridge, pancakes, pretzels, and bread.

**Soul Saturdays** are set aside for the commemoration of the dead in the Eastern Orthodox and Byzantine Catholic Churches. Saturday is a traditional day for prayer for the dead, because Christ lay dead in the Tomb on Saturday. These days are devoted to prayer for departed relatives and other faithful who would not be commemorated specifically as saints. There are several Soul Saturdays throughout the year:

- Saturday of Meatfare Week (2$^{nd}$ Saturday before Great Lent)
- The second Saturday of Great Lent
- The third Saturday of Great Lent
- The fourth Saturday of Great Lent
- The Saturday before Pentecost
- **Demetrius Saturday** (the Saturday before the feast of Saint Demetrius of Thessaloniki on October 26).
- In the Bulgarian Orthodox Church a commemoration of the dead is held on the Saturday before the feast of Saint Michael the Archangel on Nov. 8 (instead of the Demetrius Saturday).
- **Radonitsa** (Monday or Tuesday after St. Thomas Sunday, i.e. Second Sunday of Easter)

# Euphemisms for Death

The concept and symptoms of death, and varying degrees of delicacy used in discussion in public forums, have generated numerous scientific, legal, and socially acceptable euphemisms for death.

In Western culture we have found the very concept of death to be so threatening that it has been difficult for us to speak of it directly. Hence it has become customary to speak of death euphemistically, as in "passing." Here is a list of euphemisms that have been invented over the years to avoid actually saying that a person has died. Instead, we say that a dead person is:

A goner
Asleep in Christ
Bereft of life
Deceased
Departed
Done in
Feeling no pain
Hearing the final whistle
In the arms of the Goddess
In the arms of the Mother
In the arms of the Father
In the bosom of Abraham
In the Cauldron of Cerridwen
In Davy Jones' Locker
In the Elysian Fields
In Heaven
In the Land of the Dead
In the Summerlands
In the Underworld
In Valhalla
Lost
On the Other Side
Out of their misery
No longer with us
Pushing up daisies
Resting in peace
Six feet under
Sleeping with the fishes
Stretching out their legs
Taking the Big Sleep
Taking a dirt nap
Taking an early bath
Taking a long sleep
Under water
With the Ancestors
With the Ancient Ones
With the Angels
With the Departed
With the Gods
With the Lady
With the Lord
With the Spirits

*Or that they have...*

Ascended
Assumed room temperature
Been annihilated
Been carried away by angels
Been consumed
Been laid to rest
Been liquidated
Been rubbed out
Been snuffed
Been taken by the Angels
Been taken by God
Been terminated
Been translated into Glory
Been wasted
Bit the dust
Bought the farm
Breathed their last
Cashed in
Changed their form
Checked out
Come to an end
Croaked
Crossed over
Crossed over the Rainbow Bridge
Crossed over the River Jordan
Crossed over the River Styx
Departed
Discorporated
Dropped the body
Ended it all
Expired
Found everlasting peace
Given it up
Given up the ghost

Gone away
Gone to a better place
Gone to Davy Jones
Gone to their eternal rest
Gone to their eternal reward
Gone to the Great Beyond
Gone to Hades
Gone Home
Gone home to Jesus
Gone to the Happy Hunting Grounds
Gone to Heaven
Gone to the Heavenly shores
Gone to the last roundup
Gone to a new life
Gone to the Other Side
Gone to the Summerlands
Gone up into the woods
Gotten mertilized
Hit the dirt
Kicked the bucket
Left this world
Left us
Lost it
Lost the race
Made the change
Met their Maker
Moved on Up
Passed
Passed on
Passed over
Passed through the Veil
Passed into the Afterlife
Passed into Death
Passed into Memory
Passed into Shadow
Perished
Returned to dust
Ridden into the sunset
Shuffled off this mortal coil

Succumbed
Transcended
Withered away

*Food euphemisms:*

Eating dandelions by the roots
Face planting the meringue
Fettucine Al Dead-o
Filleting the soul
Gone to cultivate chili peppers
Just add maggots
Peasant under grass
Pushin' up parsley
Sleeping with the quiches
Slowly cooling to room temperature

*Or:*

It was curtains
That was all she wrote
Guess who's not going to be shopping at Wal-Mart anymore? [18]

---

[18] Some of these euphemisms appear in *The Sacred Art of Dying*, by Kenneth Kramer, pp. 14-15; some are taken from *The Last Dance,* by Lynne De Spelder and Albert Strickland, p. 19. Others—especially those involving food—are from *Death Warmed Over* by Lisa Rogak, 2004.

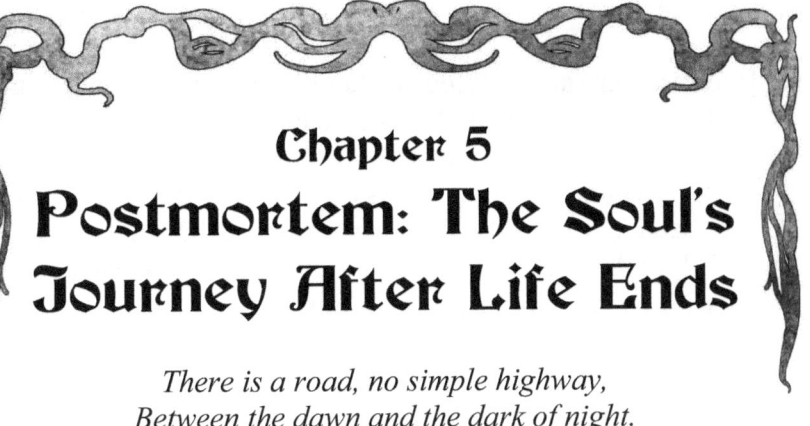

# Chapter 5
# Postmortem: The Soul's Journey After Life Ends

*There is a road, no simple highway,*
*Between the dawn and the dark of night.*
*And if you go, no one may follow;*
*That path is for your steps alone.*
~~Jerry Garcia, "Ripple"

*"To die would be an awfully great adventure!"*
~~J. M. Barrie, *Peter Pan*

*Death—the last voyage, the longest and the best.*
~~Thomas Wolfe, *Look Homeward, Angel*

HAT HAPPENS TO OUR SOUL/ SPIRIT/ CONsciousness after we die? Is our essential awareness just extinguished like a snuffed candle, or does it continue on in some invisible and ineffable realm beyond our mortal ken? This has been—throughout the entire span of human existence—the greatest of all Mysteries.

A prime indicator of our attitudes toward for the dead is how we handle the disposition of the bodies. All human cultures have developed burial ceremonies and other customs—some quite elaborate—for disposing of human remains that are very different from how they have dealt with dead animals. Burials are as old as human culture itself, pre-dating modern *Homo sapiens* to at least 100,000 years ago. In the Shanidar Cave in Iraq, in Pontnewydd Cave in Wales, and at other sites across Europe and the Near East, archaeologists have discovered Neanderthal burials with a characteristic layer of flower pollen. Those in Shanidar Cave date from 35,000 to 65,000 years ago:

[Smithsonian anthropologist Ralph] Solecki's pioneering studies of the Shanidar skeletons and their burials suggested complex socialization skills. From pollen found in one of the Shanidar graves, Solecki hypothesized that flowers had been buried with the Neanderthal dead—until then, such burials had been associated only with Cro-Magnons, the earliest known *H. sapiens* in Europe... [19]

While Solecki's thesis regarding the Shanidar Cave burials has been challenged (although the dead were clearly buried deliberately, skeptics aver that burrowing rodents might have introduced the flowers), similar funerary customs are widely documented throughout the world. Such burial customs invariably reflect attitudes of honor, respect, and even reverence for the beloved departed. For those cultures in which ancient myths have come down to us, these always include accounts of the soul's posthumous journey to some afterlife realm. The universality of the assumption that an immortal soul (however that may be understood) somehow survives the death of the physical body to go elsewhere cannot be discounted or dismissed.

But does the soul exist? Is there any scientific theory of consciousness that could accommodate such a claim? According to Dr. Stuart Hameroff, a near-death experience happens when the quantum information that inhabits the nervous system leaves the body and dissipates into the universe. Contrary to materialistic accounts of consciousness, Dr. Hameroff offers an alternative explanation of consciousness that can perhaps appeal to both the rational scientific mind and personal intuitions.

Consciousness resides, according to Hameroff and British physicist Sir Roger Penrose, in the microtubules of the brain cells—which are the primary sites of quantum processing. Upon death, this information is released from your

---

[19] Owens, Edward, "The Skeletons of Shanidar Cave," *Smithsonian Magazine*, March 2010. http://www.smithsonianmag.com/arts-culture/the-skeletons-of-shanidar-cave-7028477/#IBF7rW8H0pKWKJtq.99 accessed 6/5/16

body, meaning that your consciousness goes with it. They have argued that our experience of consciousness is the result of quantum gravity effects in these microtubules, a theory which they dubbed orchestrated objective reduction (Orch-OR).

Consciousness, or at least proto-consciousness, is theorized by them to be a fundamental property of the universe—present even at the first moment of the universe during the Big Bang. "In one such scheme proto-conscious experience is a basic property of physical reality accessible to a quantum process associated with brain activity."

Our souls are in fact constructed from the very fabric of the universe—and may have existed since the beginning of time. Our brains are just receivers and amplifiers for the proto-consciousness that is intrinsic to the fabric of space-time...[20]

Newton's First Law of Thermodynamics, also known as the Law of Conservation of Energy, stipulates that "energy can neither be created nor destroyed; energy can only be transferred or changed from one form to another."[21] If we can conceptualize "soul" or spirit as a kind of living vortex or energy field that animates our corporeal bodies, we might apply this same principle to our individual consciousness, and conclude that it too "can neither be created nor destroyed, but can only be transferred or changed from one form to another."

There do, however, seem to be many options for the soul's post-corporeal journey and destination, and these differ widely among various cultures and religions. Noting that many are not mutually exclusive, here are some of the possibilities:

---

[20] LeMind, Anna, "Quantum Theory Proves That Consciousness Moves to Another Universe After Death," originally published on www.learning-mind.com, 2014. http://www.theearthchild.co.za/quantum-theory-consciousness-moves-to-another-universe-after-death-2/ accessed 9/30/17

[21] Boundless. "The Three Laws of Thermodynamics." *Boundless Chemistry*. Boundless, 02 Jun. 2016. Retrieved 08 Jun. 2016 from https://www.boundless.com/chemistry/textbooks/boundless-chemistry-textbook/thermodynamics-17/the-laws-of-thermodynamics-123/the-three-laws-of-thermodynamics-496-3601/ accessed 4/21/17

1. The departed soul may journey on to a particular culture-specific Afterlife realm. This may be a paradisal place of reward (Heaven, Elysium, Sekhet-Aaru, Valhalla, the Summerlands, the Isles of the Blessed) or punishment (Hell, Tartaros, Jahannam, Dante's Inferno), depending on various criteria (works, faith, Grace).

2. Or the Afterlife/Underworld may be just a dumping ground for all departed spirits, regardless of the lives they had led. Afterlife realms may be vague and nebulous, or they may be mapped in considerable detail (Erebos, Irkalla, She'ol, Niflheim, the Bardos, Jannah, Xibalba, Dante's Inferno).

3. The departed soul may lose all memory of its former life (drinking from the waters of *Lethe*—forgetfulness); or it may retain full memories of its previous life and identity (drinking from the waters of *Mnemosyne*—memory).

4. The soul may pass through a gauntlet of Afterlife trials and judgements in order to prove itself worthy and deserving of its ultimate destination (Egyptian Hall of Judgement, the Bardos, Xibalba, the Christian Final Judgement).

5. The soul may pass permanently into the realm of The Dreaming, which it has visited nightly throughout its life. Or conversely, as some religions claim, we may find ("merrily, merrily, merrily") that *this* "life is but a dream," from which death is an awakening into a truer reality. "A dweam within a dweam."

6. *Apotheosis:* the soul may ascend to the realm of the Gods, to attain divinity and join the divine pantheon of ancestral spirits (Greek Heroes, Saints, Prophets, Angels, Loa).

7. The soul may just hang around in the aether, as a discarnate spirit or ghost, just on "the other side," not really going anywhere else, but generally unable to interact with the realm of the living. It may be trapped between the worlds, awaiting release of some sort in order to continue its journey. In this state,

the spirit may be contacted and consulted via mediums and *necromancy* (Spiritualism).

8. *Reincarnation:* the soul may be recycled to be reborn into another body—usually human, but not necessarily (as in Hinduism). Successive incarnations may be at higher or lower status according to how they had conducted their previous lives, or they may be more random. Reincarnation may be immediate (*transmigration*), or occur after a period of time. Souls may even reincarnate into the past, or the distant future...

9. Or, as Dr. Michael Newton,[22] Sylvia Browne,[23] and others claim, the soul may return to an elaborate and complex astral realm of further learning, reuniting with other souls who have been associated though many lifetimes, and moving up the ranks of a celestial hierarchy towards Divinity. From such a realm, the soul may choose eventual reincarnation, or remain there as a guide and mentor to other souls.

10. Released from the confines of a physical body, the soul/spirit may return, like water spilled from a broken vessel, to the vast oceanic Well of Souls (the Collective Unconscious; the Quantum Field), from whence it may in time be poured again into a new vessel.

11. According to the Quantum *Simulation Hypothesis,* all the realms, worlds, and afterlives we experience (including this one) are actually *simulations*—like 2$^{nd}$ Life, video games, and "The Matrix."[24] Gods and souls are extensions of the quantum field (which is pure consciousness), entering into these various "sim" realms via *avatars*. It is all a game, and what we call "birth" and "death" are just entries and exits as we res from

---

[22] Newton, Michael, *Journey of Souls: Case Studies of Life Between Lives.* Llewellyn Publications, Woodbury, MN, 1994.
[23] Browne, Sylvia, *Life on the Other Side: A Psychic's Tour of the Afterlife.* Berkley, 2001
[24] Merali, Zeeya, "Do We Live in the Matrix?" *Discover,* Dec. 2013, pp. 24–25.

one sim into another. As Tommy Chong says in the movie, *It's Gawd,* "This mortal world is where the Deathless come to die."

This hypothesis is remarkably compatible with most religions. And the inevitable implication is that there may be infinite levels of such sims; worlds within worlds within worlds—like Russian nesting dolls (*matryoshka*, "little matrons").

12. Or the soul may just dissipate, lose all consciousness, and fade into oblivion, like the light of a lamp when the current is turned off (Atheism). Quantum physicists and virtually all religions consider this the least likely scenario, but it may be true for some.

In all fairness, one can only conclude that all of these options must be available, and whatever any individual may experience after death is likely a product of the expectations of that person's faith, beliefs, and convictions. What you expect is what you get.

## The Near-Death Experience (NDE)

Sometimes people who—by all indications—have died, are revived or resuscitated. Many revivers report a common series of experiences that have become known as "near-death experiences," or NDEs. Such experiences have been identified in religious literature since ancient times; 95% of world cultures are documented as making some mention of NDEs. In the 19$^{th}$ century a few studies moved beyond examining individual cases—notably one in Switzerland, and another by the Mormons.

Between 1975 and 2005, close to 3,500 individual cases were reviewed in one study or another, carried out by some 55 researchers or teams of researchers. Many researchers (as well as revivers) cite the NDE as evidence that human consciousness can become separated from the body and brain under certain conditions, and glimpse the spiritual realm to which souls travel after death. Interpretation of these events tends to correspond with the cultural, philosophical, or religious beliefs of the person experiencing it.

Despite numerous culture-specific differences between various religions, the nine most frequently-reported NDE elements also recur cross-culturally. NDE researchers have found that the contents of the experiences do not vary across cultures, except for the identity of the figures encountered. For example, a Christian may see Jesus, a Hindu may encounter Yama, the Hindu god of death and others may be greeted by departed loved ones.

So, is there really a part of your consciousness that is non-material and will live on after the death of your physical body?

Dr Stuart Hameroff told the Science Channel's "Through the Wormhole" documentary: "Let's say the heart stops beating, the blood stops flowing, the microtubules lose their quantum state. The quantum information within the microtubules is not destroyed, it can't be destroyed, it just distributes and dissipates to the universe at large". Robert Lanza would add here that not only does it exist in the universe, it exists perhaps in another universe. If the patient is resuscitated/revived, this quantum information can go back into the microtubules and the patient says "I had a near death experience."

He adds: "If they're not revived, and the patient dies, it's possible that this quantum information can exist outside the body, perhaps indefinitely, as a soul."

This account of quantum consciousness explains things like near-death experiences, astral projection, out of body experiences, and even reincarnation—without needing to appeal to religious ideology. The energy of your consciousness potentially gets recycled back into a different body at some point, and in the meantime, it exists outside of the physical body on some other level of reality, and possibly in another universe. [25]

But the medical community has been reluctant to embrace or even address the phenomenon of NDEs, and most neuroscientists consider the NDE to be merely a hallucinatory state caused by various physiological and psychological factors.

Although the precise features of NDEs may vary from person to person, some common themes have been reported in most cases:

---

[25] LeMind, *Ibid.*

1. An awareness of being dead and removed or apart from the living world.
2. A sense of peace, well-being, absence of pain, and positive emotions.
3. An out-of-body experience, perceiving one's body from outside and above. Some people report observing doctors performing resuscitation efforts.
4. A "tunnel experience" of moving up or through a dark passageway.
5. Sudden immersion in a blinding light (or "Being of Light") which communicates with the person.
6. A profound feeling of unconditional love and acceptance.
7. Encountering "Beings of Light," or dressed in white. Often a reunion with deceased loved ones.
8. Receiving a life review, commonly spoken of as "seeing one's life flash before one's eyes."
9. Receiving knowledge about one's life, destiny, and the nature of the universe.
10. A decision to return to one's body, often accompanied by a reluctance to do so.
11. Suddenly finding oneself back inside one's body and wakening.

Kenneth Ring, co-founder and past president of the International Association for Near-Death Studies (IANDS), subdivides the NDE on a five-stage continuum:

1. Profound peace and contentment
2. Separation from the body
3. A passage through darkness
4. Seeing the light
5. Entering the light

Ring reports that 60% of NDErs experienced stage one (feelings of peace and contentment), but only 10% experienced stage five (entering the light). [26]

## The Journey of Souls

When hypnotherapist Dr. Michael Newton regressed his clients back in time to access their memories of former lives, he discovered that his patients were also able to tell him what their souls had experienced in the spirit world during the intervals between incarnations. In Newton's 1994 book, *Journey of Souls*, he presents 29 case studies of hypnosis interviews out of hundreds he conducted over many years, compiling an elaborate and remarkably consistent cosmology of the Afterlife. [27]

Dr. Newton's transcriptions of his clients' accounts of their journeys between lives are interesting to compare with the *Egyptian Book of the Dead,* which describes the soul's journey through the *Duat*, or Underworld, and into *Sekhet-Aaru,* the paradisal afterlife. Or the journey of the soul over the River Styx to the Halls of Hades and Persephone in the Greek Underworld of *Erebos,* and hopefully on to the Elysian Fields. Or the *Tibetan Book of the Dead,* where departed souls meet various challenges as they travel through the *Bardo* before choosing new parents for their next incarnation. Or the journey of a departed Celt to join his or her ancestors in the Isles of the Blessed. Or the retrieval of a slain Viking warrior by Valkyries to drink, feast, and fight eternally in Odin's great mead hall of *Valhalla.* Or Inanna's descent through the seven gates into *Irkalla,* the Sumerian Underworld ruled by Her dark sister, Ereshkigal. Or Dante's detailed poetic descriptions in *The Inferno* and *The Divine Comedy* of the passage of a Christian soul to Heaven or Hell. (See the following chapter.)

Dr. Newton's detailed road map of the Afterlife is described in suitably-titled chapters:

---

[26] Ring, Kenneth, *Life at Death: A Scientific Investigation of the Near-Death Experience.* Coward, McCann, & Geoghegan, New York, 1980 (p. 40)

[27] Newton, Michael, *Journey of Souls: Case Studies of Life between Lives.* Llewellyn, 1994.

1. **Death and Departure:** As with NDEs, Dr. Newton's hypnotized subjects recalling their previous deaths report a sensation of pulling away from the physical world, with a euphoric sense of freedom and brightness around them, and subsequently passing through a dark tunnel, towards a light at the end.

2. **Gateway to the Spirit World:** The tunnel is the portal into the Spirit Realm. Some see it opening close to their vacated bodies, while others must rise high above the Earth to enter it.

3. **Homecoming:** Emerging from the tunnel, most subjects report being welcomed by their personal Guide—an advanced entity who has had close connection with the subject through many lives. This might even be a soulmate, relative, or close friend.

4. **The Displaced Soul:** Some souls have been so damaged in their recent lives that they cannot accept that they are dead, and resist moving on to the Spirit World. They persist as ghosts or even "demonic spirits," who may harass the living. They have unfinished business, and are trapped between the Earthly and spiritual planes, often at a particular physical location.

5. **Orientation:** After being received and welcomed home, subjects report being taken to a place of healing and readjustment to the Spirit World. This involves a debriefing review of their former life, and counseling with their Guide.

6. **Transition:** Once past the reorientation station, returning souls arrive at a crowded "grand central station" from whence they are projected out to their proper final destinations.

7. **Placement:** Everyone is transported to a designated place in the Spirit World, where they are received into primary "cluster groups" or Inner Circles of 3-25 intimate old friends of similar awareness level. Larger secondary communities are less intimate, each with more than 1,000 souls.

8. **Guides:** All souls are assigned personal Guides as spiritual mentors and teachers. The awareness level of a soul determines

the degree of advancement of the Guide assigned to them—not only after death, but throughout life as well.

9. **The Beginner Soul:** Some souls are truly young, having incarnated only once or twice. Others may have incarnated many times, but still remain immature, at Levels I-II of their spiritual development.

10. **The Intermediate Soul:** Souls evolving into the more mature middle Levels III-IV have less association with their primary groups, and operate more independently, working with their Guides to develop skills that will qualify them to become Guides in their turn.

11. **The Advanced Soul:** Level V Guides incarnate on Earth to improve the lives of others, enhance human values, and further the ultimate enlightenment of all Beings. In Buddhist terms, they are *Bodhisattvas*.

12. **Life Selection:** Eventually, souls must prepare to leave the Spirit World to reincarnate in a living body. They may choose when, where, and to whom they wish to be reborn, and they are given preparatory exit interviews by their Guides.

13. **Choosing a Body:** Great care must be taken in selecting just the right body to serve one's purpose in the life to come. That purpose may be to learn lessons, acquire new experiences, pursue a great Mission, be reunited with loved ones from former lives, or other possibilities.

14. **Preparation for Embarkation:** Souls preparing to reincarnate must coordinate with other players in the coming life drama. They go to a place of recognition, where they learn how to recognize and connect with those they wish to be with in their next life.

15. **Rebirth:** This is the last chance for souls to enjoy the omniscience of knowing just who they are before they must adapt to a new body in a new life. They return to Earth via the same tun-

nel as they departed in death. The shock of re-entry (birth) can be greater than that of death!

In the next chapter we will explore some descriptions of the Afterlives of various cultures and religions.

**La Calavera Catrina** ("Dapper Skeleton," "Elegant Skull"): A 1910–1913 zinc etching by famous Mexican cartoonist José Guadalupe Posada. The image depicts a female skeleton wearing a fancy hat befitting the European upper class of the early 20$^{th}$ century. She was a satirical portrait of those Mexican natives who, Posada felt, were aspiring to adopt European aristocratic traditions in the pre-revolutionary era. A modern version of *Santa Muerte* (Lady Death), she has become an icon of the Mexican *Día de Muertos,* or Day of the Dead—as well as of the Grateful Dead band.

# Chapter 6
# Netherworlds: Realms of the Dead

*That undiscover'd country from whose bourn no traveler returns.*
~William Shakespeare, *Hamlet*

    As universal as belief in spiritual realms inhabited by the Gods are concepts of an Afterlife, Hereafter, Underworld, Paradise, or Land of the Dead, inhabited by the departed spirits of those who have died. According to various ideas about the Afterlife, the essential aspect of the individual that lives on after death may be some partial element—or the entire soul or spirit—of an individual, which carries with it and confers personal identity. Belief in an Afterlife, which may be naturalistic or supernatural, is in sharp contrast to the belief in oblivion after death.

    In some mythologies, departed souls simply go to join the gods in some spiritual realm, and in others they *reincarnate,* returning to the mortal world to be reborn in new bodies and begin the life cycle over again, usually with no memory of what they have done in former incarnations. In this latter view, such rebirths and deaths may take place over and over again continuously until the individual gains entry to a spiritual realm or Otherworld. In some systems of reincarnation, such as those in the Indic religions, the nature of the continued existence is determined directly by the actions of the individual in the ended life, rather than through the decision of another being.

    Other belief systems, such as those in the Abrahamic traditions, hold that the dead go to a specific plane of existence after death, as determined by a god, gods, or other divine judgment, based on their actions during their life. [28]

---

[28] Wikipedia: "Afterlife," https://en.wikipedia.org/wiki/Afterlife 12/13/17

URIAL RITES HAVE BEEN TRACED AS FAR back as the Neanderthals, 100,000 years ago, and they seem to be a universal feature of the human species. The careful burial of people in ritual positions, dressed in their finest clothes, accompanied by food, personal belongings, and other "grave goods," implies that the deceased were expected to awaken into another life beyond the grave. Eventually, *sarcophagi* (coffins) and tombs were created—along with methods of mummification—to house and preserve the bodies for all eternity. Burial chambers commonly had fake "doors" sculpted in bas-relief or only painted on the walls for the spirits to pass through into the Underworld. Elaborate descriptions of what they would encounter in that realm formed the foundations of most of the world's religions.

One of the strongest reasons for belief in an Afterlife is the desire for justice. Life is often unfair. Many good people die young, or suffer in poverty and illness. Many evil people lead rich, long, rewarding lives. Most religions offer an Afterlife that provides the justice not found in this one. If there is a final judgment after death, and if some people go to a Hell and others go to a Heaven, then evil will ultimately be punished and goodness will be rewarded. The scales of justice will finally be balanced.

A useful way to look at all the Afterlives of different cultures and religions is to see them as virtual worlds—much like those in $2^{nd}$ Life. Created out of the collective consciousness matrix of all those who believe in them, they are all "real" in that sense, but none of them are universal for everyone. Here's a sampling of some of the most venerable and well-developed:

## Mesopotamia: The Great Below

Farming, human civilization and the art of writing first arose in the fertile garden valley of Dilmun (aka Eden), between the Tigris and Euphrates Rivers, where the ancient Mesopotamians believed their Afterlife existed in a subterranean realm beneath our world. It was to this land, known alternately as *Arallû, Ganzer,* or *Irkalla* (the "Great Below") that everyone went after death, regardless of social status or their actions performed during life. The bodies of the dead decompose in this afterlife, as they would in the world above.

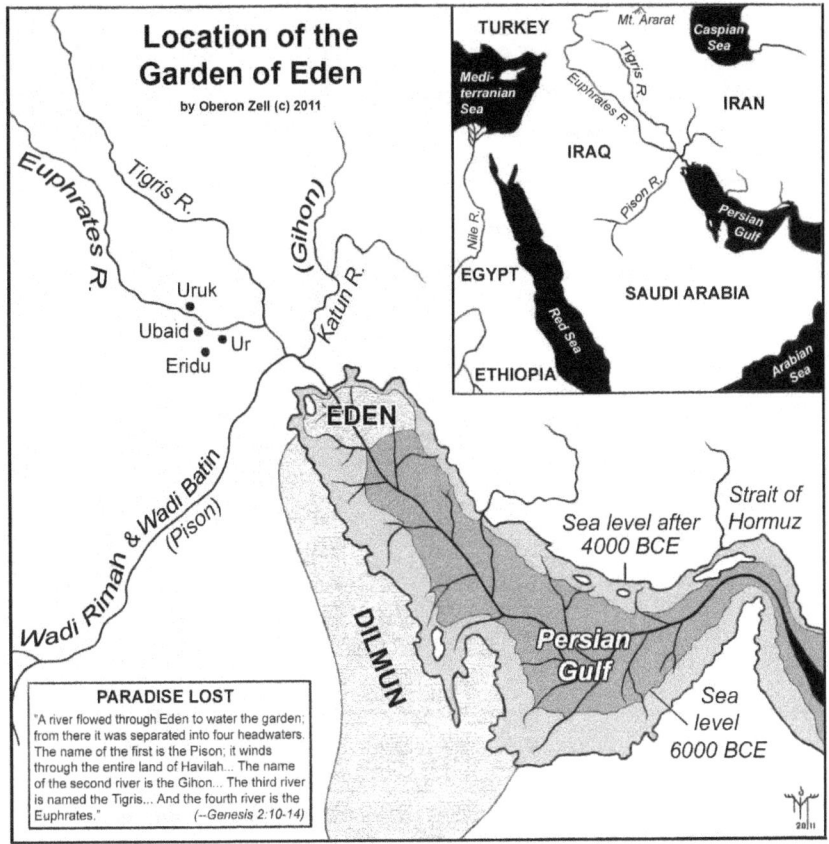

*In the Beginning: Mesopotamia and Eden (by Oberon Zell)*

*Irkalla* (Akkadian, also *Ir-Kalla, Irkalia*), *Kur* (Sumerian, also *Kurnugia*) or *Ersetu* (Akkadian, also *Erset la tari*) is the Mesopotamian Underworld from which there is no return. Kur is ruled by the Goddess *Ereshkigal* and her consort, the Death God *Nergal*.

In Babylonian mythology (620-539 BC), Irkalla was another name for Ereshkigal, who ruled the Underworld alone until Nergal, god of pestilence and destruction, was sent to her realm, where he seduced and married her. Both the deity and the realm were called Irkalla, much like how *Hades* in Greek mythology became a name for the Underworld from the god who ruled it.

The gates into and out of Irkalla lay at the equinoxes, when day and night are equal, at the opposite ends of the great arch of the Milky Way, which was called the River of Souls. After death, souls must wait for the next autumn equinox to enter Irkalla through the rising gate of Sagittarius. Return to Earth through reincarnation could only occur through the Gemini exit gate at spring equinox.

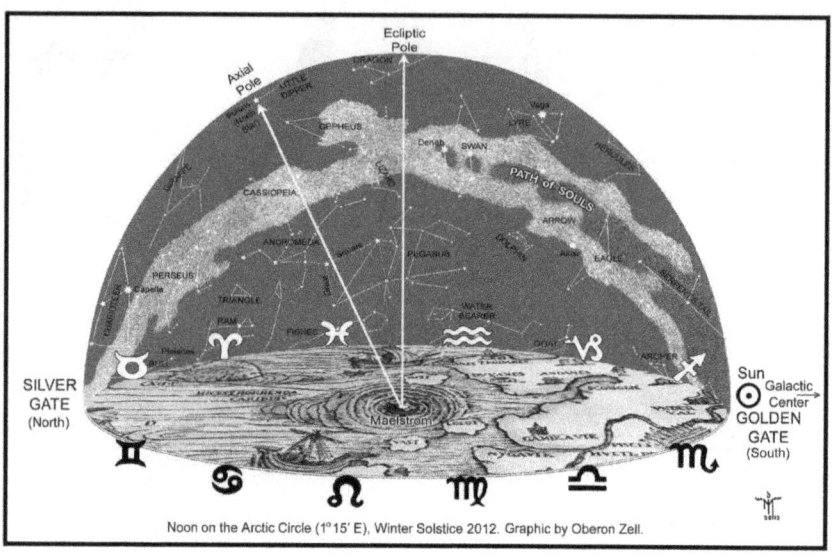

*The Milky Way as the River of Souls (by Oberon Zell)*

Irkalla was a place of neither punishment nor reward, but was just a drearier version of life above. As the subterranean destination for all who die, Irkalla was similar to the Hebrew *Sheol* or the Greek Erebus/Hades. It differed from more hopeful versions of a paradisal afterlife envisioned by the contemporary Egyptians and later in Platonism, Christianity and Islam.

The dead were considered merely weak and powerless ghosts. The myth of Inanna's descent into the Underworld relates that "Dust is their food and clay their nourishment. They see no light, where they dwell in darkness." Because the *Anunnaki* first sage, *Adapa,* unknowingly refused the gift of immortality, all men must die and true eternal life is only for the gods.

The shades or spirits of the deceased were known as *gidim* in Sumerian, and as *eṭemmu* in Akkadian. Gidim were created at the time of death, taking on the memory and personality of the dead person. They traveled to Irkalla, where they led an existence similar in some ways to that of the living. The gidim had houses and could meet with deceased family members and associates.

Gidim spent some time travelling on their journey through the portal to the Netherworld, often having to overcome obstacles along the way. They passed through seven gates, leaving articles of clothing and adornment at each gate, where guardians extracted tolls for their passage and kept anyone from going the wrong way.

The *Anunnaki,* the court of Irkalla, welcomed each gidim and received their offerings. The court explained the rules and assigned the ghosts their fate or place. Another court was presided over by the Sun God Shamash, who visited the Netherworld at night on his daily round. Shamash might punish gidim who harassed the living; he also might award a share of funerary offerings to forgotten ghosts.

The Babylonians believed that life in the Underworld could be made more tolerable if surviving relatives made regular offerings of food and drink. If the relatives failed to make such offerings, the ghosts could become restless and visit sickness and misfortune on the living. The ghosts of people who had no children to make these offerings would suffer more, while people who died in fire or whose body lay unburied in the desert would have no ghosts at all.

## Egypt: Weighing of the Heart

Ancient Egyptian civilization was based on religion; their belief in the rebirth after death was the driving force behind their funeral practices. Death was simply a temporary interruption—rather than complete cessation—of life, and eternal life could be ensured by means like piety to the gods, preservation of the physical form through mummification, and the provision of statuary and other funerary equipment. Each human consisted of the physical body, the 'ka', the 'ba', and the 'akh'. The Name and Shadow were also living entities. To enjoy the afterlife, all these elements had to be sustained and protected from harm.

Egyptians believed that being mummified and put in a sarcophagus (an ancient Egyptian "coffin" carved with complex symbols and designs, as well as pictures and hieroglyphs) was the only way to secure an afterlife. Only if the corpse had been properly embalmed and entombed in a *mastaba,* could the dead live again in the Fields of Yalu and accompany the Sun on its daily ride across the heavens. Due to the dangers the afterlife posed, the *Book of the Dead* was placed in the tomb with the body as well as food, jewelry, and 'curses.' [29]

As described in the Egyptian *Chapters of Coming Forth by Day,* often called *The Egyptian Book of the Dead,* the *ka* ("double" or astral body) of a dead person passes from the burial chamber to wander in darkness through tunnels and passages under the Earth, until at last he (or she) enters *Amenti* ("Hall of Two Truths"), the vast Judgement Hall of the Dead. *Osiris,* Lord of the Dead, sits on a great elevated throne at the far end. In his hands he holds symbols of fertility: a flail (for grain) and crook (for herds), symbolizing his power to restore all life.

In the center of the hall is a shrine with a set of scales. The ka must recite a standard 42 "Negative Confessions" of sins and evils he did not commit in life, saying before each, "I have not..." These must satisfy the 42 divine judges (one for each *Nome,* or district of Egypt) seated around the chamber, each of whom the confessor must address in turn by name. This is to assure the Gods that the soul has been truly born again, transfigured into one who could not have done these sins. Then jackal-headed *Anubis* (guardian of the dead) places the dead person's heart upon the scales, weighing it against the ostrich feather of *Ma'at,* goddess of Truth and Justice. Ibis-headed *Thoth* (god of writing) records the results.

If the deceased has spoken truly, and followed the concept of Ma'at during his life, his heart will be as light as the feather. Passing this test, he is allowed to go on to the paradisal afterlife, *Sekhet-Aaru* ("Field of Reeds")—a lovely world much like Egypt itself, with fertile fields and lakes. There the blessed dead dwell forever in the favor of Osiris, feasting with the gods on the food of

---

[29] Wikipedia: "Afterlife," https://en.wikipedia.org/wiki/Afterlife 12/13/17

immortality. But while the soul dwelt in the fields of Aaru, Osiris demanded work as restitution for the protection he provided.

But if a person's sins in life weigh heavily upon his heart (if he had lied, cheated, killed, or done anything against Ma'at), they will tip the balance. If the person has not been transformed, he or she is no better than food for animals, and that is his or her fate. His heart will be fed to a horrible monster which waits beside the shrine. A composite of hippopotamus, cheetah, lion and crocodile, she is called *Ammut*—Devourer of the Dead. From this final death there is no appeal, and no further existence.

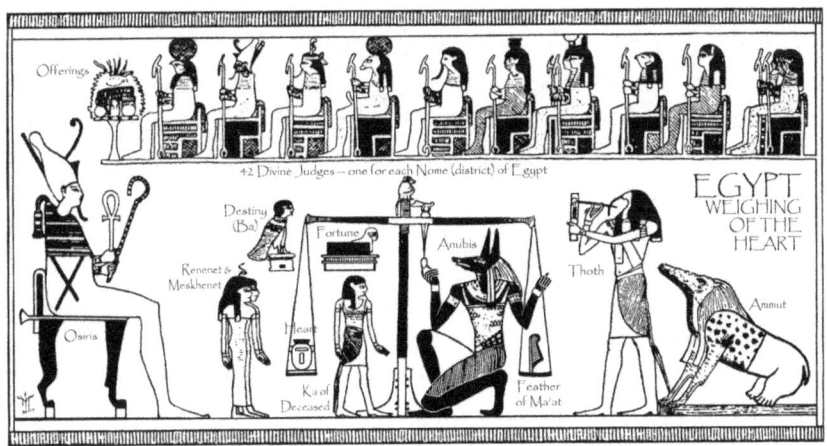

*Weighing of the Heart (by Oberon Zell, from Papyrus of Hunefer)*

However, there was a mitigating factor, as shown in the "Papyrus of Hunefer" (c. 1275 BCE), redrawn here, which illustrates the scribe Hunefer's heart being weighed on the scale of Ma'at against the feather of truth, by the jackal-headed Anubis. Acknowledging generous offerings made to the gods, Anubis crouches under the scales, and adjusts a movable weight to shift the balance in Hunefer's favor!

# Greece: Erebos, Tartarus and the Elysian Fields

The third brother of Zeus and Poseidon was assigned rulership of *Erebos,* the Greek Underworld, which is often called by his name,

*Hades*. His Queen is *Persephone,* who rules by his side for a third of the year, then returns to the upper world as the Flower Maiden for the other two thirds. Hades' realm is divided into several regions, all of which are well-mapped in myth and replicated in several underground Oracles. Except for those few heroes whom the gods chose to deify and invite to Olympus, all who die on Earth descend into the Underworld. The dead can still eat, drink, speak, and feel emotions. However, their bodies are nothing but shadows—hence they are called *shades.*

The entrance to the Underworld is in the West, and is separated from the world of the living by several rivers. The first of these is *Acheron,* river of woe, which feeds the Acherusian Lake, across which the newly-dead are ferried by *Charon,* the boatman. He requires a passage fee of the two gold or silver coins which have been placed over the eyes of each corpse (sometimes a third coin is placed between their lips). Any who cannot pay the fee must wander the shore for 100 years. The Acheron joins the river *Styx,* by which the gods swear unbreakable oaths.

Disembarking from Charon's ferry, the dead enter the region of *Erebos.* Here they pass *Lethe,* the river of forgetfulness. If they drink of its dark waters, they are relieved of their shameful deeds but lose all memory of their former lives. There is also the spring of *Memnosyne* (memory), and drinking from it ensures that one's previous life and loves will not be forgotten.

At last, the shades reach the gates of Hades' hall. These are guarded by the monstrous three-headed dog, *Cerberus,* who greets all newcomers happily but refuses to allow any to leave (he may, however, be charmed by sweet music and honeycakes). Grim Hades and stern Persephone sit on their magnificent thrones, amid the wealth of gold and jewels from the depths of the Earth.

On the Plains of Judgement, the dead are judged by kings: *Minos, Rhadamanthus,* and *Aeacus.* They decide where each pilgrim should go. Heroes and good people who did wonderful things in life go to the *Elysian Fields.* This is a place of eternal bliss where they are reunited with their loved ones. Souls who are not good enough for Elysium are sent to the *Fields of Asphodel,* where they drift unthinking and unfeeling like ghostly zombies.

People who had been particularly wicked in life—such as *Tantalus, Sisyphus,* and *Ixion*—are consigned to *Tartarus,* to endure an eternity of ironically appropriate punishment. Tartarus is the deepest and most ancient part of the Underworld, as far beneath the Earth as the Heavens are above. It is a dank and gloomy pit, surrounded by a wall of bronze, and beyond that a three-fold layer of night. Tartarus is a prison for the Titans defeated in the *Titanomachia* (Battle of the Titans)—who are guarded by the hundred-handed *Hecatonchires*. The *Cocytus,* river of tears, and *Pyriphlegethon,* the river of fire (molten lava), surround Tartarus and flow into the Acheron.

*Erebos: the Greek Underworld (by Oberon Zell)*

The spirits of the dead were believed to be able to foretell the future, as well as locate lost treasures. Temples were erected in places thought to be entrances to the Underworld where pilgrims went to receive prophecies. Dedicated to Hades and Persephone, the *Necromanteion* ("Oracle of the Dead") at Epirus, in northern Greece, was the most famous of the ancient necromantic temples, and was considered to be the entrance to the Underworld. In Homer's *Odyssey*, Odysseus visits the Necromanteion to consult the ghost of the blind seer, Tiresias, seeking a way return to his home and wife on the island of Ithaca.

The Necromanteion was said to be located at the meeting point on Earth of three of the five rivers of the Underworld—the Acheron, the Pyriphlegethon, and the Cocytus (these are actual rivers in northern Greece). It was looted and burned by the Romans in 167 BCE, and was re-discovered and excavated by Greek archaeologist Sotirios Dakaris in the 1960s. Dona and I explored the site in March of 1987, and my map of Erebos—the Greek Underworld—is based on the real rivers of Epirus and the now-drained, marshy Acherusian Lake which once lay in that region.

Here is an excerpt from my journal of that adventure:

*1987.3.21.6:00 PM — Sat. (Ostara/Spring Equinox!)*
*We go to Hell and Back*
*I hardly know how to record this day's adventure. My skin is still tingling and the hairs on the back of my neck won't lie down. Today, on the Vernal Equinox—when Persephone returns from the Underworld—we stood within Her throne room in the ancient Halls of Hades by the banks of the River Acheron, where over 3,000 years ago, wily Odysseus consulted the ghost of the blind seer Tiresias. We have returned from the Land of the Dead, and I am sitting here in a hotel room in the tiny Greek town of Parga, trying to make words on paper convey some impression of our experience...*

> "Son of Laertes and the gods of old
> Odysseus, master mariner and soldier,
> You shall not stay here longer against your will;
> But home you may not go
> Unless you take a strange way round and come
> To the cold homes of Death and pale Persephone..."
> (~Homer, The Odyssey, 10.488-493)

*And so, Dona and I came to the Halls of Hades—one of the most ancient oracles known, wherein items have been found dating back as far as 2100 BCE. The oracular shrine, which in antiquity lay underground, is now open to the sky. Measuring about 150 by 200 feet, it is an uncanny place. We were immediately* impressed by the Cyclopean masonry of the retaining walls, consisting of huge irregular polygonal blocks perfectly fitted, and which I'd only seen before in photos of ancient Peruvian ruins. Around the back we passed through a perfectly formed and fitted true arch: the entrance to the actual sanctuary.

As we were led through the various labyrinthine chambers—now excavated and cleared of earth—the scale of the complex became truly astonishing, including the incongruity of the little $18^{th}$ century church and monastery still perched atop the now-exposed ancient walls, and whose floor, specially reinforced by Dakaris, now forms a ceiling for the innermost chamber of the shrine. Black lumps of hashish that Dakaris discovered by the sack full leave no doubt that clients of the oracle were drugged into a state of ultimate susceptibility for the carefully choreographed experience of communion with the dead.

In the floor of the inner sanctuary—but out from under the little abandoned church— was a rectangular hole in the ground, about two feet by four feet, with newly installed metal steps leading downward. This was the true and actual entrance to the Underworld, and the legendary Halls of Hades! With feelings of awe and anticipation I cannot describe, we descended those stairs—goosebumps rising on our flesh and chills running up our spines. We found ourselves in a rectangular chamber, maybe 50 feet long and ten feet wide, with a barrel-vaulted ceiling supported by 15 massive arches. (The true arch was supposedly unknown until it was invented by the Romans around 500 BCE.)

The opening and stairway were at one end of the chamber, which—bound at both ends by natural stone—ran back underneath the sanctuary and church above. The side walls of the chamber were hewn out of the solid rock, and pick marks were still prominent. The curved arch blocks of the ceiling, mounted atop square-cut columns hewn from the walls, rose maybe ten feet above the rough stone floor, where rainwater had collected in apparently natural hollows of some depth. Indeed, the floor and end walls appeared to have originally been those of a natural cave.

Dakaris' excavators removed a yard-deep layer of dried blood, since turned to humus, that had accumulated from the blood offerings poured down that opening above. No human foot in antiquity had trod this ground once the vault had been built, more than 4,000 years ago.

In this ancient throne room of Hades and his Queen Persephone, we gave our thanks for the lessons of this journey and left our offerings. We felt filled with indescribable sensations: that all our journeys through the caves and tombs of the Land of the Dead had brought us here—not to another necropolis or catacombs, for actual dead bodies were never entombed here—but to Hell itself, for this was indeed the place wherein we stood.

Lingering as long as we dared keep our guide waiting above, we finally ascended those stairs and came again into the light. As we were leaving the enclosure, we noticed daisies blooming in profusion all about. I turned to our guide and held up a plucked daisy, attempting to convey my thoughts about the return of Persephone on this, Her day of the Vernal Equinox. "Persephone," he smiled, pointing at the daisy. Indeed. Evoe Kore!

## Celts: Annwfn & the Western Isles

In Celtic tradition, everything non-mortal existed in the Otherworld—which was always located to the West. These realms, as well as their rulers, were an important source of Underworld mythology. After the influence of Christianity, the Otherworld was transformed into an Underworld, namely to punish and lower the power of the old Pagan gods in the eyes of the European peoples.

The Cave of Cruachan in Connaught, Ireland has been called the Gateway to the Underworld. In the old legends, Cruachan is a gateway through which dead armies of zombies come to attack the living. Christians updated the tales, claiming that it is through the cave that condemned human souls enter the Underworld.

*Annwfn,* the Celtic Otherworld, is often called the kingdom of shades. It is a series of coexisting realms, like an archipelago of separate islands in a mystical sea. These are the astral plane equivalents of Britain's most remote island groups, the Isles of Scilly, variously described as "the Fortunate Isles" or "the Blessed Isles," owing to their beauty and relatively mild climate. Lying 28 miles off the coast of Land's End, the isles are Britain's most southwesterly lands, and consist now of 54 islands. Only five are inhabited—relatively sparsely.

These realms contain many different beings, gods, and spirits—as well as the dead. The three major regions are *Caer Wydyr, Caer Feddwid,* and *Arran.* These different sectors are separated by seas, mountains, rivers, and impassable chasms.

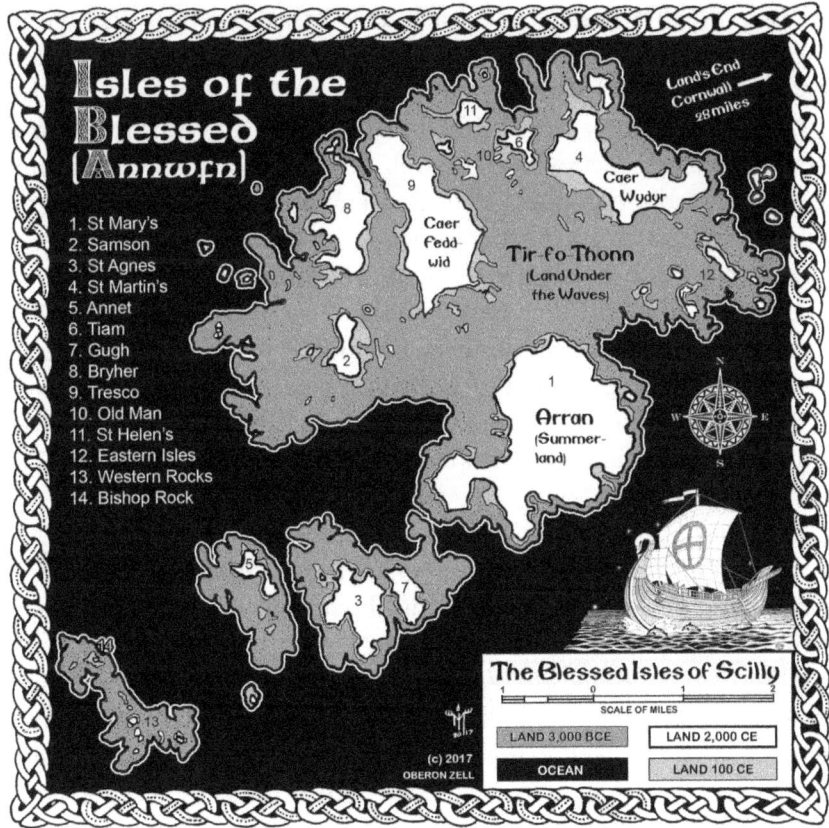

*Isles of the Blessed (Annwfn) (by Oberon Zell)*

*Arran* is considered the most divine of the three lands. It is a land of eternal Summer—with lush, grassy fields and sweet flowing rivers. In Arran is found the Cauldron of Plenty, which is linked to the Holy Grail. Only those who are pure of heart, self-sacrificing, and spiritual are allowed to enter here. This is the "Summerland" most identified with modern Wiccans, as well as Theosophists. It is a place of peace and beauty, where everything people hold close to their hearts is preserved in its fullest glory for eternity.

*Caer Feddwid* ("castle of revelry") is ruled by Arianrhod of the Silver Wheel (the Moon), Goddess of time, space, and energy. It is also known as *Caer Rigor* or *Caer Siddi*. The air is filled with enchanting music and a fountain flows with magick wine which grants eternal youth and health.

*Caer Wydyr* ("castle of glass"), also called *Nennius*, lies within a glass fort. It is a dark and gloomy place inhabited only by silent lost souls. It is the least desirable place to end up after death.

*Mag Mell/Magh Meall* ("plain of joy") is a mythical realm in Irish mythology achievable through death and/or glory. Mag Mell is a pleasurable paradise, identified as either an island far to the west of Ireland or a kingdom beneath the sea, accessible only to a select few. Furthermore, Mag Mell, like numerous other mystical islands said to be off the coast of Ireland, was never explicitly stated to be an afterlife. Rather, it is a paradisal location populated by deities, which is occasionally visited by some adventurous mortals. A place of eternal youth and beauty, it is said to be ruled by the Fomorian King *Tethra,* or more often *Manannan mac Lir*

Different gods or lords ruled in various national regions of the Celtic Otherworld. The most ancient of these is *Cernunnos* ("horned one"), who rules the dead. Images of the horned shaman, etched into cave walls in France, date back to 9,000 BCE. He is also known as *Herne the Hunter,* leading the Wild Hunt on Samhain Eve. Cernunnos became identified with Satan when Christianity spread to the Celtic regions. After the conversion of Ireland, Cernunnos was increasingly linked with a dark and foul Underworld, the dwelling place of evil spirits and souls of the damned.

A similar hunter god of the Underworld is *Gwynn,* who preys on souls, claiming them for Annwfn. Gwynn is associated with Fairies, who have been called "the Hosts of Hell" by Christians.

*Donn* ("brown one") is the Irish god of the dead who was drowned by the Goddess Eriu after he insulted her. He is the keeper of the first guidepost on the journey to the Otherworld. His realm is a small rocky island, called *Tech Duinn* ("house of Donn") off the southwest coast of Ireland, where he welcomes his descendants—the people of Ireland—who briefly visit his house just after the moment of death.

*Pwyll* was a Welsh prince who chanced to meet *Arawn,* king of Annwfn, and the two of them agreed to exchange kingdoms for a year in each other's bodies. Each ruled the other's land well, and were pleased with the arrangement when the time was completed. The full story is told in the first Branch of the Welsh *Mabinogion.*

*Mider* is a benevolent god of the Gaelic Afterworld. His wife is *Etain*. He is a just overlord whose realm is a place of tedium and sorrow rather than pain and torture. Mider had a magic caldron capable of performing supernatural feats. However, Mider's daughter betrayed him and helped the hero Cuchulain steal the cauldron.

*Bilé*, on the other hand, is an evil and vicious god who requires human sacrifices to appease his violent nature. His kingdom is a vast wasteland of crushed spirits and broken bodies who must pay him eternal homage.

*Bran* was a mortal hero in Welsh mythology. His symbol is the raven, a bird of ill omen associated with death and the grave. Bran angered the gods, was beheaded, and banished to rule in the Underworld as punishment. Bran's kingdom is filled with failed heroes who must spend eternity in regret.

The *Fomorii* are a monstrous race of creatures who dwell far below the sea. The inhabitants of this gloomy Underworld are horribly misshapen and deformed. They are ruled by Balor, who has a terrible temper and often strikes out against his subjects without provocation. Most legends agree that the Fomorii's evil caused their deformities. Balor's wrath is additional punishment for the sins of their past.

Ruled by Aor, King of the Waterfalls, the *Land Under Waves* is a twilight world reached through a sinking lake, the Red Cataract (Easaidh Ruadh). Its portal is the Shannon River in Ireland. Its beauty is seen when the surface of the sea is clear as crystal, unrippled by the wind. The seashore has sands of gold and a silver mist of light rests on the mountains. The grass is green as emeralds, with bowers of flowers in full bloom. [30]

> It is the eve of Beltaine. Between the rising and setting of the moon, that night, the loughs and the seas of Erin become gates of glass that will open to let through any person who seeks the Country-under-Wave. ...And when the gates of glass are shut behind him, he must tarry in the Under-Water Land from Beltaine until Samhain… [31]

---

[30] "Faery Places," http://www.tartanplace.com/faery/tirfothuinn.html 12/26/17
[31] Furlong, Alice & McGarry, Mary, *Country-Under-Wave*.

## Vikings: Valhalla & Hel

In Scandinavia, beliefs about the Afterlife varied from time to time and place to place. There were a number of options. Fierce Viking heroes who died in battle were received by one of Odin's *Valkyries,* or "choosers of the slain." These beautiful warrior maidens ride through the air and over the sea on flying horses, following the progress of every battle. They kiss the fallen heroes and carry their souls away to Odin's great hall of *Valhalla,* in the uppermost realm of *Asgard,* home of the *Aesir*—the Sky Gods. There the warriors spend their days re-fighting the glorious battles in which they had died and thus won eternal fame. Each night they feast on wild boar, drink mead, and carouse to their heart's content.

Women who died might go to Freyja's hall in *Vanaheim,* home of the *Vanir,* the older Earth Gods. Kings were often believed to live on in their burial mounds, where they received offerings and blessed their people. Some families lived on inside sacred hills and some continued to watch over their descendants as *alfar* (male) and *disir* (female) guardian spirits.

However, the "default" destination for non-warriors was *Niflheim,* which is the general Underworld home of the ancestors. This land of mists is described a cold and gloomy realm of icy suffering, surrounded on all sides by the river *Gioll* and steep walls impassable to the living. Like most places, it has both good and bad neighborhoods. The hall where Balder feasts is cheerful, with plenty of ale and mead. The part called *Nastrond,* on the other hand, is a terrible prison for oath-breakers and other criminals—its walls woven from snakes whose poison flows along the floor.

This region is ruled by *Hel* or *Hella,* daughter of the trickster *Loki* and the Giantess *Angrboda.* Hel is the sister of both the Midgard Serpent, *Jormungand,* who will cause the sea to flood the world with lashings of his tail, and of *Fenrir,* the phantom wolf who will swallow the sun at Ragnarok. Hel is a hideous creature; half black and half white, half human and half rotting corpse. Her domain is so far below Midgard (the Earth) that it takes Odin's eight-legged horse, *Sleipnir,* nine days and nights to reach it.

*Yggdrasil and the Nine Worlds of Norse Myth (by Oberon Zell)*

The dismal realm of Hel lies on the other side of the treacherous Echoing Bridge, where souls trying to cross are challenged by the giantess *Modgudh*. The foul-smelling entrance, *Gnipahellir*, is guarded by the fierce dog *Garm*. The ferocious monster is forever watching for Hermodr, the dark ferryman who, like the Greek Charon, conveys the dead to the Underworld. And like Cerberus, Garm also prevents the spirits from escaping Niflheim. Other souls of immoral people wash up on the haunted shore of Nastrond and are then delivered to Hel for punishment. Hel's father, Loki, is there to help. There is another gate in the east through which Odin enters to seek prophecies from the spirit of the ancient seeress.

## Judaism: She'ol

The Hebrew Scriptures themselves have few references to existence after death. *She'ol* is described as a grim and desolate Underworld to which all the dead go, both the righteous and the unrighteous, regardless of the moral choices made in life; a place of stillness and darkness cut off from life and from the Hebrew God, Yahweh.

The inhabitants of She'ol are the "shades" (*rephaim*), colorless entities without personality or strength. Under some circumstances they are able to be contacted by the living, as when the Witch of Endor raised the shade of Samuel for Saul (Deuteronomy 18:10), but such necromantic practices are forbidden.

While the Old Testament writings appear to describe She'ol as the permanent place of the dead, in the Second Temple period (ca. 500 BCE–70 CE) a more diverse set of ideas developed. In some texts, She'ol is considered to be the home of both the righteous and the wicked, separated into respective regions; in others, it was considered a place of punishment, meant for the wicked dead alone. When the Hebrew scriptures were translated into Greek in ancient Alexandria around 200 BC, the word "Hades" (the Greek Underworld) was substituted for She'ol, and this is reflected in the New Testament where Hades is both the Underworld of the dead and the personification of the evil it represents.

According to Herbert C. Brichto, writing in *Hebrew Union College Annual,* the family tomb is the central concept in understanding Biblical views of the afterlife. Brichto states that the early Israelites apparently believed that the graves of family, or tribe, united into one and that this unified collectivity is what the Biblical Hebrew term She'ol refers to—the common Grave of humans. [32]

## Christianity: Heaven, Hell & Purgatory

The Roman Catholic Church teaches that there are two main possible Afterlives, with no alternatives or escape. Nearly everyone will spend eternity (or at least until the Resurrection) in either *Heaven* or *Hell*. Heaven is a seven-tiered paradise of eternal joy and bliss—which comes from being close to God. Hell is a fiery pit of eternal torment and punishment, ruled by the Devil (Satan or Lucifer), and filled with Demons who were originally rebel Angels cast down after losing the "War in Heaven."

The Romans had a saying, *"descensus ad Avernus facile est,"* meaning that the descent to Hell was easy. In his epic "Inferno," Dante identifies the thermal Lake Avernus at the oracular site of Cumae in Baia, Italy as the entrance to Hell. [33] Excavations have revealed elaborate underground passages, leading to a subterranean body of water representing the River Styx. This Oracle of the Dead is an echo of the Necromanteion in Ephyra, Greece.

One's eventual destination is determined by their salvation status at the instant of their death. Newborns are believed to be afflicted with "original sin." An infant can be redeemed from this state only by the Church's rite of *baptism*. Once a person reaches the age of accountability, any mortal sin can cause them to lose their salvation, so that they would be "damned" and sent to Hell. However, their salvation can be restored by confessing their sins to a Priest and receiving absolution.

The souls of children who die before reaching puberty—as well as other worthy people throughout history who died without receiving salvation—go to a happy place called *Limbo*. There they must wait until the *Final Judgment* when they will be admitted to Heaven.

---

[32] Wikipedia: "She'ol"
[33] "The Oracle of the Dead at Baia," http://www.oracleofthedead.com/ 1/4/18

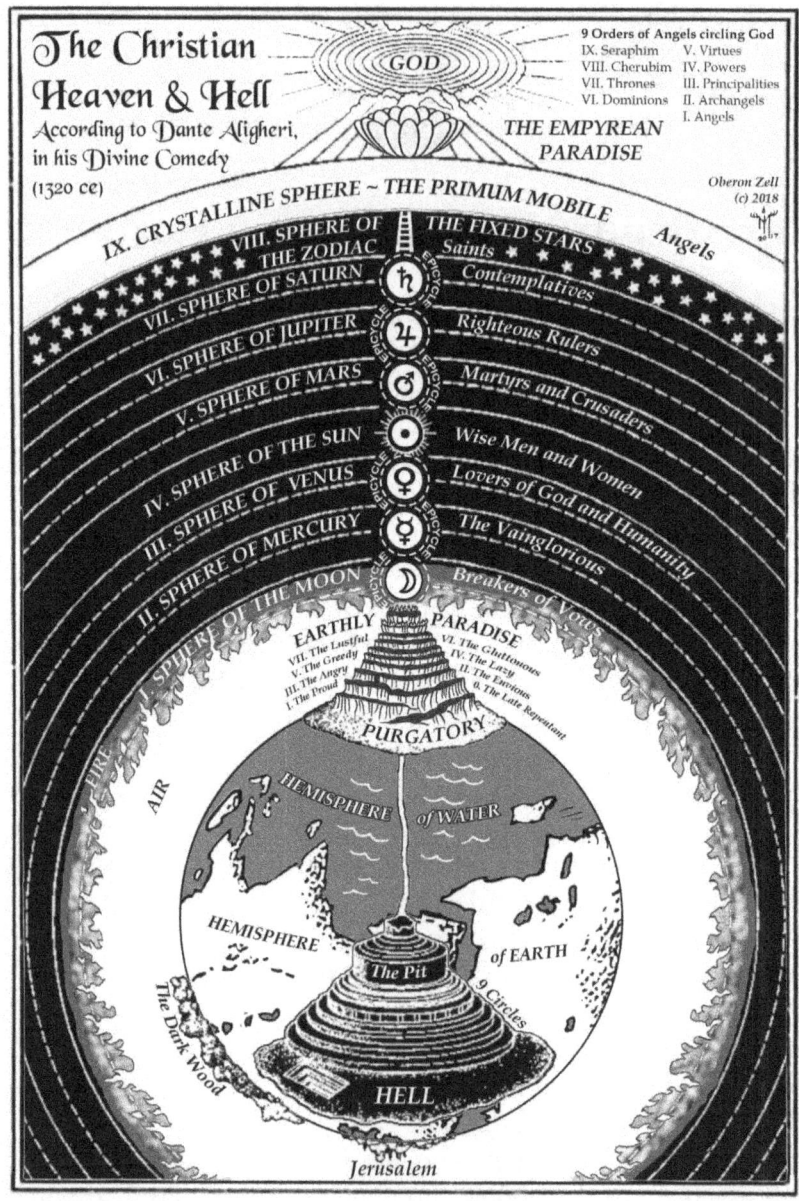

*Dante's Vision of the Christian Heaven & Hell (by Oberon Zell)*

Saints and those who have attained perfect piety are taken immediately to Heaven upon death. But most people go first to *Purgatory*, where they are systematically tortured with fire until they have become sufficiently purified to enter Heaven.

People who have committed a mortal sin which has not been forgiven or have rejected God, go straight to Hell where they will be tortured by Demons forever without any hope of relief or mercy. Dante's Hell is a vast pit with nine concentric descending circles; the damned are consigned to different levels and punishments according to their sins. Its actual entry point is the ancient Oracle of the Dead at Cumae, in Baia, Italy—near Naples. The capital city of Hell on level 5 is called *Pandemonium* ("place of all demons").

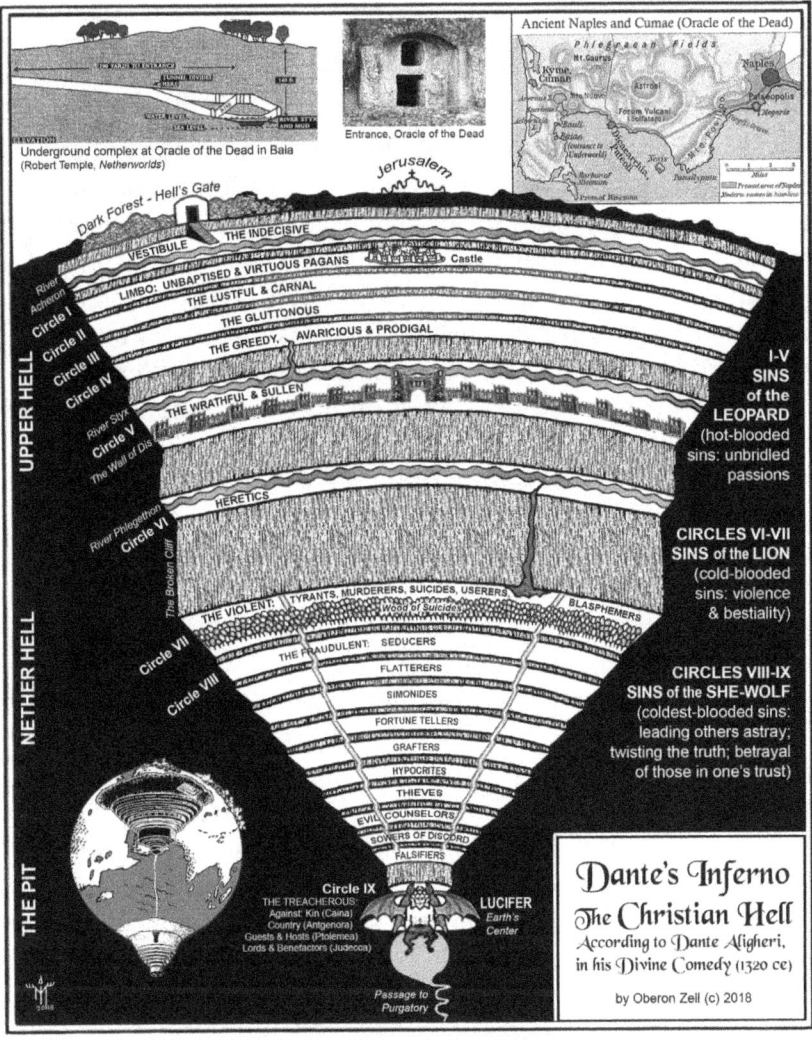

*Dante's Inferno: The nine circles of Hell (by Oberon Zell)*

Other denominations of Christianity present variations on these visions of the Afterlife, but all include the opposing destinations of Heaven vs. Hell. Protestants, however, dispense with Purgatory. Many envision Heaven as a glorious city, with streets paved with gold and a mansion for everyone. Saint Peter sits at the Pearly Gates with a great book in which is recorded all the deeds of applicants, and he assigns them their places accordingly. They become angels, with wings, robes, halos, and harps—singing praises to God in the heavenly choir for all eternity.

## Tibet: The Bardos

In both *Buddhism* and *Hinduism,* the numerous realms of the Afterlife are stages in the never-ending cycle of birth, death, and rebirth which the soul must undergo in its spiritual evolution towards eventually escaping altogether from the "wheel" of incarnations. At each death the soul goes to a paradise or hell corresponding to the way the person has behaved in their last life. After a period of reflection, they are reincarnated into a new life—either better or worse than the last one, depending on how they handled it and the lessons they learned.

The *Tibetan Book of the Dead* says that after death each soul goes before *Yama,* Lord of the Dead, who holds up a mirror in which the person's deeds in life are reflected. Yama's mirror is the soul's own memory, and so Yama's judgment is actually that of the deceased. Each person pronounces their own judgement, thus determining their next rebirth.

The Tibetan word *bardo* means literally "intermediate state," commonly referring to the state of existence in between two lives on earth. It is a concept which arose soon after the Buddha's passing, with a number of earlier Buddhist groups accepting the existence of such an intermediate state, while other schools rejected it.

According to Tibetan tradition, after death and before one's next birth, when one's consciousness is no longer connected with a physical body, one experiences a sequence of degeneration, starting from a clear perception of reality, followed by terrifying hallucinations that arise from the impulses of one's previous unskillful actions.

For the prepared and appropriately-trained individuals, the Bardo offers great opportunity for liberation, since transcendental insight may arise with the direct experience of reality; while for others it can become a place of danger as the karmically-created hallucinations can impel one into a less than desirable rebirth.

*The six Bardos (realms) of Tibetan Buddhism*

Legend has it that Buddha only ever made one drawing in his life. In the sand, he traced a wheel that described the six stages (*Bardos*) of existence:

1. **Kyenay Bardo** (This Life) is the first Bardo of birth and life. It commences at the moment of conception and continues until the final breath, when the soul leaves the body.
2. **Milam Bardo** (Dream) is the second Bardo of the dreaming state.
3. **Samten Bardo** (Meditation) is the third Bardo of meditation. It is generally experienced only by meditators, though some individuals may experience it spontaneously.
4. **Chikhai Bardo** (Dying) is the fourth Bardo of the moment of death. This Bardo commences when the onset of death is nigh and continues until the external and internal breath has completed its dissolution or transmutation.
5. **Chönyi Bardo** (Luminosity) is the fifth Bardo of the luminosity of the true nature. It commences after the final inner breath. In this Bardo visions and auditory phenomena occur, along with an upwelling of profound peace and pristine awareness.
6. **Sidpa Bardo** (Existence) is the sixth Bardo of becoming or transmigration. This Bardo endures until the inner-breath commences in the new body of the next incarnation when the Cycle begins anew.

## Arabia: The Muslim Paradise

*Jannah* ("walled garden") is the Muslim Paradise. It is a splendid oasis, comparable to the Christian Heaven—a happy place, without pain, sorrow, fear, or shame—with everything one desires and every wish fulfilled. Nearness to God is the greatest reward, surpassing all other joys.

According to the *Qur'an,* the basic criterion for salvation is the belief in the one God *(Allah)* and His Angels, revealed books, and Prophets—as well as repentance and doing good deeds. But salvation can only be granted through God's judgement.

*"Muhammed's Paradise."* Persian miniature from The History of Mohammed, *Bibliothèque Nationale de France, Paris*

Jannah is the eternal Afterlife for all of mankind, with any sinners forgiven after a time in purgatory. In contrast to Jannah, the Muslim Hell is called *Jahannam, Dozakh,* or *Nār*.

After death, one's soul will reside in the grave until the appointed resurrection on *Yawm al-Qiyāmah* or Judgment Day. The fate of the individual in the Afterlife will be according to his deeds on Earth.

Entry into Jannah is through eight gates at seven different levels (Heavens), each level being divided into 100 degrees. The second Heaven is *Firdaws* (or *Paradise*). It will be entered first by Muhammad, then those who lived in poverty, and finally the most pious. Entrants will be greeted by Angels with salutations of peace.

One day in Paradise equals 1,000 years on Earth. Inhabitants will be of the same age, and of the same standing. Their life is one of bliss—wearing sumptuous robes, jewelry, and perfumes as they recline on golden couches inlaid with precious stones and partake in exquisite banquets served in priceless vessels by immortal youths or *houris*. They will rejoice in the company of their loved ones (provided they were admitted to Paradise!).

Inhabitants of Jannah will dwell in palaces made from bricks of gold, silver and pearls, with lofty gardens, shady valleys, fountains scented with camphor or ginger, rivers of water, milk, honey, and pure drink and with delicious fruits of all seasons. There will be camels and horses of "dazzling whiteness," along with other creatures. Large trees adorn mountains of musk, with rivers flowing through valleys of rubies and pearls.

The names of the four rivers in Paradise are *Jaihan* (Amu Darya), *Saihan* (Syr Darya), *Furat* (Euphrates), and *Nil* (Nile). A spring named *Salsabil* is the source of the rivers *Al Kawthar* (abundance) and *Rahma* (mercy). A *Lote* tree marks the boundary of the 7th Heaven, beyond which no Earthly creation can pass.

*Jahannam* is one of the names for the Islamic concept of Hell. Other names for Hell (or the different gates of Hell) occurring in the Qur'an include: *Jaheem* ("Blazing Fire"), *Hatamah* ("That which Breaks to Pieces"), *Haawiyah* ("The Abyss"), *Ladthaa*, *Sa'eer* ("the blaze"), *Saqar, an-Nar*. According to the Qur'an, on the Last Day the world will be destroyed and all people (and *jinn*) will be raised from the dead to be judged by Allah as to whether they deserved to be sent to paradise (*Jannah*) or Hell. Hell will be occupied by those who do not believe in Allah, have disobeyed His laws, and/or reject His messengers. One group that will not have to wait until the Last Day to enter hell are "Enemies of Islam," who are sentenced immediately to Hell upon death. Suffering in Hell is both physical and spiritual, and varies according to the sins of the condemned. As described in the Qur'an, Hell has seven levels (each one more severe than the one above it); seven gates (each for a specific group of sinners); a blazing fire, boiling water, and the Tree of *Zaqqum*.

## Mayans: Xibalba

In K'iche' Maya mythology, *Xibalba* ("place of fear") was the lowest of the nine underworlds and the realm of the dead. The Maya believed that every cave and *cenote* gave access to this terrifying underworld. In 16th century CE Verapaz, the entrance to Xibalba was held to be a cave near Cobán, Guatemala. Other cave systems in nearby Belize have also been referred to as the entrance to Xibalba. Thousands of other entrances to Xibalba lie half-hidden in the dense scrub of the Yucatan peninsula. In some Mayan areas, the dark shadow of dust coursing through the Milky Way is viewed as the road to Xibalba.

As in Mesopotamia, the gates into and out of Xibalba lay at the opposite ends of the great arch of the Milky Way, which opened at the equinoxes. At autumn equinox, departed souls could enter Xibalba through the rising gate of Sagittarius. Return to Earth would be through the Gemini exit gate at spring equinox. (see above illus. *The Milky Way as the River of Souls*)

Xibalba is described in the *Popol Vuh* as a court below the surface of the Earth, ruled by twelve powerful gods known as the Lords of Xibalba, all of whom function in pairs. The first pair are Hun-Came ("One Death") and Vucub-Came ("Seven Death").

The remaining ten Lords (five pairs) are often referred to as demons and are given domain over various forms of human suffering—to cause sickness, starvation, fear, destitution, pain, and ultimately death. The remaining residents of Xibalba are thought to have fallen under the dominion of these Lords, going about on the Earth to carry out their assigned duties.

Xibalba is a great city, and a number of individual structures and locations within it are described or mentioned in the *Popol Vuh*. Chief among these is the council place of the Lords, the five or six houses that serve as the first tests of Xibalba—and the famous ballcourt.

Xibalba is rife with tests, trials, and traps for anyone who comes into the city. Even the roads to Xibalba are filled with obstacles: first a river filled with scorpions, then a river of blood, and finally a river of pus. Beyond these is a crossroads where travelers must choose from among four roads that speak to confuse them.

After passing these obstacles, one comes to the Xibalba council place, where visitors must greet the seated Lords. Realistic mannequins are seated near the Lords to confuse and humiliate people who greet them, and the confused are then invited to sit on a bench, which is actually a hot stove. The Lords of Xibalba entertain themselves by humiliating people in this fashion before sending them into one of Xibalba's deadly tests.

There are six deadly houses in Xibalba filled with trials for visitors. The first is Dark House, completely dark inside. The second is Rattling House or Cold House, with bone-chilling cold and rattling hail. The third is Jaguar House, with hungry jaguars. The fourth is Bat House, filled with dangerous shrieking bats, and the fifth is Knife House, with razor-sharp blades that move about of their own accord. The sixth, Hot House, has fires and heat. The purpose of this gauntlet is to humiliate and discourage those who cannot outwit the test, and are therefore uworthy.

There is also a ballcourt in Xibalba in which the heroes of the *Popol Vuh* succumbed to the trickery of the demons in the form of a deadly, bladed ball—as well as the site in which the Maya Hero Twins outwitted the Gods and brought about their downfall.

According to the *Popol Vuh*, the Xibalbans at one point enjoyed the worship of the people on the surface of the Earth, who offered human sacrifice to the gods of death. Over the period covered in the *Popol Vuh*, the Xibalbans are tricked into accepting counterfeit sacrifices, and then finally humiliated into accepting lesser offerings from above.

In 2008, a fascinating discovery was made by University of Yucatan's underwater archaeologist, Guillermo de Anda. He had spent five years searching through the 450-year-old, almost forgotten records of the Inquisition in Yucatan.

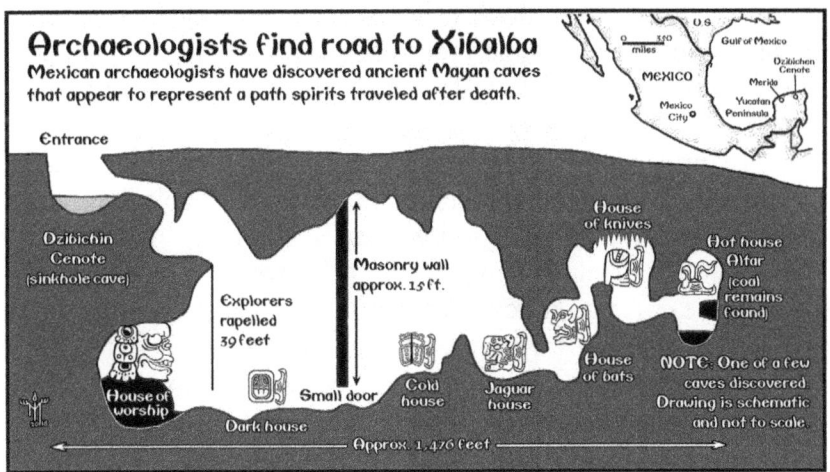

*Dzibichin Cenote: The Caves of Xibalba (source: University of Yucatan archaeologist Guillermo de Anda; redrawn by Oberon Zell*

Deep in the interior, a short distance from the modern city of Merida, de Anda came to the *Dzibichin Cenote* and the series of caves to which it gives access. There, in the light of their torches, they saw tottering ancient temple platforms, slippery staircases, and tortuous paths that skirted underground lakes littered with Mayan pottery and ancient skulls. To de Anda, this network of underground chambers, roads, and temples beneath farmland and jungle suggested that they had been fashioned to mimic the journey to the underworld.

The group explored walled-off sacred chambers that can only be entered by: crawling along a floor populated by spiders, scorpions, and toads; a broad, 100-yard smoothly-paved underground road leading to the "confusing crossroads" of the legends; and subterranean "roads" that plunge through deep pools of water that might signify the rivers of blood and pus. They also found a submerged temple and a number of walled-off stone rooms. At the center of one of the underground lakes, de Anda's team found a collapsed and submerged altar with carvings indicating it was dedicated to the ten Lords of Death.

"There are a number of elements that make us think that this road is a representation of the journey to Xibalba" de Anda said. "We think it is no coincidence that the road which comes out of the crossroads leads to the west," the direction the *Popol Vuh* describes as the way to the afterlife.

If further proof were needed, many of the chambers eerily duplicated those mentioned in the sacred book. In one, hanging stalactites and knife-sharp rocks projecting from walls made it almost impossible to move without serious injury. De Anda believes they are a representation of the feared "House of Knives." Bats with razor sharp teeth swarm everywhere, forcing visitors to dodge to avoid them. One section—so hot it leaves visitors sweating profusely—de Anda believes to correspond to the "Chamber of Roasting Heat." Cool currents of air chill frigid caves, just like the legend's "Chambers of Shaking Cold." Finally, while de Anda has not yet encountered a specific "Jaguar Chamber," the bones of that animal have been discovered in at least one cave. [34]

In January 2018, as I was completing this chapter, Dona Carter (Belladona) and I made a pilgrimage to the Yucatan to explore the Cenotes and caves associated with the legend of Xibalba. Here are a few excerpts from my journal:

*2018.1.15 – Monday*
*Journey to Xibalba*
    *Saturday Dona and I explored a cenote (sinkhole) at the Park of Two Eyes (the name of a pair of cenotes). The cenotes of the Yucatan Peninsula resulted from the shock of the big comet or asteroid of the Chicxulub impact at Meri-*

---

[34] Boyd, Mildred, "*The Pathway Through Xibalba,*" http://www.chapala.com/chapala/magnifecentmexico/path/path.html (1/9/18)

da that terminated the 150-million-year reign of the Dragons 65 million years ago.

All these hundreds of cenotes comprise a vast network of cavern systems that undermines the entire peninsula. The one we explored was called the "Mysterious Cenote," and we donned wet suits, masks and snorkels, with waterproof flashlights, for a long swim and dive through the dark water-filled caverns, the ceilings hung with needle-sharp stalactites, just as the Mayan Popol Vuh describes in the Knife House of Xibalba, with razor-sharp blades that move about of their own accord. If we'd raised our heads above the water, we'd have pierced our skulls. Fortunately, the snorkels allowed us to remain submerged.

*2018.1.24 – Wednesday*
*Perla del Oriente Maya (Mayan Pearl of the East)*
   *This trip encompasses more research for my current book on "That Undiscover'd Country," as well as adding to my materials for a future book on "History's Mysteries." In particular, I'm exploring the Mayan Underworld of Xibalba. Tomorrow we're heading off to the Mayan ruins and cenotes of Ek Balam, just a short taxi trip north of here, for more explorations.*

In modern times, Xibalba seems to have lost many of its more fearsome aspects and is merely considered to be a rather colorful Mexican afterlife, as depicted in Day of the Dead celebrations and several animated movies: *The Corpse Bride* (2005), *The Book of Life* (2014), and *Coco* (2017). In *The Book of Life*, a personified Xibalba is the ruler of "The Land of the Forgotten," while *La Muerte* (Lady Death) rules "The Land of the Remembered."

# Part III
# Intimations of Immortality

### Thanatopsis
By Willian Cullen Bryant (1794-1878)

*To him who in the love of Nature holds*
*Communion with her visible forms, she speaks*
*A various language; for his gayer hours*
*She has a voice of gladness, and a smile*
*And eloquence of beauty, and she glides*
*Into his darker musings, with a mild*
*And healing sympathy, that steals away*
*Their sharpness, ere he is aware. When thoughts*
*Of the last bitter hour come like a blight*
*Over thy spirit, and sad images*
*Of the stern agony, and shroud, and pall,*
*And breathless darkness, and the narrow house,*
*Make thee to shudder and grow sick at heart;*
*Go forth, under the open sky, and list*
*To Nature's teachings, while from all around*
*Earth and her waters, and the depths of air*
*Comes a still voice:*

*Yet a few days, and thee*
*The all-beholding sun shall see no more*
*In all his course; nor yet in the cold ground,*
*Where thy pale form was laid with many tears,*
*Nor in the embrace of ocean, shall exist*
*Thy image. Earth, that nourished thee, shall claim*
*Thy growth, to be resolved to earth again,*
*And, lost each human trace, surrendering up*
*Thine individual being, shalt thou go*
*To mix forever with the elements,*

*To be a brother to the insensible rock
And to the sluggish clod, which the rude swain
Turns with his share, and treads upon.
The oak shall send his roots abroad, and pierce thy mould.*

*Yet not to thine eternal resting-place
Shalt thou retire alone, nor couldst thou wish
Couch more magnificent. Thou shalt lie down
With patriarchs of the infant world—with kings,
The powerful of the Earth—the wise, the good,
Fair forms, and hoary seers of ages past,
All in one mighty sepulchre. The hills
Rock-ribbed and ancient as the sun, the vales
Stretching in pensive quietness between;
The venerable woods—rivers that move
In majesty, and the complaining brooks
That make the meadows green; and, poured round all,
Old Ocean's gray and melancholy waste,
Are but the solemn decorations all
Of the great tomb of man. The golden sun,
The planets, all the infinite host of heaven,
Are shining on the sad abodes of death
Through the still lapse of ages. All that tread
The globe are but a handful to the tribes
That slumber in its bosom. Take the wings
Of morning, pierce the Barcan wilderness,
Or lose thyself in the continuous woods
Where rolls the Oregon, and hears no sound,
Save his own dashings—yet the dead are there;
And millions in those solitudes, since first
The flight of years began, have laid them down
In their last sleep—the dead reign there alone.*

*So shalt thou rest, and what if thou withdraw
In silence from the living, and no friend
Take note of thy departure? All that breathe
Will share thy destiny. The gay will laugh
When thou art gone, the solemn brood of care
Plod on, and each one as before will chase*

*His favorite phantom; yet all these shall leave*
*Their mirth and their employments, and shall come*
*And make their bed with thee. As the long train*
 *Of ages glides away, the sons of men—*
*The youth in life's fresh spring, and he who goes*
*In the full strength of years, matron and maid,*
*The speechless babe, and the gray-headed man—*
 *Shall one by one be gathered to thy side,*
*By those, who in their turn shall follow them.*

*So live, that when thy summons comes to join*
 *The innumerable caravan, which moves*
*To that mysterious realm, where each shall take*
 *His chamber in the silent halls of death,*
*Thou go not, like the quarry-slave at night,*
*Scourged to his dungeon, but, sustained and soothed*
 *By an unfaltering trust, approach thy grave*
*Like one who wraps the drapery of his couch*
*About him, and lies down to pleasant dreams.*

**Calavera** (Spanish. "skull") A *calavera* [plural: *calaveras*] is a representation of a human skull. The term is most often applied to edible or decorative skulls made from either sugar or clay that are ubiquitous in the Mexican celebration of the Day of the Dead *(Dia de Muertos)* and the Roman Catholic All Souls' Day.

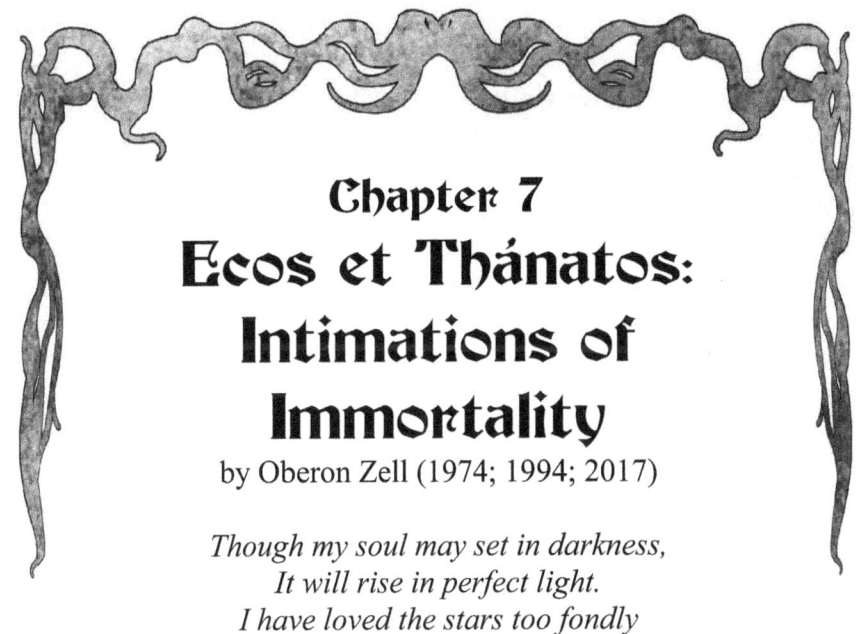

# Chapter 7
# Ecos et Thánatos: Intimations of Immortality
by Oberon Zell (1974; 1994; 2017)

*Though my soul may set in darkness,
It will rise in perfect light.
I have loved the stars too fondly
To be fearful of the night.*
~~Sarah Williams, "The Old Astronomer to His Pupil" [35]

QUESTIONS OF LIFE, DEATH, AND POSSIBLE "Afterlife" have obsessed humanity since the birth of our species. The emergence of sentience includes an awareness of mortality, and fear of oblivion has led to the hopeful invention of many concepts of afterlives and after-realms. These have formed the cornerstones of most of the world's religions. These concepts, like so many other traditional religious concepts, have been couched in metaphysical terms and language so vague and ambiguous as to be impossible to confirm or contradict. But in the greater metaphor of the Gaea Thesis, we may reach an expanded understanding of the nature of Death, as we have already reached an expanded understanding of the nature of Life.

First, of course, we need to define our terms. For the purposes of this discussion, I shall use the word "Soul" to mean one's unique conscious identity or *persona* (a combination of character,

---

[35] From "The Old Astronomer to His Pupil," by Sarah Williams, 1837-1868. *Best-Loved Poems of the American People,* Hazel Felleman, ed., Garden City Pub. Co., Garden City NY: 1936, pp. 613-614. These last lines were used as an epitaph for an Astronomer-couple buried at Alleghany Observatory.

personality, etc. which would seem to be dependent upon and inseparable from one's total memory-complex). Thus, for the "soul" to survive the death of the body in any meaningful way would require the continuity of conscious identity through memory remain unbroken. "Death" we shall thus have to understand in two senses: physical and "spiritual." Physical death obviously refers to the cessation of life-functions in the organic body; and is marked by the onset of an irreversible process of progressive decomposition with in the cellular structures of that body. "Spiritual" death would mean the termination of conscious identity through memory, and may occur independently of physical death.

Obviously, any form of "afterlife" in which one's conscious identity is lost would be of little relevance, for in that case, what we have been regarding as the essence is still obliterated. We must have some form of conscious survival, or the concept of survival becomes meaningless. Unfortunately, it is generally accepted by neuroscientists that our memory—and hence our identity—is utterly dependent upon the fragile physical structure of our corporeal bodies, especially our complex and magnificent brain and nervous system. Artificial stimulation of one or another area of the brain can result in drastic alterations of personality. Various drugs can distort memory, perception, personality—and hence identity. A blow to the head can induce amnesia, which, as far as the continuity of a person's conscious identity is concerned, is spiritual death.

## Bioenergetic Fields...

In their 1970 book *Psychic Discoveries Behind the Iron Curtain,* [36] Sheila Ostrander and Lynn Schroeder describe experiments with Kirlian photography, utilizing a field of high-intensity electricity. These experiments seem to have confirmed the existence of the *aura* and the *astral body* by recording these phenomena in all their blazing glory and in sharp enough detail to be examined

---

[36] Ostrander, Sheila & Schroeder, Lynn, *Psychic Discoveries Behind the Iron Curtain.* Prentice-Hall, 1970.

microscopically. It is now established that all living entities generate a field of energy of a unique form, apparently unrelated to the electromagnetic spectrum, which appears to conform to what the Hindus call *prana,* or Wilhelm Reich named *orgone.* Most laboratory researchers seem to prefer the term *bioplasma.* Moreover, the pattern of this energy field is both synergic and organic: the field maintains the microscopically exact configuration of the entire organism. In a living human body, "flames" of bioplasma pour out of certain specific points on the surface of the body to surround the person with a nebulous glow of diffuse radiation—the *aura.* The points of origin correspond with the acupuncture points of Chinese medicine.

Just as the pattern of the total field of energy (the "astral body") is peculiar to the exact configuration of the genetically complete individual, so is this peculiarity extended to every other living entity, including each individual cell within the body. Indeed, each organ has its own astral configuration distinct from that of its component cells or that of the larger body.

Relating these findings to the issue of immortality, we note to our dismay that in Kirlian photography of dying plants and animals the aura slowly fades with the progressive acceleration of death in each of the cells of the organism, and the astral body itself ultimately disintegrates with tiny fading sparkles (looking like the dying embers in a fireplace) until there is nothing left but dark physical matter, which begins to deteriorate thereafter. At no point in this process does the astral body appear to separate in any sense from the physical body; in fact, its disintegration actually precedes that of the physical body. This would not seem to indicate any form of survival or "discorporation" of the astral body. Indeed, it appears that the astral body is maintained solely through continuous generation by the processes of life in the physical body, and cannot exist independently. Does a magnetic field remain when the magnet is turned off, or destroyed? A generated field ceases to exist when the generator no longer continues to generate it.

In Carlos Castaneda's second book, *A Separate Reality,* the Yaqui Indian sorcerer Don Juan describes death as he has viewed it through his astral perception:

"...I shifted my eyes so I would see his personal life disintegrating, expanding uncontrollably beyond its limits, like a fog of crystals, because that is the way life and death mix and expand. That is what I did at the time of my son's death. That's all one could ever do, and that is controlled folly. Had I looked at him I would have watched him becoming immobile and I would have felt a cry inside of me, because never again would I look at his fine figure pacing the Earth. I saw his death instead, and there was no sadness, no feeling. His death was equal to everything else." [37]

# Death...

> *I find myself surprised by the thought that dying is an all-right thing to do, but perhaps it should not surprise. It is, after all, the most ancient and fundamental of biologic functions, with its mechanisms worked out with the same attention to detail, the same provision for the advantage of the organism, the same abundance of genetic information for guidance through the stages, that we have long since become accustomed to finding in all the crucial acts of living.* ~~Lewis Thomas [38]

The problem of Death is one of sudden termination; gradual discontinuity of memory and identity occurs naturally as part of our normal living, as old memories fade from mind to be replaced by new ones. In the course of our lives, every cell in our bodies "dies" and is replaced—some with quite high frequency. When nerve cells—including those in our brain—die, however, they are not replaced, but lost forever. Yet there is no sudden discontinuity, and hence we do not experience this process as "death," for our "soul" remains continuous—if not intact. Yet how fragile a thing that soul seems to be, and if it is just a field phenomenon, surely it cannot exist independently of the neurophysical miracle that generates it—the billions of interwoven cells of the living brain. It cannot even exist unimpaired if that organ is seriously damaged, let alone destroyed.

---

[37] Castaneda, Carlos, *A Separate Reality.* Simon & Schuster, 1971, p. 90.
[38] Thomas, Lewis, *The Lives of a Cell.* Viking Press, 1974, p. 51

Thus, there would seem to be no basis for the fervent contention of most religionists that something they call the "soul" somehow survives death to live on in a fancied afterlife. We could abandon our quest at this point, as many skeptics have done, and conclude that we are doomed to a brief and finite existence. We could seek consolation in the words of the Inuit Angakok shaman, Siorakidsok:

> "Now that you have covered the dead man with stones you must cancel his name from your talk and his image from your minds forever. You had five days in which to weep all the tears worth weeping for any man and to extol all the deeds any man is able to accomplish. From now on there shall be no more of that. This man should be envied for the life he led, not pitied for his finish. All lives come to an end, and whether they end a little sooner or a little later, what matters, since they end? Whatever ends is short. And is it bad that life is short? No, for it is the knowledge of its shortness that makes it valuable. And this man made the most of his. He saw his children grow up. He hunted the big bear. He ate considerable amounts of food, and usually the best. It seems he even killed a white man. May your children grow up to be as strong and as lucky." [39]

## Beyond Time and Space...

However, quantum mechanics and astrophysics have lately given birth to the new theory of *biocentrism,* which proposes that consciousness is not, in fact, generated within the human brain, but is fundamental to the universe, and immortal. According to this theory, it is consciousness that creates the material universe, not the other way around.

A 2010 book, *"Biocentrism: How Life and Consciousness Are the Keys to Understanding the Nature of the Universe,"* proposes that life does not end when the body dies, and consciousness can last forever. The author, Dr. Robert Lanza, was voted the 3rd most

---

[39] Ruesch, Hans, *Top of the World.* Pocket Books, 1971.

important scientist alive by the *NY Times*. A *US News & World Report* cover story called him a "genius" and a "renegade thinker," likening him to Einstein.

> Lanza points to the structure of the universe itself—and that the laws, forces, and constants of the universe appear to be fine-tuned for life, implying intelligence existed prior to matter. He also claims that space and time are not objects or things, but rather tools of our animal understanding. Lanza says that we carry space and time around with us "like turtles with shells." meaning that when the shell comes off (space and time), we still exist.
> The theory implies that death of consciousness simply does not exist. It only exists as a thought because people identify themselves with their body. They believe that the body is going to perish, sooner or later, thinking their consciousness will disappear too. If the body generates consciousness, then consciousness dies when the body dies. But if the body receives consciousness in the same way that a cable box receives satellite signals, then of course consciousness does not end at the death of the physical vehicle. In fact, consciousness exists outside of constraints of time and space. It is able to be anywhere: in the human body and outside of it. In other words, it is non-local in the same sense that quantum objects are non-local. [40]

## Memory Molecules...

So far, we have looked at only a part of the total picture. We must remember that we are not isolated organisms existing independently of all other organisms, but that we are actually cells in the body of a vaster Being: Gaea, our great and revered Goddess, Mother Earth. Let us examine the process of mortality from this synergic

---

[40]**LeMind, Anna,** "Quantum Theory Proves That Consciousness Moves to Another Universe After Death**," originally published on** www.learningmind.com, 2017. http://www.theearthchild.co.za/quantum-theory-consciousness-moves-to-another-universe-after-death-2/ accessed 7/15/17

and macrocosmic perspective:

When the cells within our bodies "die," they do not merely lie around inert. They are reabsorbed back into the total system; their life-forces and component chemicals being recycled into new cells. Through death, old life becomes new life. By the same token, death as we see it in the laboratory or in humans rarely occurs in Nature. Animals and plants rarely just die and lie around inert; they are killed and eaten by other animals. Even before the aura fades and the astral form disintegrates, the still-living cells of that plant or animals are being digested by another; being reabsorbed back into the total organic system of the living Biosphere. Thus, the eaten becomes the eater.

And while the individual identity of the dying one may be terminated in this process, yet the life force itself is not. Predators "kill" and eat their prey at the same occasion; they do not generally leave their kills lying around until the cells are all dead and decayed and the astral form has faded to nothingness (though some scavengers may eat meat that is pretty far gone by our standards...). Animal predators do not cook their food to kill the cells, nor do they freeze it for future consumption. The cells they eat are still alive, and that lifeforce is reabsorbed—recycled—before it has time to wither away.

> Death isn't the end—at least for some genes. Postmortem studies conducted on mice and zebrafish by geneticists at the university of Washington revealed that hundreds of the animals' genes remain active, continuing to synthesize molecules and perform other tasks, up to 96 hours after the animals' death. [41]

Some interesting experiments with rats and planaria indicate that some form of memory can be transmitted from one creature to another by the latter eating the brain of the former:

> We now know that the DNA and its associated RNA messengers carry information from generation to genera-

---

[41] "Did You Know?" *Discover,* Nov. 2016, p. 13.

tion, just as (in the human class of life) books do. Prof. Tracy Sonneborn of the University of Indiana was the first to find traces of this "molecular memory" in paramecia, which often seem to be born "knowing" certain things which earlier generations had to learn by trial and error. Dr. Ruth Sager of Columbia, in similar research, has carefully demonstrated results that rule out all other explanations of this except the theory that some memories are carried on the molecular lever, or, as science writer John N. Bleibtreu says, we possess a "molecular memory."

Prof. James V. McConnell, since 1957, has been demonstrating, over and over again, that flatworms which eat other flatworms immediately "learn" what the eaten flatworms knew. Again, learned information seems to pass on the molecular level to the "mind" of the new host-body. [42]

Georges Unger, Professor of Pharmacology at Baylor College of Medicine in Houston, delivered a paper at a scientific meeting in Atlantic City in 1973 which told of his discovery of "a whole family of 'memory molecules' in the brains of laboratory animals. Each kind of molecule represents a specific pattern of learned behavior. By injecting the molecules from one animal's brain into another, Unger reports, he has transferred the behavior pattern—in effect, a memory transplant." [43] The genetic code written into the structure of DNA governs everything humans (and all other living beings) inherit from their ancestors. The other hereditary "master molecule," RNA, serves as a messenger to carry this information out of the nucleus and into the cell body.

The first hint that one of these substances might be directly involved in the storage of nongenetic information in the brain—that is, in memory—came from the laboratory of Holger Hyden at the University of Goteborg, Sweden, in 1959. Hyden showed the production of RNA in brain cells went up markedly when an organism

---

[42] Wilson, Robert Anton, "Crowley, Leary and Genetics," *Green Egg* #60, Feb. 1, 1974.
[43] Jonas, Gerald, "The Memory Molecules," *1974 Nature/Science Annual.* Time-Life Books, 1974.

learned to do something; there were also indications that the brain produced a special kind of RNA during learning.

## Cannibals and Trees...

Interestingly, most carnivores seem to relish the brain especially, and cannibals have always regarded the brains of their slain foes of especial significance. To eat the brain of a noble enemy was to absorb his qualities of bravery and courage, and the brain was thus looked upon as sacred and to be consumed only by the slayer. The liver and heart eventually came to acquire such significance as well; but who is to say that these did not also transmit some particular chemicals that would convey the desired qualities?

Anthropologist Margaret Murray observed that "Ceremonial cannibalism is found in many parts of the world, and in all cases, it is due to the desire to obtain the qualities of the dead person; his courage, his wisdom, and so on. When a divine victim was eaten, the holy flesh thus received into the system, the worshipper became one with the deity." [44]

Is it possible that there is scientific validity in this "primitive" attitude? In *Stranger in a Strange Land*, [45] Robert Heinlein makes quite a case for ritual cannibalism among his fictional ancient "Martians," with identical motives and justification for "grokking in fullness" a discorporated water-brother. And we are all familiar with the sacramental rite of symbolic ritual cannibalism in the Christian communion ceremony!

In many horticultural villages of ancient Europe, when a member of the community died, he or she was customarily buried—unembalmed—in a shallow grave with an apple placed on his or her belly (or sometimes beneath a growing sapling). Often, a couple wanting a child would have sex upon the grave. The afterbirth of a baby thus conceived would also be buried at the root of the tree, which would then become his or her special "soul tree."

---

[44] Murray, Margaret, *The God of the Witches*. Oxford Univ. Press, 1931; 1970.
[45] Heinlein, Robert Anson, *Stranger in a Strange Land*. G. P. Putnam's Sons, 1961.

Sometimes the name of the deceased would be passed on to both the tree and the child, and their fates would be linked, as apple trees in particular have a life-span equivalent to that of humans. (It is interesting to note in passing that Orthodox Jewish law requires that bodies not be embalmed, and that they be buried immediately in a coffin made entirely of easily biodegradable materials—even metal nails are prohibited.)

The villagers practicing this custom believed that the soul—as well as the flesh of the man or woman—would pass into the tree, hence into its fruit to be rejoined with the community when they ate said fruit. Thus, a form of immortality was realized in daily life (and death) among our Pagan ancestors. The famous Chicago-area eco tactician and guerrilla saboteur of polluting industries, "The Fox," was quoted in an interview about his views on death:

> When my time comes, I hope no one drains my veins of their sustaining fluid and fills them with formaldehyde, then wastes me by putting me in a concrete box in the ground for eternity. Rather, just a simple pine box with an acorn on top of it. Find a place where a tree is needed and return me to Nature. When the acorn grows, I can nourish it and give back in some measure what I've taken. Maybe someday kids can crawl in my branches or a raccoon might curl up in my trunk or the larks can sing out from my leaves. At any rate, I would rather let an oak tree be my epitaph than a marble slab be my tombstone. [46]

Indeed, with all their emphasis on after-life, it would seem that the pious people who bury their dead in concrete and steel vaults—permanently poisoned with formaldehyde—or consign them to the life-devouring flames of the crematorium, ensure that they are perhaps the only living beings on this planet who do not achieve immortality!

---

[46] "The Fox," *Esquire,* March, 1972.

# Past Life Recalls...

> ...If the transformation [of physical death] is a coordinated, integrated physiologic process in its initial, local stages, there is still that permanent vanishing of consciousness to be accounted for. Are we to be stuck forever with this problem? Where on Earth does it go? Is it simply stopped dead in its tracks, lost in humus, wasted? Considering the tendency of Nature to find uses for complex and intricate mechanisms, this seems to me unnatural. I prefer to think of it as somehow separated off at the filaments of its attachment, and then drawn like an easy breath back into the membrane of its origin, a fresh memory for a biospherical nervous system... (~~Lewis Thomas) [47]

So let us return to the concept of immortality of the soul through continuity of memory, for we might yet discover ways in which this form of immortality may manifest.

Reincarnation is a basic tenet of many of the great religious systems of the world, and most modern Pagans affirm belief in it, though few seem to agree on exactly what is meant by the concept. As commonly understood, the word seems to connote the rebirth of the soul in a new body, following the death of the original body. That seems simple enough, but let us expand the definition a bit to include the awakening of a personality in a physical body other than the one in which that personality originated.

Russian experiments in variants of hypnosis (originated by Dr. Vladimir Raikov of Moscow, who calls his technique "suggestology") have produced clinical "reincarnation" in which art students, for example, become reincarnations of Da Vinci or Michelangelo, complete with full "memories" of the artists' childhoods, etc. During the period of the "reincarnation," which can last indefinitely, they are fully conscious and aware, but they seem to be living and creating with the reincarnated minds of other people. They may even believe they are actually living in the particular historical pe-

---

[47] Thomas, Lewis, *The Lives of a Cell.* Viking Press, 1974, p. 52)

riod of the artist's life. Moreover, their painting style and skill does clearly resemble that of the artist they have become! [48]

If these experiments seem like mere parlor games, not to be taken seriously, remember that much of the apparent "evidence" for reincarnation rests in people's having "recalls" or "memories" of former lives. If such "memories" can be so easily induced under simple lab conditions, it would be reasonable to assume they could also arise spontaneously, or during the increasingly popular New Age practice of "past life" trance regression. Should these "memories" then be dismissed as mere hallucinations?

I think not. Recalling that we ourselves are mere cells in the great body of the Mother, we should be able to draw some analogies. In our own brains, even though the particular neurons that had originally recorded certain data may have long since "died" and been recycled, it is possible, with the proper stimulation, to elicit a vivid and complete recall—visual, auditory, tactile, gustatory, olfactory—of any experience that the person has ever had, even back to the womb! Even though such experiences may have long since been lost to the actual physical cells which originally recorded them, the astral equivalents of those cells seem to be able to retain the entire pattern—like a hologram.

## The Switchboard...

Thus, while it seems to be necessary that data be available in living cells for us to have conscious access to it, our subconscious, having access to the "permanent" record in the field of our collective "astral brain," has no such limitations. Isaac Bonewits described the concept of what he calls "The Switchboard" as the final product of any and all telepathic interconnections between all people who have ever lived:

> My entire memory has been broadcast to all the world and it is now a part of your memory. Conversely, some-

---

[48] Ostrander, Sheila & Schroeder, Lynn, *Psychic Discoveries Behind the Iron Curtain*. Prentice-Hall, 1970.

where down deep inside, I have all of *your* memory as a part of *my* memory. Now, when I die, you will still have all my memories intact inside your head; and when you die, others will have your memories of my memories, *ad infinitum.*

The final result is that *each of us has, buried deeply, the memories of every living human being as well as all the memories of those who are now dead.* The vast net of billions of interlocking metapatterns with their innumerable subpatterns is what I call the *Switchboard...*

...How far back does the *Switchboard* go? Does it stop with Cro-Magnon, Neanderthal, or Pithecanthropus? Does it stop with man at all? Could it go all the way back to the first animal to have a nervous system capable of transmitting and receiving? [49]

On a macrocosmic scale, therefore, we hear encounter Jung's concept of the "Collective Unconscious," the subconscious of our whole planet, Mother Earth. And in that permanent record ("the Akashic Record," in Hindu phraseology) contained within Her vast "astral body" would be found all the patterns of all the memories of every creature that had ever lived on Earth. For all of them—all of us—have only been component cells of Her body. So, it is very reasonable that we should be able to download from Her perpetual subconscious—which is our perpetual subconscious as well, for we are Her—memories of the lives, perceptions and experiences of our predecessors. And since what we call "time" may very well be a facet of the bioenergetic spectrum, when we tap the subconscious of the Mother it is not altogether inconceivable that we may discover therein "memories" of lives and perceptions that to our own limited perceptions still lie in the "future."

Biocentrism takes this idea even further

> Today's standard science model is material based, and assumes that atoms, stars, and planets (with behavior guided by the four fundamental forces) are the basis of the cos-

---

[49] Bonewits, Philip Emmons Isaac, *Real Magic*. Berkeley Medallion, 1971, pp. 148-149.

mos. Most scientists regard consciousness as an irrelevancy, an airy-fairy sort of thing. But the surest aspect of reality is our awareness. After all, everything observed, contemplated, thought about, and experienced occurs via the simple fact of consciousness. It is the most inarguable aspect of the cosmos. So, rather than dismissing it, perhaps perception itself ought to be the starting point in our scientific explorations of reality. Therefore, let's consider an alternative model in which this is moved front and center.

By this thinking, consciousness is not merely correlative with nature, as biocentrism claims to prove, but is the sole foundational basis of the universe. For the moment, consider that perhaps awareness is eternal and never absent. Indeed, you're always conscious of something, and this always is felt to occur "right now." This never changes.

And maybe we cannot figure out how the brain creates consciousness because it has never really done that! What if the brain's job is to filter, focus and even limit the consciousness that is all-pervasive, to make the experience appropriate for the individual organism, such as yourself as a human? If this is true, then the brain's dissolution at death in no way ends the experience of awareness. Indeed, that could be what opens the floodgates to unlimited, unconfined awareness, as is experienced in mystical states such as those labeled enlightenment, samadhi, or satori. [50]

## Reincarnation...

But clearly, this form of reincarnation is not what the mystics have in mind. They envisage a soul being actually transmitted intact from a dying body to a living one. Is this possible? We can look at recorded cases for which no other explanation seems conceivable, as recorded in Ian Stevenson's book, *Twenty Cases Suggestive of Reincarnation*. [51] Many very young children have been

---

[50] Berman, Bob, "Is the universe conscious?" *Hudson Valley One,* Sept. 29, 2018 https://hudsonvalleyone.com/2018/09/29/is-the-universe-conscious/

[51] Stevenson, Ian, *Twenty Cases Suggestive of Reincarnation.* American Socie-

interviewed who recall clearly their previous death and rebirth into their new bodies. Their memories and identifications with their former lives vary from vague impressions to highly detailed; in some cases that they have actually returned to their former homes and attempted to resume their interrupted lives and relationships!

> You cannot die; you have existed forever and will continue to exist forever, for *you* are forever. You share the same soul as all the gods that have ever existed; they are aspects of the soul just as much as you are. You are the soul of the universe—and you exist here and now as a spark of that mystery. Each night as your head touches the pillow and you snuggle deeply beneath your duvet, you become the spirit you have always been. And in that state, you know of the origination of all things and the magic that you are the universe experiencing itself, swimming in the rapture of being—with no purpose other than to be. You are the beauty of the universe in perpetual motion.
> 
> Your body will die and your personality will dissolve, its memories imparted onto eternity. Your spirit will encounter other forms of existence, and it will impart those memories onto the fabric of the soul. You are a body, a soul, and a pale and mysterious thing; you are all of these and more; you have been more and will be more. Nothing is lost, it simply transforms.
> 
> Rest, close your eyes, sleep, and reach for the soul's meaning.     (~~Kristoffer Hughes, *The Journey Into Spirit*) [52]

We noted initially the prevailing scientific premise that the astral body—which has often been equated with the "soul"—cannot exist except as a generated projection of a living body; when the body dies, its aura fades and its astral form disintegrates. In this paradigm, the astral body simply cannot go wandering off on its own if the body ceases to exist. Even in "astral projection," the body still lives to supply the energy to generate that projection, hence the term. However, the records of "hauntings" indicate that orgone energy can be recorded in inanimate matter (much as light

---

ty for Psychical Research, 1966.

[52] Hughes, Kristoffer, *The Journey Into Spirit: A Pagan's Perspective on Death, Dying & Bereavement*. Llewellyn Publications, 2014, p. 229

energy is recorded on film) to be "played back" whenever stimulated by similar energy, as in a hologram. This is what Justine Glass refers to as a "gramophone ghost." [53]

From this, we can extrapolate the possibility of a dying person gathering his or her last resources of bioplasma in one final projection (made easier, perhaps, by the mind no longer having to maintain the body) to be flung forth into the æther. Countless anecdotal "ghost" stories recount a phantom of a person appearing before his or her loved ones at the exact moment of his or her distant death, in a final farewell. Usually, such phantom projections soon fade and vanish. Where do they go? Do they simply dissipate into nothingness? Or are they reabsorbed back into the "Switchboard,"—the collective unconscious of Gaea?

In the case of hauntings, that final projection seems to find a suitable recording medium in the inanimate matter of a house or other place. But in the case of reincarnation, the projected astral entity must locate another available human body in which it can be recorded and establish a new existence: ideally, the body of an unborn infant—even a mere embryo (and in some cases, such as Guru Maharaji, the body of a severely autistic person has apparently served). This new body must be accessible at the time of death or very shortly thereafter, for this projection can occur but once, and cannot go wandering around searching for long after the generating body ceases to function.

Needless to say, this can happen but rarely, and then not to everyone—but it apparently does happen. It happened to me, as the soul of my dying maternal grandfather transmigrated to the embryo growing in my mother's womb. When we really examine such phenomena, we should put them into the same category as "possession," as there seems to have been a number of recorded cases where such possession occurred while the one who was the source of the projection was still alive, and others where the recipient of the projection was far from an unborn infant, but even an adult!

In this form of reincarnation, memories (and hence, identity) may or may not make the transition intact, and of course, many of them will fade from premature brain cells before they can be per-

---

[53] Glass, Justine, *Witchcraft, the Sixth Sense.* Wilshire Book Co., North Hollywood, CA., 1965.

manently recorded and articulated. But if enough of those memories remain to convey a continuity of conscious identity, we can truly say that such a person's "soul" has survived death and been reborn. This does not, of course, guarantee "immortality" in the strict sense, for one might not make it through the next time.

## The Awakening...

Just as each of us awakened into consciousness as an infant, so too is Gaea Herself poised on the threshold of a planetary Awakening—the evolution of consciousness into the next quantum leap. In Eastern traditions this is called Enlightenment. It is a full awakening of the spirit, in which one experiences with every fiber of one's being the full connection with all other Beings, throughout all of Time and Space. It is the integration of both brain hemispheres into simultaneous consciousness, rather than the normal alternation of one or the other. We call this *Apotheosis*—literally deification or "becoming Divine."

It has been imagined that this might come about as a kind of universal telepathy. But I think the emergence and rapid evolution of the Internet is already providing the seeds of a technological vehicle of global consciousness through which this Awakening will inevitably manifest. In a 1926 interview with *Collier's* magazine, visionary genius Nikola Tesla prophesied:

> When wireless is perfectly applied the whole Earth will be converted into a huge brain, which in fact it is, all things being particles of a real and rhythmic whole. We shall be able to communicate with one another instantly, irrespective of distance. Not only this, but through television and telephony we shall see and hear one another as perfectly as though we were face to face, despite intervening distances of thousands of miles; and the instruments through which we shall be able to do his will be amazingly simple compared with our present telephone. A man will be able to carry one in his vest pocket. [54]

---

[54] Nikola Tesla, interview in *Collier's* magazine, Jan. 30, 1926.

## Coalescence of Consciousness

I believe that the two-handed coordination required for playing music and operating modern computer consoles, video games, etc. is stimulating not only a re-awakening of the dormant right brain hemispheres of humanity, but a full synchronization of both forms of mentality into a new ambidextrous consciousness that will be able to sustain the awakened mind of Gaea. And as with the awakening of consciousness in our own minds, as the billions of neurons in our brains link up synergistically, just so shall we all participate in the Awakening of Gaea Herself—and our full Apotheosis.

Scientist/philosopher Pierre Teilhard de Chardin (1881-1955) envisioned just such an awakening of planetary consciousness as the "Omega Point"—the ultimate fulfillment of the entire purpose of creation and evolution. This would be the point in time when the individual consciousnesses of all living beings on Earth coalesce into a single collective consciousness—a "noosphere." He said: "We are faced with a harmonized collectivity of consciousnesses to a sort of superconsciousness. The Earth not only becoming covered by myriads of grains of thought, but becoming enclosed in a single thinking envelope, a single unanimous reflection." [55]

> Are we all connected? Yes. We are all immersed in the Earth's magnetic field. The human species is about seven billion conductive brains all sharing the field. This field contains enough energy to store the experiences of every human being who has ever lived. [56]

And when this process of amalgamation reaches a certain "hundred monkeys" threshold (what de Chardin called "The Omega Point"), the group consciousness of these growing numbers of people will become the emergent planetary consciousness of Earth. We call Her Mother Earth, and at that point She will awaken as conscious Goddess...

---

[55] Chardin, Pierre Teilhard de, *The Phenomenon of Man*. Harper & Row, 1955.
[56] Michael Persinger; 2007 best lecture winner, Laurentian University. *Beyond (2015): Zero Point Volume IV - Left Hemisphere Edition*

# Epilogue

According to the leading thinkers in quantum physics, this "real life," as we so naively call it, is but a living virtual world simulation, like "2$^{nd}$ Life," or "World of Warcraft"—only infinitely more sophisticated than anything we are presently able to create, with many layers of sentience. More like *The Matrix, Total Recall, Jumanji*, or *Ready Player One*. Or the simulation holodecks on *Star Trek* and *The Orville*.

Humanity (i.e., *Homo sapiens*) is maybe 300,000 years old; agriculture 14,000; writing 5,000; the "Common Era" 2,020. It's been just 420 years since Giordano Bruno was burned at the stake for insisting that the Earth revolved around the sun. The United States of America is only 244 years old—close enough in recent memory to inspire a modern hit musical play: "Hamilton."

Given the accelerating rate of advances in our own lifetimes, now moving into quantum computing, try to imagine our virtual gaming worlds in another 244 years... 420... 2,020 years... 5,000... mere drops in the ocean of Eternity. Remember, *Dragons ruled the Earth for 150 million years!* And over the last *13 billion years,* how many civilizations may have arisen throughout the galaxy to our present technological level...and beyond? Maybe way, way beyond...to what? We can no more imagine than a Mayfly could contemplate metaphysics. We're just getting started on this one tiny speck of dust in an infinite cosmos!

We perceive ourselves as individual entities—just as a cup of water appears to be separate from all other cups of water. But it's only the vessels that are separate—not the universal water they contain. There is no death of the Spirit. Only a release when the vessel it contains can no longer hold it. What we think of as God or the Gods is just the next layer of Spirit of which we are extrusions.

The only difference between us and the Gods (as well as the Beloved Dead) is that They are non-corporeal (i.e., not currently animating avatars). But They are real personas just as much as the rest of us. Moreover, when we "die," our own consciousness returns ("ascends") to the next level up... And beyond the next level, there are presumably an unknowable number of further levels, like Russian nesting dolls (*matryoshka*, literally "little matrons").

Like a Fairy Circle of mushrooms springing from a common invisible mycelial network, we are extensions/projections of Universal Consciousness (Spirit; Divinity; the Quantum Field) into this realm of "materiality." We/I inhabit/incarnate/animate these marvelous avatars for a brief "lifetime" of lessons, adventures, emotions, love, family, relationships, and entanglements; agony and ecstasy, trials and tribulations; then we res out and take a little break before we/I decide to play another game with new avatars.

It's all a game, and the goal—as in any game—is to complete each level, and then advance (ascend) to the next level. Indeed, the ultimate goal is for *everyone* to advance or ascend to the next level— "Enlightenment" or "Awakening." And then perhaps to create another even more advanced game... For that is what Gods do.

John 10:34 (NLT): Jesus answered them, *"Is it not written in your Law: 'I said you are gods'?"*

Psalm 82:6 (NLT): I said, *"You are gods, and all of you are sons of the Most High."*

Thou art God/dess.

# Postscript:

*The original version of this article was written in 1974, though never published, as it was then considered too radical. Holography had just been invented, computers still used punch cards and filled whole buildings, the Internet and virtual reality were not even imagined in science fiction. 20 years later, from the perspective of 1994, I could foresee the emergence of the global Internet as the potential planetary cerebral cortex, and when we can enter into a virtual reality space in the future Internet, (perhaps even augmented by psychopharmaceuticals either traditional or yet-to-be designed) I do not think we will need to wait for the slower and less-than-inevitable process of universal telepathy to achieve the awakening of planetary consciousness. And in 2021, quantum theory and biocentrism are offering a new view of consciousness as the ultimate reality of the universe, with our individual brains more equivalent to cell phones downloading from "the cloud"—or portals into virtual realms. —OZ*

# Chapter 8
# The Village

*"I am Death, I touch all, I will come as I must,*
*Bringing comfort and rest, for your souls are my trust.*
*And reunion, my gift beyond death is the prize,*
*For your heart, for your soul, for your eyes.*

*"I will pulse in your blood, I will ring from your core,*
*When the Lady, my Love, gives you flesh once more!*
*You will meet and remember the loves of your lives;*
*For your heart and your soul are my eyes."*
~~Kathy Mar & Gwen Zak, "In Your Eyes"

UPSET BY HIS SATIRICAL BROADSIDES against the Christian establishment, a woman once asked Samuel Clemens (aka Mark Twain) whether he believed in Holy Baptism. "Be*lieve* in it?" thundered the irascible journalist; "Why, Madam, I've seen it *done!*"

This is the way the members of my expanded Family/Clan – the Ravenhearts – feel about reincarnation. It is not a matter of belief for us; it is a matter of personal experience. It is a matter of recognition (literally, "knowing again").

As Pagans, we consider the myths and legends that have been passed down to us through the generations to contain the essential stories and lessons conveyed from our ancestral selves to our present incarnations. And we Ravenhearts have a story we share amongst ourselves; a Family Myth, if you will. We call it The Village...

---

[57] Oberon Zell-Ravenheart, "The Myths of Oberon" – Editorial *Green Egg* #132, Jan. 2000.

Thousands of years ago (or Once Upon a Time, if you prefer), somewhere in central Europe, we all lived together in our little Village. We had lived there from the earliest time, from when the great walls of Ice retreated from the valley. Other villages, of course, also came into being across the Earth, all with similar stories and destinies...

We farmed the fields, hunted in the forests, picked herbs and berries on the hillsides, planted apple trees, and erected standing stones to mark the risings and settings of the Sun, Moon and stars. We learned to grind and polish stone; to fire pottery; to forge bronze—and later, meteoric iron. Our houses had ancient walls of stone and ever-renewed roofs of thatch. We honored the Earth our Mother, and celebrated the turnings of Her seasons through Summer's life, Winter's death, and Spring's rebirth. And when we died in our time, our bodies would be buried in the apple orchard, with sapling trees planted on our graves. And we would be remembered, and invited to return as children conceived by those who had loved us in our former lives.

And generation after generation, in this way we kept returning to The Village, and the ones we loved. For we were reborn among the souls we had grown to know and love, familiar beacons calling us Home to become brothers, sisters, sons, or daughters to those we had just left. And we grew strong in our love for each other, our bonds of Family, Clan, and Tribe, as well as the wisdom accumulated through countless returning lives.

Sometimes wanderers would find their way to The Village, to become part of it ever after. And sometimes some of us traveled far afield, and returned with mates from distant lands, whose lives and destinies became interwoven with The Village forevermore. These stories are also recalled and told among us.

Over the centuries, our Village suffered hard times as well as good. Periodically, raiders would cross the river to pillage and plunder, stealing what they could make off with, whether it be food, tools, goods—or women. But always we defended our homes, drove off the invaders, recouped our losses, and rebuilt our lives. And when women who had been carried off in those raids eventually came to the ends of their lives, they often returned to The Village in their next incarnations, sometimes calling to join us the souls of children they had borne far away.

And then one terrible day, the Romans came. These were not simple raiders, intent only on plunder. These were disciplined armies of conquest in the name of Empire. When we would not capitulate, they burned The Village to the ground. Most of us were killed defending our homes and families. The few survivors were taken prisoner, back to Rome, far from our destroyed home—which was lost to us forever.

For now, when we died, there was no Village to return to. No one to receive our spirits back into the welcoming wombs and arms of those who had known us and loved us. We were homeless souls, cast adrift; orphans of the storm.

And so we became scattered across the world. We took incarnation wherever we could find it, in other lands both near and far. We all have our stories of these past two thousand years, always seeking each other, through life after life, driven by love and longing. Sometimes two of us would meet, would love, would live a life together for a time. And then, death would separate us once again.

In these many lives we have lived—and in many lands—since The Village, we have each met and loved other lost souls and forged new bonds. Some of us have returned in each new life to the essential roles we had held in the Village: potter, smith, warrior, farmer, healer, hunter, herder, builder, priest/ess, storyteller, poet, wizard, witch... And some of us have lived successive lives very different one from the next.

Never quite fitting in with the societies in which we kept finding ourselves, for we carried a secret alienation deep in our souls, many of us were particularly targeted by the Witch Hunters and Inquisitors, and we were brutally tortured and murdered in life after life during the Burning Times. Only to keep returning, relentlessly—courageously—again and again.

For always we have sought each other; sought to recover the Village. Because, in our deepest heart of hearts, we remember the Home.

And now, in this time, two millennia later, some of us have found each other again. We have remembered who we truly are, and what we have always meant to each other. And we have forged a new Family—a core seed of The Village that once was, and shall be again. It is an open Family, seeking reconnection with those others of The Village who may show up. All that our Family members have done in working to create (and re-create) new (and old) religious and social movements and structures (the Church of All Worlds, Neo-Paganism, *Green Egg,* polyamory, Mythic Images, TheaGenesis, Sacred Connections, the Grey School of Wizardry...) has been towards setting up a beacon to draw Home again those of our kindred so long lost from each other.

How often have we heard the words of a newly-discovered Pagan, spoken through tears at their first Festival: "I feel like I've finally come Home! I feel like I've finally found my People!" How many of us have spoken those words? How many of us have said to another that most beautiful of all phrases, "Welcome Home, brother (or sister); welcome Home!"

And now we have a great work to do together—beyond merely finding each other and recreating The Village. We must make certain that our Home is never destroyed again, and that, once reunited, we who love each other will never be torn asunder again.

For the whole world is our Village. If our world is destroyed, there will be no Home to return to; no more wombs to receive back our sundered souls. Our task in the coming Millennium is to ensure that there will always be a Village to welcome us Home.

> *Through the Ages many races have arisen and have gone*
> *Yet disbursed among the nations of the world we linger on*
> *Now the time has come to take the sacred Cauldron of Rebirth,*
> *And fulfill our ancient pledges to the Earth!*
> (~~Gwydion Pendderwen, "We Won't Wait Any Longer")

> *And we who reach for the stars in the heavens,*
> *Lifting our eyes from the meadows and rows,*
> *Still live in the love of the Lord and the Lady;*
> *The greater the Circle, the more the love grows!*
> (~~Gwendolyn Zak, "Circles")

# Chapter 9
# Pilgrims' Progress...

*OZ's travel journal; May 25, 1986— (Ukiah, CA; home)*
*I have been back now from my European pilgrimage with Dona for almost two months. I have celebrated the bringing in of the May in the circle of my People, and have told some of my stories around the campfire. Excerpts from my journal are being published in* Mendocino Country *as a series called "Shrines of Europe." Life continues to be rich and rewarding, and I am nourished in the precious love of my extended family. I feel incredibly blessed. And it is from this perspective that I want to try and summarize the lessons of our pilgrimage in this final chapter...*

And so, led by the Tarot Trump of Death, Bella Dona and I have travelled the length of the Underworld. We have crept through the corridors of Cro-Magnon caverns, where painted ponies and bas-relief bison struggled in stone to be reborn. We have wandered through vast subterranean catacombs, where uncountable hundreds of thousands of human skeletons were stacked like cordwood from floor to ceiling. We have seen and handled human skulls that were not quite human... We have stood in the Tombs of the Tarquin Kings, and learned the meanings of the symbols in the metaphorical murals painted on the walls. We have traced the length of the Cretan Labyrinth and followed Ariadne's thread into the lair of the Minotaur. We have looked within the sarcophagi of time-lost civilizations, and have seen our former selves mirrored in crumbling mummies. We have visited the crypts of crusaders and conquistadors, lying with swords in hand beneath the floors of Medieval monasteries and gothic cathedrals. We have walked the exhumed streets of buried cities, the moment of their death frozen for millennia, and seen plaster statues encasing the contorted bones of luckless citizens. We have wandered cobblestoned paths among the burial vaults and chapels of the Paris cemetery, and paid our respects to the grave of Jim Morrison. We have trod the passages of ancient necropoli, and their secrets have been revealed to us. And we have traveled beyond the River Styx, to the very Halls of Hades and the throne room of Persephone, Queen of the Underworld, where we have traced the footsteps of Odysseus through the Land of the Dead. We have, in very fact, been to Hell and back.

And we have walked as well the halls of Heaven. We have stood within the colonnaded corridors of crumbling temples to the Gods and Goddesses of our ancestors. We have laid our offerings on ancient altars, and made our prayers of gratitude to the Great Ones. Up endless spiral staircases we have plodded, to emerge upon the roofs of towering cathedrals, with gargoyle guardians perched like pigeons on the balustrades. We have climbed the long winding way up to cloud-shrouded acropolis to gaze in wonder at the vast ruined temples upon their summits. We have embraced the Oracle Oak of Dodona, the very embodiment of mighty Zeus. We have made our pilgrimages to all the Oracles, from Dodona to Delphi, and our questions have been answered. And finally, we have drunk the holy water from the sacred Castalian spring of Gaea as it issued forth from her vaginal cleft.

And in the museums, we have examined behind glass the grave goods of a dozen dead dynasties; time capsules of the lives of individuals and races, cultures caught in time like flies in amber. We have seen their gold and ivory, their marble and pottery, their iron and copper and bronze. We have viewed their painted frescoes and read their writings on the walls.

And this we have learned, from all the honored dead who have gone before:

Death is a passage, not a destination. We are born from the womb of the Mother of Life, and to Her we eventually return, to be clothed with new flesh and born again, and again, and again. We are like drops of water spewed from a fountain, to sparkle and dance for a time in the sunlight, only to fall eventually back into the pool, from which we are continually being drawn up and sprayed forth again. There are no endings, only endless beginnings, as we cycle round and round through night and day, winter and summer, death and life.

All the symbols we learned to decipher in the tombs and catacombs were not of life's endings, but of its renewals. Trees of life, painted round the four walls of Etruscan tombs, showed the green leaves of summer, the ripening fruits of autumn, the bare branches of winter, and the flowering of spring again. Butterflies reminded us of the metamorphosis from caterpillar, through the apparent death of the mummy-wrapped cocoon (wherein the body of the lowly caterpillar dissolves into goo before being reconstituted into a beautiful new creature). Painted eggs hatched into fledgling chicks, who grew wings and flew away. Pomegranates recalled the three seeds eaten by Persephone, linking her forever to the cycle of returns. In the catacombs of Rome, where outlawed early Christians met and prayed, images of Jonah and the whale were everywhere, cast in the form of bronze candelabra and painted or etched upon the walls, as constant reminders of the story that Jonah was resurrected from the belly of the whale after three days. Three days entombment of Jesus, and three days after being bitten by a vampire to arise as the living undead... We saw guardians and monsters meant to frighten the uninitiated: gorgons and gargoyles, mantichores and minotaurs. We recognized them, gave the passwords, and were not turned away.

And we met the true Ruler of the Underworld: the Dark Mother. She sat veiled and enthroned, and She stood tall and proud, breasts bared, with serpents in her upraised hands. She wore a crown of poppies and crescent moons, and Her headdress was formed of vultures and cobras. She offered a dove and a pomegranate though Her hands were empty. Her face was radiant with incomparable beauty and She wore a fanged mask ringed with vipers. And She was thin as bones but also round-bellied and heavy-breasted with pregnancy. We have always known Her as the Queen of Life, but now we have come to know Her also as the Queen of Death. And She is our Mother, and we are Her children.

We have come to perceive ourselves as actors in a glorious cosmic drama, and we have learned to admire profoundly the competence of the Directors. The sets are magnificent, the plot is epic, with comedy and tragedy in perfect balance, and the casting is brilliant. We get to design our own costumes and write our own lines! We have come to feel that our best approach is to put on a good show; that way we will keep getting better and better parts. And all we really have to do is develop our characters, learn to pick up our cues, and be ready with snappy comebacks. And, of course, never fail to show our appreciation for being granted these roles. For this performance, Dona and I should win an Academy Award! And we cannot wait to see what offers we get for our next parts! Having been to Hell and back, neither life nor death can hold any terrors for us. The tomb is but a dressing-room where we put off our worn-out clothing of mortal flesh and pass through the painted portals of Paradise to re-enter Her cauldron womb; to sleep, perchance to dream, and eventually to reawaken clothed in new costumes for another turn on stage.

And I hereby present a mythical metaphor for your edification and amusement:

All living creatures are like cups of various sizes and shapes, with which the waters of life are scooped from the Well of Souls. And all the cups are emptied back into the pool when they are periodically broken. New cups are continually being fashioned of living clay, and are dipped in their turn into the same Well to be filled. But it is rare that a new cup will scoop up exactly the same batch of molecules as had been contained in a former cup. Usually, there will be a considerable mix. And so it is that a human may have bits of "past life" memories of several other people, as well as assorted animals—or that a human-sized cup may contain a number of entire birds and other small animals, but at most, only a fraction of a single whale. And in the proper balance of Nature, each new generation replaces the previous, so that the number of each kind of cup remains approximately constant. Now what do you suppose happens when one species proliferates greatly at the expense of others? When there are no more cups of Moa, Stellar's Sea Cow, Carolina Parakeet, Passenger Pigeon, Thylacine, Sperm Whale, Condor, Mammoth, Giant Lemur, Great Auk, Cave Bear, Megatherium, Dodo, Roc, or countless others, but the cups labelled "Human" are being produced by the geometrically increasing billions? In that case, I believe, the human soul-stuff would become increasingly diluted with other decimated species, and all the vanished animals would return in human form.

In their 1962 book, *Warriors of the Rainbow*, [58] William Willoya and Vinson Brown claimed that many years ago, the Hopi had prophesied that the spirits of all the dead Indigenous tribes would return in a single generation in the bodies of the white conquerors. This generation, they said, would be recognizable by their native affinity for the ways of those native peoples. They would wear beads and leather and feathers, let their hair grow long and hold it back with braids and headbands. They would take up the Indigenous ways, and return to the reverence of Nature and the Great Mother. They would learn the native chants, and purify themselves in sweats, fasts, and vision quests. And they would come to be known by a name similar to "Hopi," which means "the Peaceful Ones," for they would also be the Children of Peace. [59]

Around 1970, the Hopi elders declared that this prophecy had come to pass, and they summoned shamans from all the tribes to come to the Four Corners of the ancestral Hopi Land, to learn the full extent of the prophecies and to go forth and instruct those who would be receptive. This has been done.

I prophesy that the generation now being born in the 1980's will incarnate the spirits of the murdered whales. I imagine that the reason why whales always beach themselves to die is that they have a myth that they once came from the land, and that they shall return to the land in the afterlife. I believe this is true. And I believe that this new generation, who will come of age around the turn of the Millennium, will be a generation of noble heroes in an age of future legends, for it will be their task to undertake that Heroic Quest, through all manner of perils, to the Fortress of Ultimate

---

[58] Willoya, William & Brown, Vinson, *Warriors of the Rainbow*. Naturegraph Publishers, 1962.

[59] "The legend said [the Native Americans] would also be joined by many of their light-skinned brothers and sisters, who would in fact be the reincarnated souls of the Indians who were killed or enslaved by the first light-skinned settlers. It was said that the dead souls of these first people would return in bodies of all different colours: red, white, yellow and black. Together and unified, like the colours of the rainbow, these people would teach all of the peoples of the world how to have love and reverence for Mother Earth, of whose very stuff we human beings are also made." (Morton, Chris & Thomas, Ceri Louise, *The Mystery of the Crystal Skulls: A Real-Life Detective Story of the Ancient World*. Vermont, Bear & Company, 1998)

Darkness, to restore the Light, save the world, and usher in the next Golden Age of Aquarius. For this is one of those great Ages of Magic—when the fate of all living beings turns on a tiny pivot, and all things are possible. More than at any such time in all history, the choices have escalated to the ultimate: Apocalypse or Apotheosis; planetary annihilation or planetary illumination. As the character "Ozymandias" said in *The Watchmen* #11: "It's a neck-and-neck race between the Four Horsemen of the Apocalypse and the Seventh Cavalry." [60] And with such a wide range of possibilities comes the return of true Magick in the form of coincidence control through manipulation of probabilities.

There are now as many people alive at one time as have ever lived before in the entire span of human history. We're all on stage for the Grand Finale! It's been a great show, and I, for one, think we should take it on the road. I find it no coincidence that the very technology which presently threatens all life on this planet could alternately be used to build starships which could carry our children's children throughout the galaxy. We create our world by the myths we live and believe in, and for the first time in our history, we are creating myths—not just of a golden age long past, but of one yet to come. What shall it be; Star Wars or Star Trek? We're all choosing up sides...

> *Some of us will go a-sailing*
> *Through the void so deep and far.*
> *They will go with us, unfailing*
> *Plant the seeds from star to star.*
> *Hear our children's children's voices,*
> *Join with those from days of yore.*
> *Avalon is rising, is rising, is rising!*
> *Avalon is rising, to fall no more!*
> (~~Isaac Bonewits, "Avalon is Rising")

---

[60] Moore, Alan (writer); Gibbons, Dave (artist); Higgins, John (colorist), *The Watchmen*. DC Comics, 1986-1987 (issue #11).

# Appendices

## Song of the River (1941)
William Randolph Hearst, 1863-1951

*The snow melts on the mountain*
*And the water runs down to the spring,*
*And the spring in a turbulent fountain,*
*With a song of youth to sing,*
*Runs down to the riotous river,*
*And the river flows on to the sea,*

*And the water again*
*Goes back in rain*
*To the hills where it used to be.*
*And I wonder if Life's deep mystery*
*Isn't much like the rain and the snow*
*Returning through all eternity*
*To the places it used to know.*

*For life was born on the lofty heights*
*And flows in a laughing stream*
*To the river below*
*Whose onward flow*
*Ends in a peaceful dream.*

*And so at last,*
*When our life has passed*
*And the river has run its course,*
*It again goes back,*
*O'er the selfsame track,*
*To the mountain which was its source.*

*So why prize life
Or why fear death,
Or dread what is to be?
The river ran its allotted span
'Til it reached the silent sea.
Then the water harked back to the mountaintop
To begin is course once more.*

*So we shall run the course begun
'Til we reach the silent shore,
Then revisit Earth in a pure rebirth
From the heart of the virgin snow.
So don't ask why we live or die,
Or wither, or when we go,
Or wonder about the Mysteries
That only the Gods may know.*

# Appendix A.
# A Dictionary of Cemetery Symbolism

Next time you are in a cemetery, especially one with graves from the 19th and early 20th centuries, take a close look at all the designs and inscriptions carved on the headstones. See how many you can find, and collect photos. These reveal much about the deceased, if you can understand the rich symbolism. Here is what many of them mean:

**Acacia-** An evergreen, representing the immortality of the soul.

**Acorn-** Potential, life, fertility, and immortality. Acorns were sacred to Thor whose tree was the oak, and Druids believed eating them granted prophetic abilities.

**Agnus Dei-** The Lamb of God.

**Alpha & Omega-** First and last letters of the Greek alphabet. Symbolizes the beginning and the end.

**Anchor-** Often seen on sailors' graves, representing steadfastness, hope or eternal life. Anchors are a Masonic symbol for well-grounded hope, therefore they may also be found on Masons' graves.

**Angel/Cherubim-** Agent of God, often pointing towards heaven, or shown carrying or escorting the deceased to heaven. Guardian of the dead, symbolizing spirituality, divine wisdom or justice. Archangel *Michael* bears a sword. St Matthew, one of the 4 evangelists, is often represented as a winged man.

**Angel blowing a trumpet-** Archangel *Gabriel,* represents the Day of Judgment and call to the Resurrection.

**Angel of Death-** *Azrael.* Black-winged figure of Death, sometimes skull-faced, or depicted as female.

**Angel flying-** Rebirth.

**Angels gathered together in clouds-** Heaven.

**Angel weeping-** Grief, or mourning an untimely death.

**Ankh-** Egyptian symbol of eternal life.

**Ants-** Industriousness.

**Anvil-** Martyrdom. Symbolizes the creation or forging of the universe. Also found on blacksmiths' graves.

**Apples-** Salvation; sometimes sin.

**Arch, Door, Gateway-** Passing from one existence to the next. The passage to heaven. Victory in death. A draped arch symbolizes mourning.

**Ark-** Church, salvation. Noah's Ark (rare) refuge in catastrophic times.

**Armor-** Protection from evil.

**Arms outstretched-** Plea for mercy.

**Arrows-** Mortality and martyrdom. A quiver of arrows indicates warlike.

**Artillery-** Such as cannons, on a gravestone usually represents military service.

**Ash-** The mountain ash or rowan deters evil spirits from bothering the dead.

**Awen-** Three dots from under which radiate 3 vertical lines. Symbol of modern Druidry.

**Baby's Chair-** Small, empty furniture, often with tiny shoes on chair, representing the child now gone. Symbolizes unfulfilled lives of children, who will never reach adulthood.

**Bamboo-** Emblem of Buddha. The 7-knotted bamboo denotes the 7 degrees of initiation and invocation. On Japanese memorials, symbolic of devotion and truthfulness.

**Banner-** Victory, triumph.

**Bats-** (rare) The Underworld.

**Battle Axe-** Martyrdom.

**Bed-** At rest, in peace.

**Bees-** Resurrection; risen Christ.

**Beehive-** Human industry, faith, education, and domestic virtues. Often used by Freemasons and Odd Fellows.

**Bell-** Symbolizes church bell; call to worship.

**Birds in flight-** Eternal life, shown as the "winged soul" *(Ba)* from ancient Egypt. Sometimes features only wings to convey the idea of Divine mission. Often seen on graves of children.

**Black & white tiles-** Checkered pattern or similar, represents good vs. evil.

**Boat or Ship-** A voyage; crossing over to the other side. Found on graves of sailors or people who died at sea. May represent Noah's Ark, that weathered the storm against overwhelming odds. Sometimes a symbol for the Church with a cross as the mast.

**Bones-** Death, decay. One of the symbol set of M*emento Mori.*

**Book-** Bible or Book of Life, usually open, where names and accomplishments of the righteous are recorded to ensure entry into Heaven. Often seen on tombs of clergy. A pair of Holy Books on Mormon headstones indicate the *Bible* and *Book of Mormon*. The three Mormon Holy Books are the *Bible, Book of Mormon,* and *Doctrine & Covenants.*

**Bouquet of Flowers-** Condolences; grief.

**Branch or Bud, broken-** Deceased met an untimely or premature death. Usually seen on a young person's gravestone.

**Bridge-** Linking and crossing over between the Earthly and Heavenly realms, between the physical and spiritual, life and death.

**Buds-** Renewal of life.

**Bugle-** Resurrection and Military.

**Butterfly-** Resurrection; also soul leaving the body. Usually seen on graves of children.

**Caduceus-** A winged wand entwined by two serpents in the form of a double helix. Symbolizes someone who worked in the medical profession. However, this scepter of Hermes/ Mercury is actually a symbol of messengers and commerce. The proper symbol for the medical arts is the staff of Asclepius, with only one serpent. The Caduceus symbol was erroneously placed on Army medical uniforms in the early 1900's, and the misconception still prevails to this day.

**Candle with flame-** Life.

**Candle being snuffed-** Mortality.

**Candlestick-** Christ, devotion.

**Cardinal** (bird)- Passion for life.

**Chain, broken-** Symbolizes the death of a family member.

**Chalice-** The sacraments.

**Chariot-** Taking soul to heaven. "Swing low, sweet chariot…"

**Cherubs-** The graves of children.

**Cherub's Head-** The soul.

**Children-** Untimely death of the innocent. May be shown mourning a parent, but holding a skull means they are themselves dead.

**Child Sleeping-** Sleep is the realm between life and death; children are pure, artless, and innocent.

**Circle-** Eternity – no beginning, no end.

**Clock-** Mortality, death; the passage of time.

**Clouds-** God is concealed from his worshipers.

**Coat of Arms-** High social status and family lineage.

**Cobra-** Death (Egyptian).

**Cocoon/Chrysalis-** Metamorphosis. See *Butterfly*.

**Coffin-** mortality and death.

**Column-** Mortality. A draped or broken column represents a life cut short; the break from Earthly to Heavenly life. (A column or pillar was often used by the Hebrews to symbolize rulers or nobles.)

**Comedy & Tragedy Masks-** Symbol of drama and theatre. Deceased was an actor.

**Corn-** Rebirth, fertility.

**Cornucopia** ("Horn of Plenty")- An abundant, fruitful life. Symbol of harvest at the end of life.

**Cradle-** Infant or child.

**Crossed Keys-** St. Peter, Keeper of the Pearly Gates to Heaven.

**Crooks-** Shepherds' crooks, often found on graves of Odd Fellows members. Symbolizes the opening of Earth to the Heavens.

**Cross-** Salvation (Christian)

**Cross, Celtic-** A cross with a ring surrounding the intersection. A popular choice on gravestones since its revival in the 1850s. Often seen on Irish graves.

**Cross, Eastern-** Also Russian Orthodox, Greek Orthodox, and Greek Catholic. The three bars symbolize the cross Christ was crucified on: Top – title board; Middle – board on which Christ's hands were nailed; Bottom - footrest.

**Cross with Rays of Rising Sun-** Glory.

**Cross with Winding Sheet-** Descent from the cross.

**Crown-** Immortality, righteousness, victory, triumph, resurrection, symbolic of honor, glory, glory of life after death. May be shown being offered by Angels.

**Crown on Cross-** Sovereignty of the Lord.

**Curtain, Drapery, Veil-** Passing from one existence to another, on the other side of the Veil. Mourning.

**Cypress tree-** Designates hope or deep mourning. A felled cypress never grows again.

**Dog-** Loyalty, fidelity, watchfulness, and vigilance. Implies that the master was worth loving.

**Dolphin-** Resurrection (*delphin* means "womb")

**Dove-** Peace, messenger of God, symbolizing the Holy Spirit.

**Dove & Olive Branch-** Peace.

**Dragon-** In Asia, dragons protect humans from evil spirits and represent joy, health and fertility. But in Western cultures, the dragon possesses the negative traits of the snake: destruction, danger, depravity, and loss of innocence. In Jewish tradition, mythical beasts such as dragons are messianic symbols. A dragon being defeated by St. George depicts triumph over sin.

**Dragonfly-** Change and transformation, joy, and lightness. It can also symbolize a connection with Nature spirits. Japan made the dragonfly its national emblem. In some Native American traditions, it is a symbol of the departed souls.

**Eagle-** Courage and possibly a military career. Often seen on gravestones of Civil War veterans. St John, one of the four evangelists, is often represented as an eagle.

**Egg-** Regeneration, new beginning.

**Eye of Providence-** Masonic symbol of the all-seeing, all-knowing God, represented on headstones as a gateway between this world and the next. When the Eye is enclosed within a triangle it represents the Holy Trinity, and when also surrounded by a circle it symbolizes the eternity of the Holy Trinity. A sunburst surrounding the Eye symbolizes the holiness of the true God.

**Eucharist-** The body and blood of Christ. Usually found on graves of priests and nuns.

**Father Time** (Roman **Saturn**; Greek **Cronus**)- Mortality. Depicted as an old man with wings and a long beard. Also identified as Death. He carries a scythe to represent the harvest of souls, and an hourglass to denote that the sands of time have run out.

**Father Time & the Weeping Virgin-** Masonic tableau; A weeping maiden holds a sprig of acacia in one hand, and an urn in the other hand, with a broken column in front of her. Father Time stands behind her, braiding (or unbraiding) her hair. It symbolizes that time, patience, and perseverance will accomplish all things.

**Fern-** Humility and sincerity.

**Figs -** Prosperity, eternal life.

**Fish-** Christian faith.

**Flag-** Patriotism or member of armed services.

**Flame-** Eternity.

**Flowers-** In general, frailty of life. Specific meanings for each kind. See below.

**Figure with Dart-** Mortality.

**Finger-** Pointing up to Heaven. Pointing down means sudden death; God reaching down for the soul.

**Fluer-de-lis-** Trinity, Virgin.

**"Foo Dogs"** (*Shih Tzu of Fo*)- Guardians of Buddha, always a pair, often seen at gates of Chinese cemeteries.

**Fox-** Cruelty, cunning, intelligence.

**Frog-** Sin and worldly pleasures, or may represent resurrection.

**Fruits-** Eternal plenty as in the fruit of life. Fruit on vine; as Christ is to the Church.

**Garland-** Victory in death.

**Gourds-** In 17th and 18th century New England, the birth and death of earthly matters

**Grapes-** Blood of Christ, as in communion.

**Hammer-** The power of creation. It can also represent the person's profession.

**Hammer & Sickle-** Alliance of factory workers and farming peasants. Emblem of the Communist movement.

**Hands, clasped-** Unity. An Earthly farewell, a heavenly welcome or matrimony. Often used as a Masonic and I.O.O.F. symbol.

**Hands, Cohanim -** Hands with thumbs (and sometimes forefingers) touching. Jewish symbol for members of the *Cohen,* the priestly tribe of Aaron.

**Hand holding heart-** Charity. Used by Masons, Odd Fellows.

**Hand pointing up-** Deceased pointing up to heaven.

**Hand pointing down-** The hand of God reaching down from Heaven.

**Hand writing-** Writing names in the book of life. Often seen on writers' graves.

**Hands reaching towards each other-** Hand of God reaching down from Heaven, and hand of the deceased reaching up for it.

**Harp or Lyre-** References heaven, angelic music, praise to God. Occasionally used on the grave of a poet. Often carved with a broken string, symbolizing the end of life.

**Hawthorn-** Hope, merriness, springtime.

**Heart-** Love, mortality, love of God, courage and intelligence. Deceased's spirit or soul.

**Heart bleeding-** Christ's suffering for our sins.

**Heart encircled with thorns-** The suffering of Christ.

**Heart flaming-** Signifies extreme religious fervor.

**Heart pierced by a sword-** The Virgin Mary, harkening to Simeon's prophecy to Mary at the birth of Christ, "Yea, a sword shall pierce through thine own soul." Also represents charity.

**Heart, Sacred-** Found in Catholic cemeteries, refers to the suffering of Christ for our sins.

**Holly-** Foresight. People believed that holly bushes protected tombs from lightning strikes.

**Horse-** Death, courage or generosity, in honor of the crusaders. White horses represent good, while black ones represent evil.

**Hourglass-** Fleeting Time, *Tempus Fugit,* inevitability of Earthly death. Often seen in conjunction with a skull and crossed bones, symbolic of crucifixion, death, and mortality. Winged hourglasses signify resurrection of the dead. A reclining hour glass does not allow the sand to pass, indicating that time stopped prematurely, thus symbolizing the death of a young person.

**Hummingbird-** A tiny spirit. Often found on infants' gravestones.

**I.H.S.-** Sometimes looks like a dollar sign. IHS stands for the first three letters of Jesus' name in the Greek alphabet. Also stands for *in hoc signo,* Latin for "by this sign we conquer," referring to the cross.

**Ivy-** Memory, immortality, friendship, fidelity, faithfulness, undying affection, eternal life.

**Knot-** A tied knot symbolizes marriage and unity.

**Lamb-** Innocence; the "Lamb of God." Lambs are most often seen on children's graves.

**Lamp-** Wisdom, faithfulness.

**Laurel Leaves-** Special achievement, distinction, success, triumph. The "evergreen" memory of the deceased.

**Laurel Wreath-** Victory, immortality, eternity.

**Leaves, dead-** Sadness, melancholy.

**Lion-** Strength, nobility, resurrection. Guards the tomb against evil spirits. The lion also recalls the courage and determination of the souls which they guard; it manifests the noble spirit of the departed. Winged represents St Mark, one of the four evangelists.

**Maple leaf-** Long life and self-control; Canada.

**Menorah-** Jewish symbol, a candelabra with seven branches. Usually marks the grave of a righteous woman.

**Mermaids** (or Sirens)- The messengers of Persephone, sent to carry the souls of the dead to Hades.

**Moon-** Rebirth. Crescent for Virgin. A crescent moon and star (Luna and Venus) is also a symbol of Islam.

**Mortar & Pestle-** Usually found on the gravestones of pharmacists, and sometimes doctors.

**Musical notation-** Found on the graves of musicians. The music can be from a song the musician wrote, or it could be the deceased person's favorite hymn.

**Myrtle-** The evergreen myrtle represents achievement and eternal life.

**Oak tree-** Hospitality, stability, strength, honor, eternity, endurance, liberty, power, authority or victory.

**Oak leaves-** Strength, endurance, longevity, faith and virtue. Often seen on military tombs.

**Olive-** Peace; healing faith.

**Owl-** Wisdom, watchfulness.

**Ox-** Patience, strength. Winged ox represents St. Luke the Evangelist.

**Palette & Brushes-** Usually found on artists' gravestones.

**Palm tree or frond-** Spiritual victory, success, eternal peace, Christ's victory of death.

**Peacock-** Immortality, the incorruptibility of flesh. Also a symbol for pride.

**Pelican-** Charity, sacrifice. A symbol of the atonement and the Redeemer often found in Christian iconography.

**Pentagram** (5-pointed star in a circle)- 5 Elements, 5 senses. Modern Witch or Wiccan.

**Phoenix-** Resurrection, beauty of soul, immortality, the incorruptibility of flesh.

**Piano-** Deceased played the piano.

**Pineapple-** Hospitality, good host.

**Pine Tree-** Evergreen, eternal. Fertility, regeneration, fidelity.

**Pitcher-** Often found on graves of prohibitionists. Represents virtue and control. On a Jewish grave, it symbolizes a Levite, a person who was responsible for cleaning the hands of the Temple Priest.

**Plow-** Harvest; the reaping of life.

**Pomegranate-** Immortality, resurrection, unity, nourishment of the soul. Associated with Persephone, Queen of *Erebos,* the Greek Underworld.

**Poplar-** Where other cemetery trees promise immortality, the poplar grants us only memories and the sorrows that accompany them.

**Portrait-** Usually a portrait of the deceased.

**Pyramid-** The completed work of creation, eternal, with a solid foundation.

**Rabbit-** Humility, gentleness, self-sacrifice.

**Ram-** Sacrifice. (The ram was a common sacrificial animal to the ancient Hebrews.)

**Rifle-** Found on the graves of military members and hunters.

**Ring, broken-** Family Circle severed.

**R.I.P.-** *Requiescat in pace* (Latin) "Rest in Peace."

**Rooster-** Awakening, the Resurrection, vigilance, calling attention to the person's death.

**Rosary-** Devotion to Mary and constant prayer for the deceased. Almost always found on Catholic gravestones.

**Scales-** Often marks the grave of someone who was in the legal profession. Sometimes shown with statue of Themis (Justice), or St Michael, who weighs the souls of the departed.

**Scarab-** Egyptian symbol of spontaneous creation. Also symbolizes the renewal of life.

**Scroll-** Symbolizes the Scriptures.

**Scythe-** Reaping of life.

**Shoes-** Empty shoes symbolize the loss of a child. Usually one shoe is overturned.

**Sheep & Goats-** Christians vs. non-believers

**Squirrel with a nut-** Religious meditation or spiritual striving.

**Shells-** Journey through death to rebirth. Left on graves to signify that the deceased had not been forgotten. Most common is a scallop, representing the baptism of Christ. A child cradled in a scallop shell was popular in the 19th century. The conch was regarded by many cultures as a symbol of reincarnation and wisdom. In Buddhism, the shell's call can awaken one from ignorance; in Chinese Buddhism it signifies a prosperous journey; and in Islam it means hearing the divine word.

**Skull** (sometimes with crossbones)- Death and mortality. A winged skull symbolizes the ascension into heaven. A skull wearing a wreath represents victory of death over life.

**Sleeping child-** Victorian symbol for death.

**Squirrel with a nut-** Religious meditation or spiritual striving.

**Snake-** Sin, Satan, fall of man. A snake eating its tail (Ouroboros) represents eternal life – no beginning, no end.

**Soldier on Horse-** A soldier's grave. If the horse has both front legs in the air, the person died in battle. If only one leg is raised, the person died as a result of wounds. And if the horse has all four legs on the ground, the person died of natural causes.

**Sphinx-** Guardian; strength and protection.

**Stag-** Virility, wisdom, regeneration and growth. Also faithfulness, thirsting for God, or Christ slaying Satan. Because its antlers resemble branches, the stag has been associated with the Tree of Life; and because it regrows its antlers, it's a symbol of regeneration. During the Middle Ages, the stag was often shown with a crucifix between its antlers, representing purity and solitude, and was the enemy of Satan, the serpent. The Celts believed the stag led lost souls through the darkness. In Buddhism, the golden stag represents knowledge. The Chinese regard it as a symbol of virility and happiness.

**Star-** A 5-pointed star represents the Star of Bethlehem. A 6-pointed star represents creation.

**Star of David-** Jewish sign of Divine Protection.

**Sun-** The soul rising to heaven.

**Swallow-** Represents a child or motherhood.

**Swastika-** Common Buddhist symbol representing the seal of the Buddha's heart; doctrine of Buddha; the round of existence.

**Sword-** Martyrdom. Crossed swords are often seen on the gravestones of veterans, especially officers.

**Tablets-** Usually two tablets joined, representing the Ten Commandments.

**Thistle-** Earthly sorrow. Also, the thorns on a thistle symbolize the crown of thorns and the Passion of Christ. In addition, it is found on many Scottish gravestones.

**Thor's Hammer-** Modern Asatru, or Norse religionist.

**Torch or Flame-** Eternity. An upside-down torch symbolizes an extinguished life.

**Tree or log-** Used for carpenters, builders, lumbermen, or to suggest a life cut off in its prime. May represent head of the family, and occasionally contains a nest with birds suggesting children of the deceased.

**Tree Trunk/Stump-** Marks the graves of Woodmen of the World members. Usually includes other symbols such as anchors, lilies, vines, etc. Broken branches on the tree symbolize a life cut short.

**Tree, fallen -** Mortality, Death.

**Urn-** The Soul. A symbol of death, used to collect tears of the mourners.

**Vine-** The sacraments, God's blood, God.

**Wheat-** Long life, productive and abundant. Cycle of the seasons and of life. Resurrection, fertility, bread and wine (Christian). A sheaf of wheat represents harvest, usually found on older peoples' gravestones.

**Willow Tree-** Sadness or mourning. In ancient Greece, the Willow was associated with Persephone, Queen of the Underworld. When Orpheus went to the Underworld to retrieve his beloved Eurydice, he brought along a willow branch. This apparently helped him gain his gift of poetry.
**Willow, Weeping-** Nature's lament, a symbol of sorrow and mourning.
**Winged Solar Disc-** An Egyptian symbol of a solar eclipse that represents the journey of the sun and the spiritual attributes of the heavens. Also a Zoroastrian symbol of the soul, and divine power. The three rows of feathers represent good words, good thoughts, and good deeds.
**Woman Clinging to Cross-** Faith. Usually found with the verse "Rock of Ages cleft for me" or "Simply to the cross I cling." A person lost in the sea of sin, whose only hope is to cling to Christ's cross.
**Woman Holding Anchor-** Hope.
**Woman Holding Cross-** Faith.

**Woman Weeping-** Mourning, sorrow.
**Wreath-** Symbol of victory. Memory, passed to eternal life.
**Wreath, Bridal-** A young bride.

**XP, overlapped-** The *Chrisma,* one of the oldest Christian symbols. XP (*Chi-Rho*) are the first letters of the Greek word for Christ.

**Yew tree-** Sadness, eternal life.

# Flowers

Owing to their fragile beauty, flowers convey transience, love, grief, happiness and other emotions. Victorian floral symbolism became so popular that almost every flower had a symbolic meaning in "The Language of Flowers." Here are the ones most often found on gravestones:

**Acacia-** Immortality of soul.
**Acanthus-** Heavenly garden. Associated with the rocky ground of ancient Greek cemeteries, it is the most common motif found on memorials.
**Almond-** Divine favor, virgin birth.
**Anemone-** Those the color of blood represent the transience of life.

**Asphodel-** The classic flower of death said to grow in *Erebos*, the Greek Underworld.
**Bellflower-** Constancy, gratitude.
**Buttercup-** Cheerfulness.
**Calla lily-** Majesty, beauty, marriage.
**Century plant-** Immortality; everlasting life.
**Cherry-** The non-fruiting Japanese cherry blossom (*Sakura*) represents perfection of virtue and existence.
**Chrysanthemum-** Where in Europe this flower represents the harvest, the Japanese see the sun, immortality, and the perpetuity of the Imperial Family.
**Cinquefoil-** Maternal affection, beloved daughter.
**Clover or Shamrock-** Irish, or for luck in a gambler.
**Crocus-** Youthful gladness.
**Daffodil-** Death of youth, desire, art, grace, beauty, deep regard.
**Daisy-** Innocence, gentleness, purity of thought, the "day's eye." Grave of young child.
**Dogwood-** Resurrection, sacrifice, eternal life.
**Easter Lily-** Purity, chastity, virginity. Typically associated with the Virgin Mary. Modern symbol of the Resurrection.
**Forget-me-not-** Remembrance.
**Honeysuckle-** Bonds of love, generosity and devoted affection.
**Lalla-** Beauty, marriage.
**Lily-** Majesty, purity, resurrection, restored innocence of the soul. Often seen on women's graves.

**Lily of the Valley-** Innocence, happiness, purity, humility. One of the first Spring flowers.
**Lotus-** Creation, purity, resurrection, evolution, potential. Common in ancient Egypt and India, it is sacred in Buddhism.
**Madonna Lily-** Purity
**Marigold-** Ubiquitous in Mexico's Day of the Dead, where the seasonal blossoms decorate graves and altars.
**Mistletoe-** The "golden bough." Living far above the ground, Druids considered it sacred and an ingredient of immortality.
**Morning Glory-** Resurrection, mourning, youth, brevity of life, farewell, departure, mortality.
**Narcissus-** "Numbness." Popular in ancient Greece as a decorative border for graves.
**Pansy-** Remembrance, humility.
**Passion Flower-** Christ's passion.
**Poinsettia-** A death occurring near Christmas.
**Poppy-** Peace, rest, sleep, eternal sleep, consolation.
**Rose-** Universal symbol of love, beauty, hope, unfailing love. Queen of flowers, seen most often on graves of women. A red rose symbolizes martyrdom and a white rose purity and virginity. How open the rose is indicates how old the person was at the time of death:
**Rose bud-** A child 12 or under.
**Rose in partial bloom-** An adolescent girl.
**Rose in full bloom-** A woman who died in the prime of life.

**Rose, Tudor** (sometimes called the Union Rose)- The traditional floral heraldic emblem of England. May indicate the deceased was of English descent.

**Rosemary-** Remembrance. It was put in coffins and given to mourners as a favor.

**Snowdrops-** Hope.

**Sunflower-** Devotion to God. Life fulfilled.

**Thistle-** Earthly sorrow, Christ's crown of thorns, Scotland as country of origin.

**Tulip-** Love, passion. It represents immortality, because it continues to grow after it is cut.

# Fraternal Orders, Lodges, and Associations

Many old cemetery graves contain members of various organizations, and the distinct iconography and names (or initials) of those organizations may be seen on their headstones:

**American Legion-** Found on graves of people who were American Legion members, an organization for veterans.

**A.O.U.W.-** Ancient Order of United Workmen, a benefit society.

**A.R.-** Arbeiter Ring, an American Jewish fraternal organization committed to social justice. Later became the Workmen's Circle.

**B.P.O.E. with Elk-** Benevolent Protective Order of Elks, a fraternal organization.

**BRT with a Train-** Brotherhood of Railroad Trainmen. A fraternal organization for men who worked as trainmen.

**Canadian Legion of British Empire Service League-** Usually seen with a maple leaf. A Canadian organization formed in the 1920's for war veterans and their dependents.

**Colonial Daughters of the 17$^{th}$ Century-** An organization for women who descended from an ancestor who served in the Colonial wars from 1607 to 1699.

**Crown & Cross-** Both victory and Christianity. May be a member of York Rite Masons.

**D of P-** Degree of Pocahontas (sometimes seen as the Daughters of Pocahontas), organized in 1885. The female auxiliary for the patriotic Improved Order of Redmen.

**D.A.R.-** Daughters of the American Revolution, a women's organization for descendants of American Revolutionary War veterans.

**Eagle, double-headed-** Masonic symbol, part of the Scottish Rite, where it symbolizes the 32$^{nd}$ degree.

**Eagle with FFC-** Symbol of the Improved Order of Red Men, a patriotic society. Their motto: "Freedom, Friendship, Charity."

**Eagle with FOE-** Symbol of the Fraternal Order of Eagles, a fraternal organization.

**Eagle with TOTE-** Symbol of the Improved Order of Red Men, a patriotic society. TOTE = Totem of the Eagle.

**F of A** - Foresters of America, founded in 1895 to provide life and disability insurance to members. Usually contains an eagle, crossed flags, and a deer. Their motto was Liberty, Unity, Benevolence, and Concord.

**F.A.T.A.L.** (with 5-pointed star)- Motto of the Order of the Eastern Star; means "Fairest Among Thousands, Altogether Lovely."

**F.C.B. with Shield & Suit of Armor-** Symbol of the fraternal Knights of Pythias. FCB stands for "Friendship, Charity, and Benevolence."

**F.C.I.-** "Fraternity, Charity, and Loyalty." Motto of the Women's Relief Corp.

**G.A.R-** Grand Army of the Republic. A fraternal organization for men who fought and were honorably discharged from the Union Army during the Civil War.

**I.O.M.-** Independent Order of Mechanics, formed in 1868. Their symbols include Jacob's Ladder and an ark.

**M.W.A.-** Modern Woodmen of America. This was the original name for the Woodmen of the World organization.

**Jr. OUAM-** Junior Order of United American Mechanics. Founded in 1853 in Philadelphia, PA, it is the oldest fraternal order still active in the US.

**Keystone with letters HTWSSTKS-** The Masonic Keystone, mark of an Ancient Grand Master. HTWSSTKS stands for "Hiram The Widow's Son Sent To King Solomon."

**K of C-** Knights of Columbus, a fraternal organization for Catholic men.

**K.O.T.M.-** Knights of the Maccabees, a fraternal organization.

**Moon with Seven Stars, the letter "R", and a dove-** The Daughters of Rebekah, the female auxiliary of the Odd Fellows.

**OES, 5-Pointed Star-** Order of the Eastern Star, the largest fraternal organization in the world to which both women and men may belong. A woman must be related by birth or marriage to a Mason in order to become a member of OES, and a man must be a Mason to join.

**O.S.C.-** Order of Scottish Clans. A fraternal and benevolent society founded in 1878. They provided life and disability insurance to Scottish immigrants. They became a part of Independent Order of Foresters in 1971.

**P of H-** Patrons of Husbandry, aka the National Grange. An agricultural organization.

**P.A.P. with Moose-** Loyal Order of Moose (LOOM), a fraternal organization. P.A.P. stands for motto: Purity, Aid, Progress.

**PLEF, sometimes with crown and shield-** Symbol of the Pythian Sisters, a fraternal organization for women. Letters PLEF stand for motto: "Purity, Love, Equality, and Fidelity."

**R.N.A.-** Royal Neighbors of America. A fraternal organization that offers life insurance, annuities, and medicare supplement for women. Formed on March 21, 1895, it is still active.

**Saint Aldemar Commandery-** A Knights Templar organization. Masonic.

**S.A.R.-** Sons of the American Revolution, a fraternal society organized in 1889 for male descendants of American Revolutionary War veterans.

**Snake on a cross with "In Hoc Signo Vinces"-** The Masonic brazen serpent, a symbol of the 25th Degree Masons. Ref. Numbers 21:9 "And Moses made a serpent of brass, and put it upon a pole, and it came to pass, that if a serpent had bitten any man, when he beheld the serpent of brass, he lived." *In Hoc Signo Vinces* ("In this sign I conquer") was the injunction given to Constantine the Great in a dream to place the Cross upon his battle standards.

**Square & Compass-** Usually has the letter "G" in the middle. Found on gravestones of Freemasons.

**Star, Cross, and Shepherd's Crook-** Symbol of the White Shrine of Jerusalem. Often seen with the phrase *In Hoc Signo Spes Mea,* ("In this Sign (the Cross) is my hope.") A society for women who are related to a Master Mason. Founded 1894.

**Sunburst with star and cross, Monstrat Viam-** Symbol of the First Corps of Cadets, now the 211th Military Police Battalion. *Monstrat Viam* is Latin for "It Points the Way."

**SV-** Sons of Veterans of the USA, formed in 1881. Changed their name to the Sons of Union Veterans of the Civil War in 1925.

**Sword, Crescent, and Sphinx-** Symbol of the Shriners (The Imperial Council of the Ancient Arabic Order of the Nobles of the Mystic Shrine). Group was founded in 1872.

**Tent-** A symbol used by the Independent Order of Odd Fellows. The tent symbolizes their encampments, the three highest degrees attainable before reaching the highest branch.

**T.R.H.-** The Royal Highlanders, a fraternal insurance organization formed in 1896 in Aurora, NE. Often seen with the letters P.F.V., which is their motto: "Prudence, Fidelity, and Valor."

**Triangle with square, spade, and keys-** Symbolizes the York Rite of Masonry.

**Triangle with a star in the center-** Order of the Sons of Temperance, a fraternal organization that promoted the temperance movement (abstinence and prohibition of alcohol). Their motto: "Love, Purity, Fidelity."

**Triangle with three T's joined at base-** Symbol of the Royal Arch Masons (RAM).

**Trowel or Spade-** Symbolizes mortality and death. Also used as a Masonic symbol; a trowel is used to spread the cement of Friendship and Brotherly Love.

**U.O.A. Druids-** United Order of Ancient Druids, a fraternal organization.

**U.V.L.-** Union Veterans League, an organization for Union Civil War veterans.

**Veteran of the Cross-** A veteran member of Methodist Church.

**W.B.A.-** Woman's Benefit Association, a club for women that provided life insurance. Part of the Order of the Maccabees.

**W.C.-** Woodmen Circle, the female auxiliary to the Woodmen of the World.

**Woodmen of the World-** An insurance company and fraternal organization.

**Woodmen Circle-** Ladies auxiliary to Woodmen of the World.

**W.R.C.-** Women's Relief Corp. Female auxiliary for the Grand Army of the Republic.

# References

"Gravestone Symbolism," Grave Addiction, http://www.graveaddiction.com/symbol.html

"Gravestone Symbols and Carvings- Meaning and Inspiration," Stoneletters, https://stoneletters.com/blog/gravestone-symbols

Eye of Providence symbolism, http://www.ancient-symbols.com/symbols-directory/eye_of_providence.html

"Historic Cemetery Symbols: What do Seashells Mean?," Tui Snider, http://tuisnider.com/2015/08/11/historic-cemetery-symbols-what-do-seashells-mean/

"Hourglass Symbolism," Words on Stone, https://wordsonstone.wordpress.com/2017/08/28/hourglass-symbolism/

The International Association of Cemetery Preservationists, Inc.

"Symbolism in Stone," Friends of Oak Grove Cemetery, https://friendsofoakgrovecemetery.org/category/mourning-art/

"Victorian Funeral Symbolism," Friends of Oak Grove Cemetery, https://friendsofoakgrovecemetery.org/category/victorian-funeral-symbolism/

# Appendix B.
# Encyclopedia of the Afterlife

In researching and compiling this extensive Glossary, I was struck with the universality of certain themes and memes: survival of the conscious soul/spirit after death; the existence of an Afterlife realm, usually with separate regions for various denizens—such as underworlds and paradisal domains; guides *(psychopomps)* to escort (or ferry) the newly dead to their respective afterlife destinations; the anthropomorphic personification of Death itself as a sentient entity (the Angel of Death, the Grim Reaper); and powerful supernatural beings (gods or demons) who rule/preside over the dead in their respective Netherworlds.

I do not believe that the universality of these memes can be dismissed as mere coincidence; but rather I regard this phenomenon to be validation of the concept of continuity of consciousness after death, and the existence of an immaterial "Undiscover'd Country" in which departed spirits may sojourn until their possible (though not inevitable) return to the world of the living in new incarnations.

That each of the Afterlives described by various cultures reflects the unique characteristics of those respective cultures, while still maintaining certain elements common to all, is further validation of the proposition that indeed, consciousness is not simply extinguished upon the death of the body, but rather—as attested by every human culture since the dawn of time—continues on a "great adventure" divorced from the constraints of mortal flesh, which is shed as an emerging butterfly sheds the chrysalis (another universal motif).

So here is an alphabetical catalog, "who's who," and guide to the Other Side of the Veil...

**Acheron** (Gr. "joyless"): The River of Woe in *Erebos* (the Greek Underworld), across which the newly-deceased are ferried by *Charon* the ferryman, who requires as passage fee the coins that have been placed over the eyes or in the mouth of the corpse. The Acheron joins the more famous river *Styx* (actual rivers in Greece).

**Adlivun** (Inuit, "those beneath us;" also known as **Idliragijenget**): The Inuit (Polar Eskimo) Underworld, located beneath the land and the sea. *Sedna, Tornarsuk* and the *tornat* (spirits of animals and natural formations) and *tupilak* (souls of dead people) live in Adlivun, which is a frozen wasteland. The *psychopomps Pinga* and *Anguta* bring the souls of the dead to Adlivun, where they must stay for one year before moving on. Adlivun is ruled by *Sedna,* who purifies the souls in preparation for the next stage of their journey to the Land of the Moon *(Quidlivun),* where they enjoy eternal rest and peace.

**Aed/Aodh**: Prince of the *Daoine Sidhe* and a god of the Underworld in Irish mythology. He was the eldest son of *Lir,* High King of the T*uatha de Dannan,* and *Aobh,* a daughter of *Bodb Dearg.*

**Aita/Eita:** Etruscan equivalent to the Greek *Hades,* ruler of the Underworld.

**Aizsaule/Viņsaule:** The Latvian world of the dead, described as similar to the world of living. Its entrances are located in forests, swamps, rivers, graveyards, caves, under rocks and in the sea. The devil steals people away to take them to his world. The dead, called *Veļi* (also *Iļģi, Dieviņi, Pauri*), visit their old homes during autumn from *Miķeļi* (Sept. 29) to *Mārtiņi* (Nov. 10).

**Aken:** In Egyptian mythology, Aken was the custodian of the boat named *Meseket* that carried the souls of the dead into the Underworld. He remained in a deep sleep when he was not needed, and had to be woken by the Ferryman, *Mahaf,* when his services were required. Depicted as a sailor standing in the stern of a papyrus boat, he was not worshipped, and had no cult center, but he is referred to a number of times in the *Book of the Dead.* The Egyptian word for part of the soul, *Ba,* also meant *ram*. Therefore, Aken was usually depicted as being ram-headed.

**Aker** ("one who curves"): Lord of the Horizon in Egyptian mythology, and one of the earliest gods worshipped. Since the horizon was where night became day, Aker was said to guard the entrance and exit to the *Underworld,* opening them for the sun to pass through during the night. The dead had to request Aker to open the Underworld's gates, so that they might enter.

**Akh** *("magically effective one"):* A concept of the dead that varied over the long history of ancient Egyptian belief, the Akh was intellect as a living entity. Following the death of the *Khat* (physical body), the *Ba* and *Ka* would be reunited to reanimate the Akh.

**Ala** (also known as *Ani, Ana, Ale,* and *Ali* in varying dialects): Goddess of the Earth, morality, fertility and creativity, and the most important *Alusi* (deity) in the Igbo pantheon of Nigeria. Ala rules over the Underworld, and holds the deceased ancestors in her womb. Her name literally means "ground," denoting her status as the Earth itself, and her husband is *Amadioha,* the sky god. As goddess of morality, Ala is in charge of Igbo law and customs, and judges human actions. Her agent and messenger is the python. In art, Ala is represented as a regal figure seated on a throne, surrounded by her family.

**Allatu:** Original Sumerian version of the later Babylonian Goddess *Ereshkigal,* she was the ancient dark Earth Goddess, Queen and Keeper of the Underworld.

**All Saints' Day** (Nov. 1): A Catholic Christian festival in honor of all the saints, known and unknown, famous or obscure, including individuals who may have personally led one to faith in Jesus.

**Amenti:** The Judgment Hall of the Dead in ancient Egyptian religion, presided over by *Osiris,* Lord and Judge of the Dead.

**Am-heh:** A minor god in the Egyptian Underworld, whose name means either "devourer of millions" or "eater of eternity." Depicted as a man with the head of a dog who lived in a lake of fire, Am-heh could only be controlled by the god *Atum.*

**Ammut/Ammit** ("devourer of the dead"): In ancient Egyptian religion, she is a hideous composite of hippopotamus, cheetah, lion and crocodile who eats the hearts of any who are found unworthy in the *Weighing of the Heart,* thus terminating their existence.

**Angels** ("messengers"): Supernatural beings found in various religions and mythologies. In Zoroastrianism and Abrahamic religions *angels* are celestial beings who serve as messengers and intermediaries between *Heaven* and Earth. Their roles include protecting and guiding human beings, and carrying out God's tasks. Some Christians believe that good people become angels after death. The theological study of angels is known as "angelology."

**Ankh** ("eternal life"): The *ankh,* also known as breath of life, the key of the Nile or *crux ansata* (L, "cross with a handle"), was the ancient Egyptian hieroglyph for "life." The ankh appears in hand or in proximity of almost every deity in the Egyptian pantheon (including Pharaohs). Thus it is widely understood as a symbol of early religious pluralism: all sects believed in eternal life, and this is the literal meaning of the symbol..

**Annwfn** ("the Blessed Isles"): The Celtic Afterworld, consisting of an archipelago of separate islands in a mystical sea. The three major regions are *Arran, Caer Wydyr,* and *Caer Feddwid.*

**Anubis:** Jackal-headed Egyptian god of embalming and the Underworld, son of *Nepthys* and *Set.* Adopted by *Osiris* after Set's defeat by *Horus,* Anubis became Osiris' messenger to the world of the living, spirit guide *(psychopomp)* for the dead, and personal guardian during sleep and astral travel. He weighs the hearts of the dead to determine their ultimate fate..

**Apotheosis/Apotheasis** (Gr, "to deify;" also called **divinization** and **deification**): The glorification of a subject to divine level. In theology, *apotheosis* refers to the idea that an individual has been elevated to godlike stature, or even become a deity (*theos*=god; *theas*=goddess). In art, the term refers to the treatment of any subject in a particularly grand or exalted manner. See *Ascension.*

**A'raf** ("the heights"): Muslim borderland between heaven and hell, described as a high wall with a gate. Here dwell souls who witness both the terror of hell and the beauty of paradise. They yearn to enter paradise, but their sins and virtues are evenly balanced. Yet with the mercy of God, they will be among the last people to enter paradise.

**Arawn:** King of *Annwfn,* the realm of the dead in Welsh mythology. He agreed to exchange kingdoms for a season with the Welsh prince *Pwyll;* both were pleased with the arrangement at its end.

**Arran/Avalon:** A land of eternal summer in Celtic religion, with green grassy fields and sweet flowing rivers. Arran hosts the Cauldron of Plenty, which is also linked to the Holy Grail. Avalon is closely associated with the Arthurian legends. Only those who are pure, self-sacrificing, and spiritual are allowed to enter this region.

**Arsay:** Canaanite Goddess of the Underworld, she is the third daughter of *Baal* at Ugarit. She equates with the goddess *Allatu.*

**Ascension:** Entering into Heaven directly without dying first. An Ascended Master is a spiritually enlightened being who in past incarnations was an ordinary human, but who has undergone a series of initiatory spiritual transformations. In some New Age teachings, Ascension refers to the spiritual transformation of the Earth

**Asphodel Meadows:** A neutral region of *Erebos,* the Greek Underworld, where ordinary souls whose work is done were sent to live after death. Edith Hamilton suggests that the asphodel of these meadows are not exactly like those of our world but are "presumably strange, pallid, ghostly flowers." Others suggest that they were actually narcissi.

**Asgard** (Old Norse: *Ásgarðr*; "Enclosure of the Æsir"): In Norse mythology, Asgard is one of the Nine Worlds and home to the Æsir tribe of gods. Odin and his wife Frig, are the rulers of Asgard. One of Asgard's best-known locations is *Valhalla,* Odin's great mead-hall, where slain Viking warriors feast and fight eternally.

**Astral body:** A body composed of a subtle material, intermediate between the intelligent soul and the mental body. The concept derives from the philosophy of Plato, and is related to an *astral plane* consisting of the planetary heavens of astrology. The term was adopted by 19th-century Theosophists and neo-Rosicrucians.

**Astral plane:** The world of the celestial spheres, crossed by the soul in its *astral body* on the way to being born and after death, and generally said to be populated by *angels, spirits* or other immaterial beings. The term was popularized in the late 19th and early 20th centuries by Theosophy and neo-Rosicrucianism.

**Astral projection/Astral travel:** An interpretation of out-of-body experience (OBE) that assumes the existence of an *astral body* separate from the physical body and capable of travelling outside it in an *astral plane.*

**Avaiki:** The netherworld in the mythology of *Mangaia* (Cook Islands), described as the interior of a vast coconut shell. *Varima-te-takere,* the mother of *Vatea,* lives in the lowest depths of the hollow of this shell.

**Avernus:** A volcanic crater near Cumae, Italy, west of Naples. Within the crater is Lake Avernus, on the shore of which is the grotto of the *Cumaean Sybil.* Avernus was believed to be the entrance to the Underworld, and is so portrayed in Virgil's *Aeneid.* The name is Greek, meaning "without birds," because according to tradition, any birds flying over the lake were doomed to fall dead—likely due to toxic fumes that the crater gave off. In later times, Avernus became an alternate name for the Underworld, and excavations of the grotto confirm its use as a *necromanteion,* or oracle of the dead.

**Azrael:** Black-winged Angel of Death in Judeo-Christian myth. The *Grim Reaper* whose scythe cuts free the souls of the dying.

**Ba** ("personality"): Ancient Egyptians believed that a human soul was made up of five parts: the *Ren,* the *Ba,* the *Ka,* the *Sheut,* and the *Ib.* The Ba was everything that makes an individual unique, similar to the notion of "personality." The Egyptians believed the Ba would live after the body died, and it is sometimes depicted as a human-headed bird flying out of the tomb to join with the Ka in the afterlife.

**Bardo** (Tibetan, "transitional state"): In Tibetan Buddhism, the state intermediate between two lives on Earth, after death and before one's next birth, when one's consciousness is not connected with a physical body.

**Bardo Thodol:** The *Tibetan Book of the Dead*.

**Baron Cimitière** (Fr. "Baron Cemetery"): One of the *Guédé loa* in Haitian Vodou, a spirit of the dead, along with *Baron Samedi* and *Baron La Croix*. He is the male guardian of the cemetery, protecting its graves. His "horses" (possessed worshippers) wear a tuxedo or tails and a top hat. They have expensive tastes, smoking cigars and drinking wine or fine liquor. They are just as crass as the other Guede, but mock polite manners and upper-class airs.

**Baron La Croix** (Fr. "Baron the Cross"): One of the Guédé, a Vodou *loa* of the dead and sexuality. He is the ultimate suave and sophisticated spirit of Death—quite cultured and debonair. He has an existential philosophy about death, finding death's reason for being both humorous and absurd. Baron La Croix is the extreme expression of individuality, and offers to you the reminder of delighting in life's pleasures.

**Baron Samedi** (Fr. "Baron Saturday"): Vodou *loa* of the dead, he is the head of the *Guédé*. His wife is *Maman Brigitte*. He is usually depicted with a top hat, black tuxedo, dark glasses, and cotton plugs in the nostrils, as if to resemble a corpse dressed and prepared for burial in the Haitian style. He has a white, skull-like face, and speaks in a nasal voice. He is noted for disruption, obscenity, and debauchery, with a particular fondness for tobacco and rum infused with hot peppers. He is also the Loa of *resurrection,* in which capacity he is often called upon for healing by those near or approaching death, as it is only Baron Samedi who can accept an individual into the realm of the dead.

**Barzakh** (Arabic, "obstacle"): In Islamic eschatology, al-Barzakh is the barrier between the physical and spiritual worlds, in which the soul awaits after death and before resurrection on *Qiyamah* (Judgment Day). In Barzakh, the spirit is separate from the body, freed to contemplate the wrongdoings of its former life, but unable to act.

**Batara Kala:** God of the Underworld in Javanese and Balinese mythology, ruling over it in a cave along with *Setesuyara,* Goddess of the Underworld. Batara Kala was also the creator of Light and the Earth, as well as the god of Time and Destruction, who devours unlucky people. Related to the Hindu concept of *Kala*, or Time, he causes eclipses by trying to eat the Sun or the Moon.

**Bifrost:** (See *Rainbow Bridge*)

**Bilé:** An evil Afterworld ruler in Celtic mythology whose kingdom is a vast wasteland of crushed spirits and broken bodies who must pay him eternal homage.

**Bridge of Judgement:** A bridge in the Afterlife in Zoroastrian (Pharsee) religion. The soul travels to it by one of two paths: the Endless Light, where the good dead eat "the butter of early spring." Or the Wicked Underground, where the wicked are condemned to eat only spoiled rotten food until the Resurrection.

**Bran:** A mortal hero in Welsh mythology who angered the gods, was beheaded, and then banished to rule in the Underworld as punishment. His symbol is the raven, associated with death and the grave. Bran's kingdom is populated with failed heroes who spend eternity in regret.

**Caer Feddwid** (Welsh, "castle of revelry"): Also known as *Caer Rigor* or *Caer* Siddi, this is a paradisal place in *Annwfn,* ruled by *Arianrhod of the Silver Wheel* (i.e. the Moon), goddess of space, time, and energy. The air is filled with enchanting music, and a fountain flows with magick wine that grants eternal youth and health.

**Caer Wydyr/Nennius** (Welsh, "castle of glass"): A dark and gloomy place in *Annwfn,* inhabited only by lost souls. It is the worst place to end up after death.

**Cerberus:** The son of *Typhon* and *Echidna,* Cerberus is a monstrous dog with three heads and a serpentine tail who guards the entrance to *Erebos,* the Greek Underworld. He is friendly enough to the spirits who enter, but if any try to leave he seizes them and holds them fast. However, *Orpheus* found that Cerberus could be charmed with sweet music and honey cakes.

**Cernunnos** ("horned one"): Ancient Celtic ruler over the dead, depicted with stag antlers; also known as *Herne the Hunter,* he leads the Wild Hunt on *Samhain* Eve.

**Channeling:** A form of *mediumship* in which the channeler goes into a trance, or "leaves their body," allowing a departed soul or other spirit entity to borrow the channeler's body and talk through them. Channelers may open their eyes, smile and utilize facial expressions when channeling. They can also walk and behave normally. But the rhythm and the intonation of their voice may change completely.

**Charon:** The son of *Erebos* and *Nyx* (night), a gloomy, sullen old man who ferries the souls of the dead across the Acherusean Lake and River into the realm of shadows. The souls are brought down from the upper world by *Hermes,* and must pay Charon an *obolos*, coins placed for this purpose onto the eyes or into the mouths of the dead.

**Charun:** A *psychopomp* of the Etruscan Underworld; he leads the dead to enjoy a happy afterlife. He is often portrayed with *Vanth,* a black-winged Death Goddess also associated with the Underworld.

**Chepi:** A ghost or fairy in the mythology of the Narragansett tribe of Native Americans from the Narragansett Bay region of Rhode Island, Connecticut, and eastern Massachusetts. Chepi is an avenging spirit of the dead who shares knowledge with medicine people in dreams or visions, and can be called upon by the *pawwaw* or medicine person, to destroy an enemy.

**Chthonic** (Gr. "subterranean"): Adjective for deities or spirits of the Underworld, especially in Greek religion. The Greek word *khthon* is one of several for "earth," referring to the underground, rather than the living surface (*Gaea*) or the land as territory (*khora*). It evokes abundance and the grave.

**Cocytus** (Gr. "river of tears"): A branch of the River Styx in the Greek Underworld.

**Cave of Cruachan:** A cave in Connaught, Ireland that has been called the Gateway to the Underworld, through which armies of zombies come to attack the living. Christians claimed that condemned human souls enter Hell through Cruachan.

**Culsu/Cul:** A female underworld demon associated with gateways in Etruscan myth. Her attributes included a torch and scissors. She was often represented next to *Culsans,* god of doors and doorways, corresponding to the two-faced Roman god *Janus.*

**Cŵn Annwfn** (Welsh, "hounds of Annwfn"): The spectral hounds of *Annwfn,* the Welsh Otherworld. They were associated with the Wild Hunt, presided over by either *Arawn,* king of Annwfn in the First Branch of the *Mabinogi,* or by *Gwyn ap Nudd,* the Underworld king and king of the Fair(y) Folk in later medieval lore. According to Welsh folklore, their growling is loudest when they are at a distance, growing softer and softer as they draw nearer. Their coming is generally seen as a death portent.

**Dea Tacita** ("the silent goddess"): A Roman goddess of the dead, equated with the Earth Goddess *Larunda,* and honored in the *Larentalia* festival on Dec. 23. These silent goddesses were the personification of the terror of obscurity (being forgotten), invoked to destroy a hated person.

**Death/Grim Reaper:** The concept of *Death* as an anthropomorphic personification has existed in many societies since the beginning of recorded history. In 15th century Europe, Death was depicted as a skeletal black-cloaked figure carrying a scythe, while the title of "the Grim Reaper" is first attested from 1847. In Jewish tradition, Death was referred to as the **Angel of Life and Death** (*Malach HaMavet*) or the **Angel of Dark and Light**, from Talmudic lore. The Spectre of Death is a *psychopomp,* who severs the last ties between the soul and the body and escorts the deceased to the next world, without having any part in the victim's actual demise. In some stories, the Grim Reaper may be bribed or outwitted in order to retain one's life. In many languages (including English),

Death is personified as male, while in others it is perceived as female (as in Slavic and Romance languages). See *Mors, Thanatos*.

**Dewi Sri/Shridevi** (*Dewi/devi* means "goddess"): The Javanese, Sundanese, and Balinese pre-Hindu and pre-Islamic goddess of rice and fertility, with dominion over the Underworld and the Moon. She is still widely worshipped on the islands of Bali and Java. After the adoption of Hinduism in Java in the 1$^{st}$ century, Dewi Sri was associated with the Hindu goddess *Lakshmi*, as both grant wealth and family prosperity.

**Día de Muertos** (Spanish, "day of the dead"): A popular Mexican festival to remember and honor beloved family members and friends who have died. It is celebrated from Oct. 31-Nov. 2 and presided over by *la Muerte* (Lady Death), originally the Aztec goddess *Mictecacihuatl,* who has been popularized in modern times as *la Catrina*.

**Di Inferi** (L. "the gods below"): A shadowy collective of ancient Roman deities associated with death and the Underworld. The epithet *inferi* is also given to the mysterious *Manes,* a collective of ancestral spirits whose name means "good" or "kindly"—a euphemistic way to speak of the inferi so as to avert their potential to cause harm or fear.

**Dionysian Mysteries:** A ritual of ancient Greece and Rome which used intoxicants and other trance-inducing techniques (like dance and music) to remove inhibitions and social constraints, liberating the individual to return to a natural state. It also provided some liberation for the marginalized: women, slaves and foreigners. In their final phase the Mysteries shifted their emphasis from a *chthonic,* Underworld orientation to a transcendental, mystical one, with *Dionysus* changing his nature accordingly.

**Dis Pater:** A Roman god of the Underworld, later subsumed by *Pluto* or *Hades*. Originally a *chthonic* god of riches, fertile agricultural land, and underground mineral wealth.

**Divinization:** In Christian theology, *divinization* (also *deification,* making divine, or *theosis*) is the transforming effect of divine grace, the Spirit of God, or the atonement of Christ. It literally means to become more divine, more like God, or take upon a divine nature. See *apotheosis*.

**Diyu:** The Chinese Hell or *purgatory*, which serves to punish and renew spirits in preparation for *reincarnation*. It is a subterranean maze with various levels and chambers to which souls are taken after death to atone for the sins they committed when they were alive. The exact number of levels or courts in Diyu and their associated judges differ from 3-18 between various Buddhist and Taoist interpretations. Each court deals with a different aspect of atonement and punishment; sinners are subjected to gruesome tortures until their "deaths," after which they are restored to their original state for the tortures to be repeated.

**Donn** (Gaelic, "brown one"): Irish God of the Dead. Donn was drowned by the Goddess Eriu after he insulted her, after which he became the keeper of the first guidepost on the journey to the Otherworld. His realm is *Techn Duinn* ("house of Donn"), the assembly place for the newly dead, located on a small rocky island southwest of Munster off the coast of Ireland, where he welcomes his descendants, the people of Ireland, to come when they die.

**Duat:** The ancient Egyptian Underworld.

**Duzakh:** The Zoroastrian Persian Hell, described as a deep well, terrifyingly dark, stinking, and extremely narrow. The smallest of the *xrafstars* (harmful creatures) are as big as mountains, and all devour and destroy the soul of the damned. Horrible punishments and tortures are adapted to the sins committed by the damned. There is much emphasis on sexual crimes, but also on other sins disapproved of by *Mazdean* ethics. Duzakh is the residence of *Ahriman,* the demons, and the *drujes*. All atmospheric calamities are associated with it: snow, cold, hail, rain, burning heat, etc.

**E Bukura e Dheut** ("beauty of the Earth") A crafty Fairy in Albanian folklore. Her sisters are *E Bukura e Detit* (Beauty of the Sea) and *E Bukura e Qiellit* (Beauty of Heaven). *E Bukura e Dheut* is beauty itself, golden-haired, but may also appear with black skin. She may be a good spirit or (more often) evil, with magical powers that derive from her dress. She lives in the underworld, where her palace is guarded by a three-headed dog, a *kuçedra* and other weird and creatures. She is always ready to help, and so powerful that she can undertake tasks that would normally be the province of God or an angel. Many stories describe heroes who attempt to gain a strand of her golden hair. If one succeeds at all the labors she requires, she will become his faithful wife.

**Ectoplasm** (Gr. "something formed or molded"): A spiritual product formed by trance mediums and excreted as a gauze-like substance from bodily orifices. Spirits are said to drape this substance over their nonphysical bodies, enabling them to interact in the physical realm. However, examined ectoplasm was revealed to be faked from cheesecloth, butter, muslin and cloth, and most parapsychologists doubt whether genuine examples ever existed.

**Edimmu:** A type of *utukku* in Sumerian mythology, similar in nature to the *preta* of Vedic religion or the *kiangshi* of Chinese mythology. The ghosts of those who were not buried properly, they were considered vengeful toward the living and might possess people if they did not respect certain taboos, such as the prohibition against eating ox meat. They were thought to cause disease and inspire criminal behavior in the living, but could sometimes be appeased by funeral repasts or libations. The edimmu were also thought to be completely or nearly incorporeal, "wind" spirits that sucked the life out of the susceptible and the sleeping (most commonly the young).

**Egyptian Book of the Dead:** An ancient Egyptian funerary text, used from the beginning of the New Kingdom (ca. 1550 BCE) to around 50 BCE. The Egyptian name for the text may be translated as "Book of Coming Forth by Day," or "Book of Emerging Forth Into the Light." This is a loose collection of magick spells intended to assist a dead person's journey through the *Duat*, or Underworld, and into *Sekhet-Aaru*, the paradisal afterlife, and was compiled by many priests over about 1,000 years.

**Eingana:** A creator goddess in Australian Aboriginal mythology, and the mother of all water, animals, and humans. She is a snake goddess of death who lives in the *Dreamtime*. She has no vagina;

she simply grew in size and, unable to give birth to the life inside her, had the god *Barraiya* open a hole with a spear near her anus, so that labor could commence. Eingana holds a sinew that is attached to every living thing; if she lets go of one, the attached creature dies.

**Eleusinian Mysteries:** Initiatory ceremonies held every year at Eleusis, Greece, in honor of *Demeter* and her daughter *Persephone*. The Mysteries represented the abduction of Persephone by *Hades,* Lord of the Underworld, and her return in the spring. The rites were kept secret and preserved since the Mycenaean period. Since they involved visions of an Afterlife, some scholars believe that their power derived from psychedelic agents. As Christianity gained in popularity in the $4^{th}$-$5^{th}$ centuries, Eleusis's prestige began to fade. Julian, the last Pagan emperor of Rome, who reigned from 361-363 after 50 years of Christian rule, attempted to restore the Mysteries and was the last emperor to be initiated into them. Emperor Theodosius I closed the sanctuaries in 392 CE, and their last remnants were destroyed in 396 CE, when Alaric, King of the Goths, invaded accompanied by Christians "in their dark garments," bringing in Arian Christianity and desecrating the old sacred sites.

**Éljúðnir** ("sprayed with snowstorms"): Hall of the Norse goddess *Hel,* located in *Helheim.*

**Elysian Fields** (or **Elysium**): A lovely paradisal region in *Erebos,* the Greek Underworld, where good people are reunited with their loved ones to dwell happily until their next incarnation together.

**Enmesarra**: An Underworld god of the law in Sumerian and Akkadian mythology. He is also described as a Sun god, protector of flocks and vegetation, equated with *Nergal.*

**Erebos:** The ancient Greek Underworld; often called *Hades*, the name of its ruler.

**Erecura:** An ancient Celtic *cthonic* goddess, represented with the attributes of *Proserpina* and associated with the Roman Underworld god *Dis Pater.* Depicted with such symbols of fertility as the cornucopia and apple baskets, she may originally have been an Earth Goddess. Images of Erecura are found in the Danubian area of Southern Germany and Slovenia, as well as in Italy, Great Britain, and France.

**Ereshkigal** ("great lady under the earth"): Babylonian version of the earlier Sumerian *Allatu,* she was the ancient dark Earth Goddess, Queen and Keeper of *Irkalla,* the land of the dead or Underworld. She struck down her younger sister *Ishtar/Inanna* for her hubris, but was later tricked into allowing her to be resurrected. Sometimes her name is given as **Irkalla**, similar to the way the name *Hades* was used in Greek mythology for both the Underworld and its ruler.

**Erlik/Erlig**: In Turkic and Mongolian mythology, Erlik is the god of evil, darkness, lord of the lower world, and judge of the dead. Erlik was the first creation of *Tengri* or *Ulgan,* the creator god, but Erlik's pride led to rebellion, and he was banished to the Underworld. Evil spirits created by Erlik cause misfortune, sickness, and death. Besides these, his nine sons and daughters assist their father in his evil ways. If people refuse him sacrifice, Erlik takes them away to his lower world and makes them his slaves.

**Etheric body:** The innermost layer in the "human energy field" or *aura.* Analogous in usage to *spirit,* it is in immediate contact with the physical body, sustaining and connecting it with higher bodies. According to Theosophists, the etheric body inhabits an etheric plane corresponding to the four higher subplanes of the physical plane. It is often confounded with the related concept of the *astral body*—the early Theosophists had called it the "astral double."

**Exaltation:** The Church of Jesus Christ of Latter-Day Saints (LDS or Mormons) believe in *apotheosis* along the lines of the Christian tradition of *divinization* or *deification*, but in the LDS church it is referred to as "exaltation" or eternal life, and is accomplished through "sanctification." Mormons believe that humans may live with God through eternity in families and eventually become gods themselves, though remaining subordinate to God the Father, the Son, and the Holy Spirit (the Mother). Mormons believe that one purpose for Christ's mission is the exaltation or Christian deification of humans. However, only those who are sufficiently obedient and who accept the atonement and the grace and mercy of Jesus Christ before the resurrection and final judgment will be "exalted" and thereby achieve deification. A popular Mormon quote, attributed to the early Mormon leader Lorenzo Snow in 1837, is "As man now is, God once was: As God now is, man may become." See *Apotheosis*.

**Exorcism** (Gr. "binding by oath"): The practice of evicting demons, ghosts, or other spirit entities from a person or an area they are believed to have possessed. This may be done by an elaborate ritual, making the entity swear an oath, or simply by commanding it to depart in the name of a higher power.

**Feng-Du:** The Chinese Underworld.

**Feralia** (Feb. 21) A midnight ritual of placation and exorcism held in ancient Rome, culminating the 9-day *Parentalia,* when the paterfamilias addressed the malevolent, destructive aspects of his *Manes*. It functioned as a cleansing ritual for *Caristia* on the following day, when the family held a banquet to celebrate the amity between themselves and their benevolent ancestral dead (*Lares*).

**Final Judgement:** In the Abrahamic religions and Zoroastrianism, this is the final and eternal judgment by God of every nation. Christian Futurists believe it will take place after the Resurrection of the Dead and Second Coming of Christ, while Full Preterists believe it has already occurred.

**Flins:** The God of Death in Wendish (Slavic) mythology.

**Fólkvangr** ("field of the host"): A meadow or field in Norse mythology, presided over by the goddess *Freyja*, where half of those slain in battle go upon death, while the other half go to *Odin's* feast-hall, *Valhalla*.

**Fomorii:** A monstrous and misshapen race who dwell in a gloomy Irish Underworld far beneath the sea. They are ruled by *Balor,* who has a terrible temper, and often strikes out against his subjects without provocation. Most legends agree that the Fomorii's evil caused their deformities, and Balor's wrath is punishment for the sins of their past.

**Fortunate Isles** (or **Isles of the Blessed**): Heroes and other favored mortals in Greek and Celtic mythology were received by the gods into a blissful paradise of eternal summer. According to Greek mythology, the islands were reserved for those who had chosen to be reincarnated thrice, and managed to be judged as especially pure enough to gain entrance to the Elysian Fields all three times. These islands were thought to lie in the Western Ocean near the encircling River Oceanus; Madeira, Canary Islands, Azores, Cape Verde, Bermuda and Lesser Antilles have sometimes been cited as possible matches. See *Summerland*.

**42 Negative Confessions:** A litany of 42 sins and evils that the deceased must deny having committed in life before the 42 divine judges (one for each *Nome*, or district of Egypt) in *Amenti*, the Egyptian "Judgment Hall of the Dead."

**Gallus** (also called **gallu demons** or **gallas**): Great demons/devils in Sumerian and Akkadian (Babylonian and Assyrian) mythology, they hauled unfortunate victims off to the Underworld. They were one of seven kinds of devils ("the offspring of hell") of Babylonian theology that could be appeased by the sacrifice of a lamb.

**Garm/Garmr:** The blood-stained watchdog who guards *Gnipahelli*, the foul-smelling opening of Niflheim, the Norse Underworld. This ferocious monster is forever watching for *Hermodr*, the dark ferryman who brings the dead to the underworld. Garm also prevents the spirits from escaping Niflheim.

**Gehenna:** A place outside ancient Jerusalem called in the Hebrew Bible the *Valley of the Son of Hinnom;* one of two principal valleys surrounding the Old City, where apostate Israelites and followers of Canaanite gods sacrificed their children by fire (2 Chr. 28:3, 33:6). In Abrahamic scriptures, Gehenna is an afterlife destination of the wicked. In the Qur'an, *Jahannam* is a place of torment for sinners and non-believers, or the Islamic equivalent of *Hell*.

**Ghost** (also **spectre, phantom, apparition** or **spook**): The soul or spirit of a dead person or animal that can appear to the living in visible form or other manifestation. Descriptions of ghosts vary widely—from an invisible presence to translucent or barely visible wispy shapes, to realistic lifelike spectres. The deliberate attempt to contact the spirit of a deceased person is known as *necromancy*, or in *Spiritualism* as a *séance*. Certain religious practices—funeral rites, exorcisms, and some practices of Spiritualism and ritual magic—are specifically designed to rest the spirits of the dead. Ghosts are generally described as solitary essences that haunt particular locations, objects, or people they were associated with in life, though phantom armies, ghost trains, phantom ships, and even ghost animals have also been reported.

**Gidim:** *Ghosts* in Mesopotamian religions, comparable to the shades of the deceased in the Underworld of Classical myth. Gidim were created at the time of death, taking on the memory and personality of the dead person. They traveled to the Netherworld, *Irkalla,* where they were assigned a position, and led an existence similar in some ways to that of the living. Relatives of the dead were expected to make offerings of food and drink to the dead to ease their conditions. If they did not, the ghosts could inflict misfortune and illness on the living.

**Gimlé** ("lee-of-fire"): In Norse myth, a place where the survivors of *Ragnarök* are foretold to live. In the *Prose Edda* and *Völuspá* it is described as the most beautiful place on Earth, more beautiful than the Sun. In *Asgard,* the realm of the gods, Gimli is the golden roof of a building where righteous men go when they die.

**Ginen:** In Haitian Vodou, the dead body, or *Corps cadavre,* is regarded as merely the vessel for the two components of the soul: the *gros bon ange* ("great good angel"—the life force) and the *ti bon ange* ("small good angel"—the personality). Upon death, the *gros bon ange* is sent to Ginen, the place where the Haitian ancestral spirits reside. The *ti bon ange* hovers around the body for nine days after death, and must be banished by trapping it in a jar and then burning it. If this is not done properly, the *ti bon ange* will haunt and harass the living.

**Gjallarbrú** ("Gjöll bridge"): A bridge spanning the river *Gjöll* ("noisy") in Niflheim, the Norse underworld, which must be crossed in order to reach *Hel*. A covered bridge thatched with gold, it figures in the story of *Baldr,* when *Hermód* is sent to retrieve the fallen god from the land of the dead. Arriving at the bridge Hermód was challenged by the guardian of the bridge, the giant maiden *Módgud* ("furious battler"), who demanded that he state his name and business before allowing him to pass.

**Gnipahelli:** The dark, foul-smelling opening of *Niflheim,* the Norse Underworld. It is guarded by the ferocious dog *Garm*.

**Guédé** (also spelled Gede or Ghede): In Haitian Vodou, the Guédé are the family of Loa that embody the powers of death and fertility. Guédé spirits include *Ghede Doubye, Ghede Linto, Ghede Loraj, Ghede Masaka, Guédé Nibo, Guédé Plumaj, Guédé Ti Malis,* and *Guédé Zaranye.* All are known for the drum rhythm and dance called the "banda."

**Guinee:** The spirit world in Haitian Vodou.

**Gwyn ap Nudd:** The king of the *Tylwyth Teg* or "fair folk" and ruler of *Annwfn,* the Welsh Otherworld. Described as a great warrior with a "blackened face," Gwyn leads the Wild Hunt, where he claims souls for *Annwfn*. His retinue of Fairies have been called the "Hosts of Hell" by Christians.

**Hades:** In Greek mythology, he is the elder brother of *Zeus* and *Poseidon,* and ruler of the Underworld, the dead, the wealth of mines, and all things buried. His part-time Queen is *Persephone.* In Rome he was called *Pluto,* and his Queen was *Proserpina.* Eventually his name became identified with the Underworld itself.

**Hallowe'en** (Oct. 31): (also **All Hallows' Eve** or **All Saints' Eve**), is Christianized version of the old Gaelic *Samhain*. Activities include trick-or-treating, costume parties, carving pumpkins into jack-o'-lanterns, bonfires, apple bobbing, divination games, playing pranks, visiting haunted attractions, telling scary stories and watching horror films.

**Hawaiki**: The original home of the Māori, before they travelled across the sea to *Aotearoa* (New Zealand). It also features as the Underworld in many Māori stories.

**Heaven** ("sky," "firmament"): A transcendent abode of gods, angels, saints, and/or venerated ancestors. It is believed that heavenly beings can descend to Earth or *incarnate,* and that Earthly beings can ascend to Heaven in the afterlife; or in exceptional cases, enter Heaven alive. In Christian religion, Heaven is the seven-tiered paradise of eternal bliss reserved for those who have been "saved" by Grace or through accepting *Jesus Christ* as their personal savior.

**Hekate:** Ancient Greek Titaness who sided with the Olympians in the *Titanomachia* ("Battle of the Titans"). Known to the Romans as *Trivia* ("three ways"), she stands at each fork in the road and holds up two torches to illuminate the choices before us. She also stands at the threshold between Life and Death, facilitating the passage between, as *psychopomp* and midwife. She is the collective spirit and patroness of all women who have died in childbirth.

**Hel/Helheim** ("concealment"): General home of the non-warrior ancestors in Norse religion, a realm of icy suffering ruled by the goddess *Hel*. Located in *Niflheim*, the ninth world, Hel has both good and bad regions. The Hall of *Baldur* is a cheerful place, with plenty of ale and mead. *Nastrond,* on the other hand, is a terrible prison for oath-breakers and other criminals. Hel lies beneath one of the three roots of the world tree *Yggdrasil*, on the other side of the treacherous Echoing Bridge over the river *Gjöll* ("Noisy"), where souls are challenged as they try to cross.

**Hel/Hella** ("concealer"): The Ruler of *Hel* in Norse religion, she is the daughter of the malevolent trickster *Loki* and the giantess *Angurboda*. She is a terrible icy cold keeper of the unworthy dead, half fleshy and half blue-black rotting corpse, with a gloomy, downcast aspect. Hel has a great hall called *Éljúðnir*, with huge walls and gates, where she dispenses lodging and items to those who died of disease or old age.

**Hell:** The nine-tiered fiery pit of eternal torment and punishment in Christian religion, ruled by the Devil *(Satan* or *Lucifer)*, and populated with demons who were originally rebel angels cast down from Heaven.

**Hermodr:** The dark ferryman who brings the dead to the *Niflheim,* the Norse underworld.

**Hine-nui-te-pō** ("great woman of night"): A goddess of night and death and the ruler of the Underworld in Māori mythology. She fled to the Underworld in shame when she discovered that *Tāne,* whom she had married, was also her father. The red color of sunset comes from her.

**Hubur** ("watercourse" or "netherworld"): The river of fertility in the Sumerian Underworld, identified with the Euphrates.

**Hypocephalus** (L. "under the head"): A solar disc Placed under the head in an Egyptian mummy's coffin, and inscribed with scenes from Spell 162 of the *Egyptian Book of the Dead;* meant to "bring a flame" and keep the head warm.

**Ib** ("heart"): An important part of the Egyptian soul was the *Ib,* or heart, believed to have been formed at conception from one drop of the mother's heart-blood. To ancient Egyptians, the heart was the seat of emotion, thought, will and intention—and the key to the afterlife, where it gave evidence for or against its possessor. During the *Weighing of the Heart* ceremony, the heart was examined by Anubis and the deities. If the heart weighed more than the feather of *Ma'at* (truth), it was immediately consumed by the monster *Ammut,* thus terminating the deceased's existence.

**Iblīs:** The Islamic Devil, Iblis is a *Jinn* or *Angel* who refused to bow to Adam. He has no power other than the ability to cast evil suggestions into the minds of humans and Jinn.

**Irkalla:** The Babylonian Underworld, ruled by the goddess *Ereshkigal* and later, her consort, the death god *Nergal.* Irkalla was originally another name for Ereshkigal, who ruled the Underworld alone until Nergal seduced her. Both the deity and the location were called Irkalla, much like how *Hades* is both the name of the Greek Underworld and the god who ruled it. Irkalla was a place for the bodies of the deceased to exist after death. One passed through seven gates on their journey to Irkala, leaving items of clothing and adornment with the guardian at each gate. Irkalla had no punishments or rewards, being merely a drearier version of life above, with Erishkigal as both warden and guardian of the dead rather than a sinister ruler like Satan or the death gods of other religions.

**Iriy/Irij/Vyriy:** A paradisal place in Slavic mythology where birds fly for the winter and souls go after death. Snakes have their own underground *iriy* where they retreat for the winter.

**Isles of the Blessed**: See *Fortunate Isles*.

**Iyatiku:** The Corn Goddess of the Keresan Pueblos. From *Shipap*, her underground realm, humanity first emerged, and from there infants are born and to there go the dead. To provide food for them, she planted bits of her heart in the four directions. Later the pieces of Iyatiku's heart grew into fields of corn.

**Izanami** ("She who invites"): Japanese Goddess of both Creation and Death, as well as the former wife of *Izanagi,* the creator god.

**Jabru:** Elamite god of the Underworld and father of all Elamite gods. Jabru's Akkadian counterpart was *Anu.*

**Jahannam:** One of the names for the Islamic concept of Hell. Other names for Hell (or the different gates of Hell) occurring in the Qur'an include: *Jaheem* ("Blazing Fire"), *Hatamah* ("That which Breaks to Pieces"), *Haawiyah* ("The Abyss"), *Ladthaa, Sa'eer* ("the blaze"), *Saqar, an-Nar.* According to the Qur'an, on the Last Day the world will be destroyed and all people (and *jinn*) will be raised from the dead to be judged by Allah as to whether they deserved to be sent to paradise (*Jannah*) or Hell.

**Ka** ("vital spark"): In ancient Egyptian myth, the Ka was the concept of vital essence, that which distinguishes a living from a dead person, with death occurring when the *ka* left the body. This resembles the concept of *spirit* in other religions. The Egyptians also believed that the *ka* was sustained through food and drink, offerings of which were presented to the dead, although it was the *kau* within the offerings that was consumed, not the physical aspect.

**Lemurs:** Latin term for *ghosts* in ancient Rome.

**Lethe** ("oblivion"): A spring and river in *Erebos,* the Greek Underworld, in which the souls of the dead drink to forget their Earthly existence.

**Libitina** (also **Libentina** or **Lubentina**): Roman goddess of funerals and burial. Her name was used as a figure of speech for death, and undertakers were known as *libitinarii*. Libitina was associated with Venus, and the name appears in as an epithet of Venus.

**Limbo:** An in-between place in the Roman Catholic afterlife reserved for babies who die unbaptized, as well as other worthy people throughout history who died without receiving salvation through Christ. There they must abide until the Final Judgment, when they will be admitted to Heaven.

**Loa:** The spirits of Haitian and Louisiana Vodou. They are also referred to as Mystères and the Invisibles, in which are intermediaries between *Bondye,* the Supreme Creator, who is distant from the world, and humanity. Unlike saints or angels however, they are not simply prayed to, they are served. They are each distinct beings with their own personal likes and dislikes, distinct sacred rhythms, songs, dances, ritual symbols, and special modes of service. But the loa are not deities in and of themselves; they are intermediaries for, and dependent on, a distant Bondye.

**Lua-o-Milu:** The land of the dead in Hawaiian myth, ruled by *Milu*. Dead souls enter Lua-o-Milu through a trail called *Mahiki*. The spirits of the dead can watch what the living do and turn them to stone by staring at them.

**Lucifer Rofocale:** First of the Fallen, leader of the rebel angels in the War in Heaven, ruler of the Christian Hell, administrator of justice, demon of the concealers. In modern mythos, Lucifer has closed down Hell and now wanders the world in mortal guise, still administering justice to the wicked.

**Ma'at:** Goddess of Truth and Justice in ancient Egyptian religion. In the *Weighing of the Heart,* the heart of the deceased is weighed against the ostrich feather of Ma'at.

**Mag Mell/Magh Meall** ("plain of joy"): A mythical realm in Irish mythology achievable through death and/or glory. Mag Mell was a pleasurable paradise, identified as either an island far to the west of Ireland or a kingdom beneath the sea. A place of eternal youth and beauty, it is by the Fomorian King *Tethra,* or more often *Manannan mac Lir.*

**Maalik:** A grim Angel in *Jahannam*, the Islamic Hell, who administrates the Hellfire, assisted by 19 mysterious guards known as *az-zabānīya.*

**Mahaf:** Ferryman of the dead in Egyptian mythology.

**Makeatutara:** The father of *Māui* and guardian of the Underworld in Māori mythology; his wife is *Taranga*. Makeatutara made mistakes as he recited the dedicatory incantations over Māui, who was thus doomed to die. As a result, humankind is mortal.

**Maman Brigitte:** A Vodou death *loa* and the wife of *Baron Samedi*. She drinks rum infused with hot peppers and is symbolized by a black rooster. Like Baron and the *Ghede*, she uses obscenities. She protects gravestones in cemeteries if they are properly marked with a cross.

**Mamitu:** The goat-headed Goddess of Destiny in Mesopotamian mythology, who decrees the fate of the new-borns. She was also worshipped as Goddess of the Oath, later a Goddess of Fate and a judge in the Underworld, where she lives with the *Anunnaku*. She is occasionally regarded as a consort of *Nergal*. In some passages, she is referred to as a demon of irrevocable curses.

**Manes:** In Hinduism, these are spirits of dead relatives who must be appeased in the funerary rite of *Shraddha*. The manes are gratified with *pinda* (boiled rice balls), which are thrown out the door after each meal.

**Man/Mani:** Etruscan class of spirits representing "the dead," but not the same as a *hinthial,* "ghost." From the Mani came the Latin *Manes*, which are both "the good" and the deified spirits of the dead.

**Manannán mac Lir:** Also known simply as Manannán or Manann, he is a sea deity in Irish mythology ('Mac Lir' means "son of the sea"). He is also seen as a *psychopomp* and is associated with the Otherworld and the veil between the worlds.

**Marzanna** (Polish), **Morė** (Lithuanian) or **Morena** (Czech, Slovak, Russian) or also *Mara, Maržena, Morana, Mora or Marmora:* A Baltic and Slavic goddess of death, winter and nightmares who is associated with seasonal rites based on the death and rebirth of Nature. Some medieval Christian sources compare her to the Greek goddess *Hecate,* associating her with sorcery, or to *Ceres,* the Roman Goddess of Agriculture.

**Medium:** In *Spiritism* and *Spiritualism* the medium is an intermediary between the world of the living and the world of Spirit. Mediums claim that they can relay messages from spirits, or that they can allow a spirit to control their body and speak through it directly or by using automatic writing or drawing. Investigations during Spritualism's heyday in the late 19th century revealed widespread fraud—with mediums employing the techniques of stage magicians—and the practice thus lost much credibility.

**Merau**: Polynesian Goddess of death and the Underworld.

**Mictlan:** The Aztec Underworld. Most people who died went to Mictlan, although other possibilities existed. Located far to the north, Mictlan had nine distinct levels. The journey from the first level to the ninth was difficult and took four years, but the dead were aided by the canine *psychopomp, Xolotl.* The dead had to pass many challenges, such as crossing a mountain range where the mountains crashed into each other, a field with wind that blew flesh-scraping knives, and a river of blood with fearsome jaguars. Mictlan was ruled by King *Mictlantecuhtli* and his Queen, *Mictecacihuatl.*

**Mider:** A benevolent god of the Gaelic Afterworld. His wife *Etain* was abducted by *Angus.* Mider is a just overlord whose realm is a place of tedium and sorrow rather than pain and torment.

**Miru:** A Polynesian goddess who lives in *Avaiki* (the Underworld) beneath Mangaia, in the Cook Islands. She intoxicates the souls of dead people with *kava* and then burns them eternally in her oven (also called Avaiki). The *Tapairu* are her daughters.

**Mnemosyne:** The personification of memory in Greek mythology, source of the word *mnemonic.* A *Titanide,* or Titaness, she was the daughter of *Uranus* and *Gaea,* and the mother of the nine *Muses* by *Zeus.* Mnemosyne presided over an eponymous pool or well in *Erebos,* counterpart to the river *Lethe* (oblivion). Dead souls drank from Lethe to forget their past lives when they reincarnated. Initiates of the Mysteries were encouraged to drink from the well of Mnemosyne rather than Lethe, so they would remember.

**Mori Karaeng:** Place of the dead among the Manggarai tribe of the Flores Islands in Indonesia. An afterlife "Bizzaroworld," everything there is the total opposite of what the dead loved or hated in life. Therefore the surviving relatives smash dishes, bowls, and cups so that the dead will have good ones to use in the afterlife.

**Mors** (also known as **Letum**) (L. "death"): The Roman personification of *Death* equivalent to the Greek *Thánatos.* The Latin term is feminine gender, but ancient Roman art does not depict Death as a woman.

**Mot** (West Semitic "death"): An ancient West Semitic god of the dead and of all the powers that opposed life and fertility. He was the favorite son of the supreme god El, and the implacable enemy of Baal, god of springs, sky, and fertility.

**Mystai:** Initiates of the Mysteries (of *Eleusis, Dionysos, Orpheus, Attis, Adonis, Mithra, Osiris, etc.*).

**Naraka/Niraya:** A term in Buddhist and Jain cosmology usually referred to in English as "hell," "hell realm," or "purgatory." The Narakas of Buddhism are closely related to *diyu*, the hell of Chinese mythology. A Naraka differs from the Christian hell in two respects: firstly, beings are not sent to Naraka as the result of a divine judgment and punishment; secondly, the length of a being's stay in a Naraka is not eternal, though it is usually very long—measured in billions of years. A soul is born into a Naraka as a direct result of his or her previous *karma* (actions of body, speech and mind), and resides there for a finite length of time until his karma has achieved its full result. After his karma is used up, he may be reborn in one of the higher worlds as the result of an earlier karma that had not yet ripened.

**Náströnd** ("corpse shore") A place in the Norse *Hel* inhabited by *Niðhöggr* (the dragon who gnaws at a root of the world tree) who chews on corpses. It is for those guilty of murder, adultery and oath-breaking (considered the worst possible crimes).

**Nav/Navi:** The immaterial world, the world of the dead, in Slavic mythology. Stars, which are the souls of the dead, as well as *Svarga* and *Irij*, are parts of Nav.

**Necromancy** (Gr. "divination of the dead"): A form of magick involving communication with the deceased—either by summoning their spirit as an apparition or raising them bodily—for the purpose of *divination,* or to discover hidden knowledge.

**Necromanteion** (Gr. "oracle of the dead"): An ancient Greek temple of *necromancy* devoted to *Hades* and *Persephone,* where devotees came to talk with their dead ancestors. Located in Epirus, near the city of Ephyra, it was believed to be the entrance to the Underworld. Discovered in 1958 and excavated by archaeologist Sotirios Dakaris, the site is at the meeting point of the *Acheron, Pyriphlegethon* and *Cocytus* rivers, which flow through and water the kingdom of Hades. In Homer's *Odyssey,* the Necromanteion was where Odysseus made his *nekyia.* Although other ancient temples such as that of Poseidon in Taenaron as well as those in Argolis, Cumae, and Herakleia in Pontos also housed oracles of the dead, the Necromanteion of Ephyra was the most important.

**Nekyia:** In ancient Greek cult-practice, a *nekyia* is a rite of *necromancy* by which ghosts were called up and questioned about the future. A *nekyia* is not necessarily the same thing as a *katabasis,* which is the actual physical journey to the Underworld undertaken by several heroes in Greek and Roman myth.

**Nephthys** ("Lady of the [Temple] Enclosure"): A member of the *Great Ennead* of Heliopolis in Egyptian mythology, a daughter of *Nut* and *Geb.* Nephthys was typically paired with her sister *Isis* in funerary rites because of their role as protectors of the mummy and the god *Osiris* and as the sister-wife of *Set.*

**Nergal:** Sumerian god of pestilence and destruction, he married *Allatu* to become Lord of the Underworld.

**Neter-khertet** ("divine place underground"): The Underworld in Egyptian mythology. See *Duat.*

**Neti:** A minor Underworld god in Mesopotamian mythology, the chief gatekeeper of the Netherworld, and the servant of the goddess *Ereshkigal.* Neti features prominently in the myth of *Inana's Descent into the Underworld* when he opens the 7 gates of the realm and admits the Goddess, removing one emblem of her power at the threshold of each gate.

**Nga:** God of death among the Nenets people of Siberia, as well as one of two demiurges, or supreme gods.

**Niflheim** ("mist home"): The ninth of the *Nine Worlds* of Norse mythology, described as a dreary, dark place of everlasting winter where a poisonous fountain spews rivers of ice. Souls of those who die by any means other than battle are sent to Niflheim. The entrance to Niflheim is *Gnipahelli,* a dark, foul-smelling opening that is guarded by the ferocious dog *Garm.*

**Niflhel** ("Misty Hel"): A location in Norse mythology which overlaps with the notions of *Niflheim* and *Hel*. The spirits of just men will live forever in *Gimlé*, whereas those of evil men will live forever in Niflhel. Properly, Niflhel is the lowest level of Hel where the evil dead suffer torment, whereas Niflheimr is the primordial realm of icy mist, yet some early manuscripts consistently confuse these two names.

**Nine Worlds:** The cosmology of Norse mythology has nine homeworlds, supported in the branches and roots of the cosmic world tree *Yggdrasill*. Each is home to a specific family of beings. Different sources assign different names, but in general, from top to bottom, these are:
   1. *Aesir* (new Sky Gods): *Ásgarð*
   2. *Vanir* (old Earth Gods): *Vanaheim*
   3. *Menn* (Humans): *Miðgarð*
   4. *Jötnar* (Giants): *Jötunheim*
   5. *Álfar* (Elves): *Álfheim*
   6. *Dvergar* (Dwarves): *Svartálfaheim*
   7. Primordial Fire: *Múspellsheim*
   8. Primordial Ice: *Niflheim*
   9. *Náir* (the Dead): *Helheim*

**Orcus:** An Etruscan god of the Underworld, punisher of broken oaths. As with *Hades,* the name of the god was also used for the Underworld itself. In the later tradition, he was conflated with the Roman *Dis Pater*. Orcus was chiefly worshipped in the countryside, where he survived long after the more prevalent urban gods ceased to be worshipped. He survived as a folk figure into the Middle Ages, and aspects of his worship were transmuted into the wild man festivals held in rural parts of Europe into modern times.

**Orpheus:** A legendary musician, poet, and prophet in ancient Greece, he could charm all living things and even stones with his music. His wife, *Eurydice,* was killed by a serpent on their wedding day, and Orpheus descended into the Underworld to bring her back. His music charmed *Cerberus,* as well as *Hades* and *Perseph-*

*one,* who allowed him to lead Eurydice back to the Earth. But he was told not to look back to see whether she was following him. Of course, as they were almost out, he did turn to look back, and she was immediately sucked away. Orpheus was the prophet of the *Orphic Mysteries,* and a collection of *Orphic Hymns* still survives.

**Orphic Mysteries:** Initiatory rites associated with the Greek poet *Orpheus,* who descended into *Erebos* and returned. Orphics also revered *Persephone* (who annually descended into Erebos for a season and then returned) and *Dionysus* or *Bacchus* (who also descended into Erebos and returned). Orpheus was said to have invented the Mysteries of Dionysus. Poetry containing distinctly Orphic beliefs has been traced back to the $5^{th}$ or $6^{th}$ century BCE.

**Osiris:** Egyptian god of the Underworld and Judge of the Dead. He was depicted as a green-skinned man with a pharaoh's beard, partially mummy-wrapped, wearing a distinctive crown with two large ostrich feathers at either side, and holding a shepherd's crook and harvesting flail.

**Pacha** (Quechua, "world"): An Incan concept for dividing the different spheres of the cosmos. There were three different levels of *pacha*: the *hanan pacha* or *hanaq pacha* ("world above"), *ukhu pacha* ("world below"), and *kay pacha* ("this world"). These realms were simultaneously spatial and temporal. The Earth Mother is *Pachamama.*

**Pana:** The Inuit god who cares for souls in the Underworld *(Adlivun)* until they are reincarnated.

**Pandemonium** ("place of all demons"): The capital city of *Hell* in Roman Catholic myth.

**Parentalia** (or ***dies parentales,*** Latin, "ancestral days") (Feb. 13-21) A 9-day festival held in ancient Rome in honor of family ancestors. Sacred offerings of flower-garlands, wheat, salt, wine-soaked bread and violets were made to the *Manes* (shades of the dead) at family tombs, outside Rome's sacred boundary. These rites were meant to strengthen the mutual obligations and protective ties between the living and the dead, and were a lawful duty of the *paterfamilias* (head of the family). Parentalia concluded Feb. 21 in the midnight rites of *Feralia*.

**Paradise** ("walled garden"): An afterworld of eternal joy and bliss as conceived in various religions.

**Patala/Patal**: According to Hindu cosmology, the universe is divided into three worlds: *Svarga* (Heaven: six upper regions), *Prithvi* (Earth) and *Patala* (the underworld and netherworld, which are located under the Earth). Patala is composed of seven regions or *lokas;* the seventh and lowest of them is also called Patala or *Naga-loka,* the region of the Demons and *Nagas* (snake-people).

**Peckols/Patollo:** A scary and ruthless god of the dead and the Underworld in Prussian mythology. He was portrayed as an old man with a white beard and white turban. He would haunt and taunt the living if they disobeyed their Pagan priests or buried the dead without proper sacrifices to the gods.

**Persephone** (Roman *Proserpina*): Flower maiden *(Koré),* daughter of Grain-Mother *Demeter* and *Zeus,* who is abducted by *Hades/ Pluto* in the fall, to reign as his Queen in Erebos until spring equinox, when she returns to bring new life to the Earth.

**Phlegethon** and **Pyriphlegethon** ("burning coals"): Two rivers in *Erebos,* the Greek Underworld. They surround the infernal regions, then unite and join the waters of the *Acheron.*

**Pokol:** The Hungarian Underworld.

**Pulotu:** The Underworld, the world of darkness (as opposed to the human world of light) in the mythology of Tona and Samoa in western Polynesia. Pulotu may be represented as the paradise from which the gods came and to which the souls of deceased chiefs go (commoners did not have souls). In some accounts, Pulotu is a jumping-off place of spirits on their way to the Underworld.

**Psychopomp:** (Gr. "guide of souls") One who escorts newly-deceased souls into the Afterlife. Examples are *Charon, Hermes,* and *Anubis.* In tribal cultures, the shaman serves as a psychopomp, who may also help at birth to introduce the newborn child's soul into the world. In Jungian psychology, the psychopomp is a mediator between the unconscious and conscious realms, symbolically personified in dreams as a wise man or woman, or sometimes as a helpful animal.

**Pure Land:** A concept in Chinese Buddhism involving rebirth in the Western Paradise, or "Pure Land" (*jingtu*), of Amitabha Buddha. Unlike the ordinary realm of the ancestors, which mirrors the world of the living, the Pure Land is desired for ways in which it differs from this world. It is inhabited not by relatives, but by wise and compassionate teachers of the Buddhist Dharma, and it is free of the impurities and sufferings of the mortal realm. For some it is not a place at all, only a symbol of the peace of *nirvana* (the enlightened state beyond cyclical existence).

**Purgatory:** An interim place in Roman Catholic religion where the newly-deceased are systematically tortured with fire until they have become sufficiently purified to enter *Heaven*.

**Rainbow Bridge:** In Norse mythology, **Bifröst** is a rainbow bridge reaching between *Midgard* (Middle Earth) and *Asgard,* the realm of the gods. The *Eddas* alternately refer to the bridge as *Ásbrú* ("Æsir's bridge"). The bridge ends in Asgard at Himinbjörg, the residence of the god Heimdallr, who guards it from the Jötnar (Giants). Scholars have proposed that the bridge may have originally represented the Milky Way and have noted parallels between Bifröst and *Gjallarbrú,* another bridge in Norse mythology.

**Rarohenga:** Underworld and realm of the spirits in Māori mythology. Inhabitants of Rarohenga are called *turehu*, governed by *Hine nui te Po.*

**Reincarnation:** Being reborn in a new body. (**Reintarnation:** Being reborn as a hillbilly.)

**Resurrection:** Physically coming back to life after being dead. As a religious concept, it is used in two distinct respects: a belief in the ongoing resurrection of individual souls, or a singular resurrection of the dead at the end of the world.

**River of Souls:** The Milky Way, which according to Sumerian belief was the path of souls across the heavens. The entryway into the heavens only opened at autumn equinox, in the rising gate of Sagittarius. Reincarnation back into the living world could only occur at the opposite end of the year, at spring equinox, in the rising gate of Gemini.

**Rohe:** The wife of the demi-god *Māui* in a tradition of the Moriori people of the Chatham Islands. Beautiful Rohe was a sister of the sun, and her face shone. A quarrel arose after Rohe remarked that Māui's face was ugly. Māui then decided that they should change faces. Afterwards Māui used magic to kill Rohe, but her spirit returned and destroyed him. Thus were black magic and death introduced into the world. After her death, Rohe ruled as the goddess of the *pō* (spirit world), where she gathered in the spirits of the dead. Evil influences were attributed to her.

**Samhain** ("summer's end"): The 7-day Festival of the Beloved Dead in Celtic Pagan tradition, starting Nov. 1. The central rite is the "dumb supper," eaten in silence, and shared with the beloved dead whose names are called in invitation and memory. Many ancient Samhain traditions are popularly retained in Hallowe'en customs, and most authentically in the Mexican festival of *Dia de Muertos* ("Day of the Dead").

**Santa Muerte** (Spanish "Holy Death") Female personification of death in Mexican folk religion, associated with healing, protection, and safe delivery to the afterlife. A continuation of the Aztec goddess of death *Mictlancihuatl* (Nahuatl for "Lady of the Dead").

**Satan/Shaitan** ("adversary"): The Lord of Lies who rules along with his twin *Moloch* over *Shahul,* the "triple hell" or grave hell of supernals in Christian myth. He was an *angel* who rebelled against

God, and was cast down to Earth, where he now has power in the material world, seducing humanity into sin and damnation.

**Séance:** A *necromantic* ritual conducted by a *medium,* in which the living attempt to communicate with the spirits of the dead.

**Sedna:** Goddess of the sea and marine animals in Inuit mytho, also known as the Mother of the Sea or Mistress of the Sea. The story of Sedna, which is a creation myth, describes how she came to rule over *Adlivun,* the Inuit Underworld. The varying legends each give different rationales for Sedna's death, but in each version, her father takes her to sea in his kayak and pushes her overboard, chopping off her fingers, which become seals and walruses. She sinks to the Underworld, becoming ruler of the monsters of the deep, worshiped by hunters who depend on her goodwill to supply food.

**Sekhet-Aaru** ("field of reeds"): The paradisal afterlife in ancient Egyptian religion—a lovely realm with fertile fields and lakes, much like Egypt itself. There the blessed dead dwell forever in the favor of Osiris, feasting with the gods on the food of immortality. Souls who qualified had to undergo a long and perilous journey before reaching Aaru. Once they arrived, they had to enter through a series of 15 or 21 gates guarded by evil demons armed with knives. Aaru was located in the east, where the Sun rises.

**Shabti/Ushebti:** Small wooden models of servants empowered with spells to care for the deceased in the Egyptian afterlife.

**Shamayim:** The term for Heaven in the *Tanakh* (the canon of the Hebrew Bible), located above the *firmament* (a solid transparent dome which covered the Earth and separated it from the "waters" above). The God of Israel (*Yahweh*) lived in a Heavenly palace. His dwelling on earth was Solomon's Temple in Jerusalem, which was a model of the cosmos and included a section which represented Heaven.

**She'ol** ("grave," "pit"): Hebrew term for the place of the dead, the common grave of humans, or Underworld of the Torah. It is a place of darkness to which all the dead go, both righteous and unrighteous, regardless of the moral choices made in life, a place of stillness and darkness cut off from life and from *Yahweh,* the Hebrew God.

**Sheut** ("shadow"): Ancient Egyptians felt that a shadow contains something of the person who cast it. The shadow also represented Death, or a servant of Anubis, and was depicted as a small human figure painted completely black. Some pharaohs had a shadow box in which part of their *Sheut* was stored.

**Shinjed:** Tibetan dread Lord of Death.

**Shiryō:** Japanese term for the soul of the dead, the antonym of *ikiryō* (soul of the living).

**Six Realms of Existence:** Within the larger realm of Desire, Buddhist cosmology typically identifies six domains or realms of existence: *gods, demi-gods, humans, animals, hungry ghosts* and *hells*. These realms can be described briefly as follows:

- **God realm:** the gods lead long and enjoyable lives full of pleasure and abundance, but they spend their time pursuing meaningless distractions and never think to practice the *dharma* (teachings of the Buddha). When death comes to them, they are totally unprepared, as they have completely exhausted their good *karma* (for which they were reborn in the god realm) and they suffer through being reborn in the lower realms.

- **Demi-god realm:** the demi-gods have almost as much pleasure and abundance as the gods, but they suffer from constant fighting and jealousy, and from being killed and wounded in their perpetual wars with each other and with the gods.

- **Human realm:** humans suffer from hunger, thirst, heat, cold, not getting what they want, and getting what they don't want. They also suffer from birth, old age, sickness and death. Yet the human realm is considered to be the most suitable for practicing the dharma, because humans are not completely distracted by pleasure (like the gods or demi-gods) or by pain and suffering (like the beings in the lower realms).

- **Animal realm:** wild animals suffer from being attacked and eaten by other animals; they generally lead lives of constant fear. Domestic animals suffer from being exploited by humans.

- **Hungry ghost realm:** hungry ghosts suffer from extreme hunger and thirst. They wander constantly in search of food and drink, only to be miserably frustrated any time they come close to actually getting what they want.

- **Hell realm:** hell beings endure unimaginable suffering for eons of time. There are 18 different types of hells, each inflicting a different kind of torment. In the hot hells, beings suffer from unbearable heat and other torments of various kinds. In the cold hells, beings suffer from unbearable cold and other torments.

**Soku-no-kumi:** The *yomi* (Underworld) in Japanese mythology ruled by the god *Amatsu-Mikaboshi*. The realm reflects the bitterness of the goddess *Izanami* after she died giving birth to the fire god *Kagutsuchi* and ended up in the Underworld where she remained, trapped behind a boulder that the horrified *Izanagi* placed there. Soku-no-Kumi residents are the *Shitidama,* souls of the sinful, who are violent beings more demonic in nature than human. Occasionally these spirits escape from Soku-no-Kumi and cause havoc on Earth. Due to his contempt for humankind, Amatsu-Mikaboshi does nothing to bring them back.

**Soul/Spirit:** The incorporeal and immortal essence of a living being, which survives death of the body to *reincarnate* or enter an *Afterlife*. Avicenna defined the soul as nothing other than "what a human indicates by saying 'I'." Although the terms "soul" and "spirit" are sometimes used interchangeably, "soul" can denote a more worldly and less-transcendent aspect of a person.

**Spirit guide**: A term used by Spiritualist Churches, mediums, and psychics to describe an entity that remains a disincarnate spirit in order to act as a guide or protector to a living human being. Spirit guides were often stereotyped ethnically, with Native Americans, Chinese, Tibetans or Egyptians being popular for their perceived ancient wisdom. Other common guides were saints or other enlightened individuals. In recent years, extraterrestrial guides have become popular. Some spirit guides live as energy, in the cosmic realm, or as light beings, which are very high-level entities. Some spirit guides have lived many former lifetimes, paid their *karmic* debts, and advanced beyond a need to reincarnate. The term can also refer to totems, *angels* or Nature spirits.

**Spiritism:** A branch of *Spiritualism* developed the 19th century by the French educator Allan Kardec and today found mostly in Continental Europe and Latin America, especially Brazil. Spiritism postulates that humans are essentially immortal spirits who temporarily inhabit physical bodies for several incarnations to attain moral and intellectual improvement. It also asserts that spirits, through mediumship, may have influence in the physical world.

**Spiritualism:** A belief that spirits of the dead have both the ability and desire to communicate with the living. The *spirit world* as seen by Spiritualists is an afterlife realm of hierarchical "spheres," through which spirits continue to evolve. More advanced than the living, spirits can provide useful knowledge of moral and ethical issues, as well as the nature of God—often referred to as "Infinite Intelligence." Many Spiritualists have *spirit guides* upon whom they rely for guidance. Spiritualism reached its peak in membership from the 1840s to the 1920s. By 1900, Spiritualism had more than 8,000,000 followers in the US and Europe, mostly drawn from the middle and upper classes, but its credibility was shaken by accusations of fraud perpetrated by *mediums.*

**Styx:** The most famous river of *Erebos,* the ancient Greek Underworld, this is a tributary of the *Acheron,* across which the newly-deceased are ferried by *Charon.* The Gods swear unbreakable oaths by the Styx.

**Sulis:** The Romano-Celtic Underworld goddess, concerned with knowledge and prophecy. She is the tutelary goddess of the thermal waters at Bath, England, and is linked with the Roman goddess, *Minerva.*

**Supay:** Incan and Aymara God of Death and ruler of *Ukhu Pacha*, the Incan Underworld, as well as a race of demons. Supay is associated with miners' rituals.

**Summerland:** The name given by Theosophists, Wiccans and some contemporary Pagans to their conceptualization of an Afterlife. All people, except spirits who remain behind lost and wandering, go to the Summerland, even the wicked. There, they can be reunited with their loved ones, look over those they left behind on Earth, and take time to recuperate from life.

**Svarga/Swarga** (aka **Swarga Loka**): Any of the 7 *loka* or planes located on and above *Mt. Meru* in Hindu myth, where the righteous dwell in a paradise before their next incarnation. During each *pralaya,* the great dissolution, the first 3 realms, *Bhu loka* (Earth), *Bhuvar loka,* and *Swarga loka,* are destroyed. Below the 7 upper realms lie 7 lower realms of *Patala,* the Underworld.

**Tartarus:** The deepest and darkest region of the Greek Underworld, where the rebel *Titans, Cyclopes* and *Centimani* were imprisoned by *Zeus* after the *Titanomachia* ("Battle of the Titans"). As far below *Erebos* as the Earth is below the Heavens, *Tartarus* is where souls are judged after death and those who had been particularly wicked are consigned to an eternity of ironically appropriate punishment. Like other primal entities (such as Earth, Night and Time), *Tartarus* was also considered to be the unbounded first-existing entity from which Light and the Cosmos were born.

**Ta'xet:** The Haida god of violent death, whose counterpart is *Tia,* the goddess of peaceful death.

**Te Uranga-o-te-rā**: In Māori mythology, the fifth lowest level of the Underworld, ruled by *Rohe,* the wife of *Māui.*

**Thanatos** ("to die;" "be dying"); The Greek personification of *Death.* He was a minor figure in Greek mythology, often referred to, but rarely appearing in person.

**Theosis** ("deification"): In Eastern Orthodox theology, *theosis* is a transformative process whose goal is likeness to or union with God. As a process of transformation, *theosis* is brought about by *katharsis* (purification of mind and body) and *theoria* ("illumination" with the "vision" of God),.*Theosis* is the primary purpose of human life, achievable only through a synergy (or cooperation) between human activity and God's uncreated energies (operations).

**The Three Realms:** There are three realms or worlds in Buddhist cosmology into which a being wandering in *saṃsāra* (the repetitive cycle of birth and death) may be reborn. These are the *desire realm,* the *form realm,* and the *formless realm.* In Indo-Tibetan *Mahāyāna* Buddhism there are six domains within the desire realm, while in *Theravada* Buddhism there are only five, because the domain of the *asuras* is not regarded as separate from that of the *devas*. Taoism also features the five domains.

**Tibetan Book of the Dead:** The *Bardo Thodol* ("liberation through hearing during the intermediate state") is a text from a larger body of teachings by Karma Lingpa (1326-1386). Known in the West as the *Tibetan Book of the Dead*, it is a guide through the experiences that the soul has after death, in the *bardo,* the interval between death and the next rebirth. The text also includes rituals to perform when death is closing in or has taken place.

**Tír na nÓg** ("Land of the Young") or **Tír na hÓige** ("Land of Youth"): A realm of everlasting youth, beauty, health, abundance and joy in the Irish Otherworld, inhabited by the *Tuath Dé,* the gods of Pagan Ireland. Various Irish mythical heroes visited Tír na nÓg after a voyage or an invitation from one of its residents. They reached it by entering ancient burial mounds or caves, or by going under water or across the sea.

**Tlālōcān** ("place of Tlaloc"): An Aztec paradise, ruled over by the rain deity *Tlaloc* and his consort *Chalchiuhtlicue,* who took in those who died through drowning or lightning, or as a consequence of diseases associated with rain. Among modern Nahua-speaking peoples of the Gulf Coast, Tlalocan survives as an all-encompassing concept embracing the Underworld and its denizens.

**Totenpäss** (plural *Totenpässe*) (German, "passport for the dead"): Inscribed tablets or metal leaves found in burials of initiates into Orphic, Dionysian and some ancient Egyptian and Semitic Mysteries. *Totenpässe* are placed on or near the body as a phylactery, or worn around the neck as an amulet. The inscription instructs the initiate on navigating the Afterlife, including directions for avoiding underworld hazards and responses to the Underworld judges.

**Transmigration of the Soul:** Passage of a soul upon death from one body directly into another.

**Tuonela/Manala:** Realm of the dead in Finnish and Estonian mythology. The fate of good and bad people is the same and the dead wander the Afterlife as shadowy ghosts. *Tuoni* and his wife *Tuonetar* rule Tuonela. At times living people visited Tuonela to gather information and spells. The trip there required trekking in a desert, and crossing of a river with the help of a ferryman (similar to *Charon* in Greek mythology). Shamans could visit Tuonela by falling into a trance and tricking the guards.

**Underworld/Netherworld:** Thought to be deep beneath the surface of the world in most mythologies, this is an afterlife or a realm of the dead where the souls of the departed go. *Chthonic* is the technical adjective for things of the Underworld.

**Urshanabi:** Ferryman of the *Hubur,* river of the Underworld in Mesopotamian myth. His Greek equivalent was *Charon.*

**Utukku:** Spirits or demons in Sumerian mythology that could be either benevolent or evil. The evil utukku were called *Edimmu*; the good utukku were called *shedu.*

**Valkyries** ("choosers of the slain"): A host of beautiful females in Norse mythology who choose among those who will die in battle and those who will live. The Valkyries bring their chosen heroes to *Valhalla,* Odin's great feast-hall of the slain (the others go to *Freyja's* afterlife realm *Fólkvangr*). Valkyries also appear as lovers of heroes, where they are often described as princesses.

**Valhalla** (from Old Norse *Valhöll* "hall of the slain"): The great feast-hall of *Odin* in Norse mythology, where warriors who have died in battle *(einherjar)* spend their days fighting over and over the glorious battles in which they had died, and feasting each night on wild boar and mead (honey wine).

**Vanaheimr** ("home of the Vanir"): One of the Nine Worlds of Norse mythology, and home of the *Vanir,* a group of old gods associated with fertility, wisdom and divination.

**Vanth/Vanthi:** Black-winged Etruscan goddess of the Underworld, often depicted in the company of *Charun*. She appeared at the moment of death, and guided the deceased to the Underworld. See *Azrael, Death, psychopomp*.

**Veles:** Major Slavic deity of Earth, Waters and the Underworld. Associated with dragons, cattle, magic, musicians, wealth and trickery, he is the opponent of the supreme thunder-god *Perun*, and the battle between the two of them constitutes one of the most important Slavic myths.

**Vichama:** God of Death in Incan myth, and the son of *Inti*, the Sun God. His mother was murdered by his half-brother *Pacha Kamaq*, the Creator God, and Vichama took revenge by turning the humans created by Pacha Kamaq into rocks and islands. Afterwards he hatched three eggs from which a new race of humans was born.

**Viduus** ("divider"): Roman god who separated the soul and the body after death. See *Grim Reaper*.

**Vingólf** ("friendly door"): The hall of the Norse goddesses where righteous men and those slain in battle go after death.

**Weighing of the Heart:** In the Egyptian afterlife, the *Ka* (spirit) of the dead person comes to *Amenti*, the Judgment Hall of the Dead, where *Anubis* places his heart on the scales of *Ma'at* (Truth,Justice). If the deceased's heart is lighter than Ma'at's feather, he may pass on to *Sekhet-Aaru* ("Field of Reeds"), the paradisal afterlife. But if the heart weighs more than the feather, it is immediately eaten by the monstrous *Ammut*.

**Whiro/Hiro:** Lord of Darkness and embodiment of all evil in Māori myth. He is the brother and enemy of *Tāne*. He inhabits the Underworld and is responsible for all ills. When people die, their bodies descend into the Underworld, where they are eaten by Whiro. Each time Whiro eats a body, he becomes stronger. He will eventually become sufficiently powerful to break free of the underworld, at which point he will come to the surface and devour everything and everyone on it. Cremation is recommended to prevent this, because Whiro cannot gain strength from ashes.

**World Tree:** Also called *axis mundi* ("world axis"), this is the celestial and geographic pole, represented as a vast metaphorical tree that connects the Heavens, the Earth, and the Underworld in a number of belief systems. Most famous is the Norse *Yggdrasil.*

**Xibalba** ("place of fear"): The Underworld in *K'iche'* Maya mythology, ruled by the Mayan death gods and their helpers. The entrance to Xibalba was traditionally held to be a cave in the vicinity of Cobán, Guatemala; the area is still associated with death. Cave systems in nearby Belize have also been referred to as the entrance to Xibalba. In some Maya areas, the Milky Way is viewed as the road to Xibalba.

**Xolotl:** Aztec god who aided the dead on their journey to *Mictlan,* the Underworld. God of fire and lighting, sickness and deformities, Xolotl was the dark personification of Venus, the evening star, and the twin of *Quetzalcoatl,* the pair being sons of the virgin *Coatlique.* Xolotl guarded the sun when it traveled through the Underworld at night. He also assisted Quetzalcoatl in bringing humankind and fire from the Underworld. His two animal forms are the *Xoloitzcuintli* dog breed and the *axolotl* salamander.

**Yama:** Hindu Lord of the Dead, who takes mortals into his realm until they are reincarnated. He holds a mirror (the soul's own memory) in which the deceased's deeds in life are reflected. Each person pronounces their own judgment, thus determining their next rebirth. In East Asian mythology, Yama is a wrathful god said to judge the dead and preside over the *Narakas* ("hells" or "purgatories") and the cycle of rebirth. The Buddhist Yama has developed different myths and different functions from the Hindu deity.

**Yan Luo:** Chinese God of Death and ruler of *Feng-Du,* the Chinese Underworld.

**Yomi** or **Yomi-no-kuni** ("yellow springs/ wells"): Japanese land of the dead (World of Darkness) in Shinto mythology. Yomi is neither a paradise of reward, nor is it a hell of punishment for past deeds; rather, all the deceased carry on a gloomy and shadowy existence in perpetuity regardless of their behavior in life.

**Yomotsu-shikome:** ("Ugly-Woman-of-the-Underworld"). In Japanese mythology, she was a hideous hag sent by the dead *Izanami* to pursue her husband *Izanagi,* for shaming her by breaking his promise to not see her in her decayed form in the Underworld.

# Appendix C.
# Elegies: Funerary Songs & Poems

It is customary at funerals of all cultures to sing (or play recordings of) hymns, songs, chants and poetry. Called *dirges, elegies, laments, burial hymns, threnodies,* or *requiems,* these are traditionally somber songs or lamentations for the dead, expressing mourning or grief. But in Pagan funerary ceremonies, as well as in New Orleans, China, India and elsewhere, they are more likely to be positive, upbeat, hopeful, life-affirming, and celebratory, commonly referencing themes of rebirth.

Here are some of the chants, invocations, ritual elements and elegies used in Pagan funeral ceremonies and memorial services:

## Funeral Homily
*Morning Glory Zell, 1948-2014*

Though words cannot express
What words cannot express…
…We feel in our hearts
The sorrow of your loss.

Surely death and loneliness
Are the cruelest gifts of lifelong
    love.

Yet we who choose such love must
Drink deeply from the bitter cup
Believing in the end that it will
    leave
Behind a taste of lingering
    sweetness.

May She be with you
In Her dark-winged form.
    Blessed Be.
\*\*\*

## Circle Casting and Invocation
*Marylyn Motherbear Scott
(for Morning Glory Zell in devotion to her life and her work)*

I cast the circle near and far
From thy beloved Earth to the
    distant star,
That star that holds thy light aloft,
Binding thy work in sacred troth,
So all may know and all may see
The blessings of thy work and thee

From those of us upon the rim,
Protecting thy path as you circle in,
To those who've passed this way
    before.
Who stand beyond, on the
    shadowed shore,
Arms outstretched, to enfold thee
    and kiss
As you enter a land hid in
    magickal mist.

Fivefold the kiss upon thy feet,
Remembrance of a bliss so sweet,
A kiss upon thy knees, womb,
    breasts,
To thy lips, sealed so, in the West,
We dance with thee, thy spirit hail,
May thy soul be content,
May thy wisdom prevail.
    And so it is.

\*\*\*

## Calling Elements and Ancestors (2017)
*Oberon Zell*

O ancient powers of sea and flames
Of winds and stones,
We call Thee forth;
Protect our Circle, guard our rites,
Our journey hence from Death to
    Birth.
Ancestors all, we call to you,
Across the misty veils of Time;
Our lineage deep continues on
From ancient past to future line…

\*\*\*

## Take Me Down
*Bird Brother/Barton Stone*

When the Morning Star arises
I can see Her spirit fly.
    Take me down, take me down.
When She spreads the dawning
    day
Across the crystal sky.
    Take me down, take me down.

*Ch:* Take me down in Your
    embrace,
    Where I see my truest face.
    Take me down into my soul,
    Take me down and make me
    whole.

In childlike trust and innocence
We face the Southern lands,
    Take me down, take me down.
Where my Lady rides a tiger,
Golden apples in Her hands.
    Take me down, take me down.

*Ch:*

When the setting sun descends
Behind the belly of the Earth,
    Take me down, take me down.
There we'll contemplate the
    Mysteries
Of death and rebirth.
    Take me down, take me down.

*Ch:*

Old Woman of the North
She rides Her broom across the sky
    Take me down, take me down.
With Her basket full of diamonds
And a twinkle in Her eye.
    Take me down, take me down.

\*\*\*

## The Wheel Turns
*Starhawk*

Where there is Fear there is Power;
Passion is the Healer
Desire cracks open the door,
When you're ready it'll take you
    through!
But nothing lasts forever,
Time is the Destroyer.
The Wheel turns, again and again;
Watch out or it'll take you
    through!
But nothing dies forever,
Nature is the Renewer.
The Wheel turns, again and again;
When you're ready it'll take you
    through!

\*\*\*

## Do Not Stand at My Grave and Weep (1942)

*Mary E. Frye, 1905-2004* [61]

Do not stand at my grave and weep
I am not there. I do not sleep.
I am a thousand winds that blow.
I am the diamond glints on snow.
I am the sunlight on ripened grain.
I am the gentle autumn rain.
When you wake in the morning hush,
I am the swift, uplifting rush
Of quiet birds in circling flight.
I am the soft starlight at night.
Do not stand by my grave and mourn.
I am not there, I am reborn!

\*\*\*

## A Tree Has Been Cut Down (June 2003)

*Ralph Metzner, 1936-2019*

The giant trees stand in a circle
Silently communing with the One
Who lies felled on the forest floor.
"One of us has been cut down".

The form but not the Being within the form.
Your freedom is our loss, beloved friend.
No longer do you stand with us on the Earth path,
Your precious, beautiful, human form destroyed

But You, Immortal Soul, dancing freely now,
Moving as lightning, or wind, or winged Spirit,
Communing with us in our earth-body sleep.

Farewell, dear friend.
As you depart for that unknown country,
We can remember
The Oneness of all Being. [62]

\*\*\*

## Well Song (round)

*Starhawk, Rose May Dance, Raven Moonshadow*

We will never, never lose our way
To the we-ell, of Her memory
And the power, of the living flame,
It will rise, it will rise again!
Like the grasses, through the dark,
Through the storm,
Towards the sunlight, we shall rise again!
We are searching, for the Waters of Life,
We are moving, we shall live again!

\*\*\*

---

[61] Frye made and circulated many copies privately. She never published or copyrighted the poem, and it is often published as "anonymous."

[62] In memory of Phyllis Jackson, colleague and friend, who was murdered in 2003 in San Francisco by her demented stepson. Dedicated to all who die a violent death.

## Born in the Fire, Never Dying (1980)
*Gwydion Pendderwen 1946–1982*

There is no life but the one
Handed down from sunrise
Whispered through moonset
Carried on the wind
Born in the fire, never dying.

I am desire risen up
From the land of shadows
Broken by dreaming
Born in the fire, never dying.

Sing of weeping that has washed
The rancor from my heart
Here in this new land
I am the Phoenix
Born in the fire, never dying.

Lost in silence let me sing
The message of my life
Hallowed by hunger
Let me carry rain
Born in the fire, never dying.

\*\*\*

## Metempsychosis (1980)
*Gwydion Pendderwen 1946–1982*

I doubt all, save the survival
Of some unquenchable fire within me;
I seek no immortality,
For it comes without search.
I live with the joy of my senses,
Knowing that this part will surely perish,
Leaving only that which came before.
To live here and now, without that certainty,
Without the acceptance of Death
As the unveiling of the one,
Is to forget, forever,
The secret name that is whispered at birth
Beyond the hidden gates.

\*\*\*

## Rainbow Bridge
Lyrics and Melody (1996)
© 2009 e.v. Gypsy
*From Spirit Nation, 2010*
*For Jack and All our Dear Ones*

They say there is no death
Just passing through a door
And we will meet again
The ones who've gone before
They say there is a way
To let our souls take flight
And we'll be guided through
To the light

Be not afraid
We mortals seldom know
What lies ahead
What's waiting for us when we go
Through the veils
Beyond the sky
Beyond our dreams
As we sail
To the Isle Across the sea

Memories may survive and stay
  with those we love
And we will watch and guide from
  above
Our families and our friends may
  have to stay behind
But they will journey through in
  their time

We're not alone
Every one of us must go
Returning home
We enter through the Gates of Dream

The Otherworld we journey to
when it's our time
The Mother waits and we'll be
reborn again
And we'll meet and know and love
again
In Avalon (x4)

\*\*\*

## The Bridge

*(4/17/14) Susa Morgan Black
(contemplating Morning Glory's
death)*

Dying, our world grows cold, dark
and empty
And we fear the endless void
Where we will disappear forever
Forgotten and unknown.

And yet, by these desolate signs
we know that we are close
To the boundary between
Life and Death.

We tread upon that final bridge.
The Bridge of Mortality, or
The Bridge of Immortality?

At the mortal end,
The boundary is in dark shadow,
As we face our final fears on that
bridge
Over the bottomless chasm of
obscurity.

Here we lay aside our concerns,
our memories,
Our dreams, our plans, our
relationships,
Our purpose, our journey in this
world.

And yet, we dare to take the step
On the bridge, and cross over

With each step we take, we grow
lighter
Until we shed our body's senses
And mind's emotions
And realize that the darkness is an
Illusion of mortality, a delusion of
fear.

The bridge becomes the Rainbow
Bridge
Taking us to the Other Realm.
A realm of spirit, warmth and
color, the
Opposite of how we see Death.

The illusion of Death shatters
Into sparkling shards of Sacred
Truth.
The Delusion of Darkness becomes
Eternal Light.

On the railings of the bridge are
carved
these immortal words from C. S.
Lewis:
"We do not have souls.
We *are* souls. We have bodies."

And we have crossed the bridge
Across that immortal bridge,
All we have loved welcomes us.
All we have hated forgives us.

As we shed our old personality
And looking into a celestial mirror
We embrace our true selves.
And we are once again, The Fool.

\*\*\*

## I'll Be Reborn (1982)

*Gwydion Pendderwen 1946–1982*

When I grow old, my time is near
And all my friends have gathered
'round,

O don't you weep, and don't you mourn,
'Cause you can't keep a good man down!

And in the Spring, yeah, I'll be back
Like the grass in yonder field.
I'll be reborn into this wo-o-orld
When the Lady's will is revealed.

Now when my body is in the ground
Well, there ain't nothing can keep me down;
I'll come with the blossoms and the growing grain
And then you'll know I'm back again.

Now I've had freedom, and joy and tears;
I'm proud I've learned each lesson well,
So when I come back in the Springtime
I won't repeat this lifetime's hell.

When I come back, I may be a baby
Or a bird high in a tree,
But you will know me if you still love me
'Cause I'll be born both wild and free!

Well, life's a burden, but death's a lie
And there ain't no reward up in the sky;
Just let me cast off this robe of mortal pain
And pick up where I left off again.

Now I ain't perfect, my soul ain't clean:
I done some things I ain't put right.
But all that karma will be forgotten
In a blaze of eternal light!

Now put my body beneath the ground
Don't plant no headstone on my grave;
Just plant an acorn and pass the whisky
And then you've know that I've been saved.

Now seal the Circle, and dance and sing,
And let my spirit pass through the ring;
But don't you worry, and don't you weep and mourn
'Cause I've been promised, I'll be reborn!
I'll be reborn, I'll be reborn…

\*\*\*

## Return, Return
*Morning Glory Zell, 1948-2014*

Return, return, return to the womb of the Mother
Return, return, return to the womb of rebirth.
Return, return, return to the love of each other
Return, return, return to the love of the Earth.

## Weaver, Weaver

*New words by Starhawk
(Traditional Irish lament
"Mo Ghile Mear")* [63]

Weaver, Weaver weave our thread,
Whole and strong into your web.
Healer, Healer, heal our pain,
In love may we return again .

We are dark and we are bright;
We are formed from earth and
    light.
From joy and pain our lives are
    spun,
But all too soon the spinning's
    done.

Weaver, Weaver weave her thread,
Whole and strong into your web.
Healer, Healer, heal her pain,
In love may she return again.

No one knows why we are born;
A web is made, a web is torn.
Like wandering seabirds we alight,
To rest one moment, then take
    flight.

Weaver, Weaver weave his thread,
Whole and strong into your web.
Healer, Healer, heal his pain,
In love may he return again.

So may we find the hidden way,
Beyond the gates of night and day,
To that sweet land where apples
    grow,
And endless healing waters flow.

Weaver, Weaver weave their
    thread,
Whole and strong into your web.
Healer, Healer, heal their pain,
In love may they return again.

And at that spring may we drink
    deep,
And wake to dream, and die to
    sleep,
And dreaming weave another
    form,
A shining thread of life reborn.

Weaver, Weaver weave our thread,
Whole and strong into your web.
Healer, Healer, heal our pain,
In love may we return again.

\*\*\*

## Circle Opening

*Gwydion Pendderwen, 1946-1982*

All from Air into Air,
Let the misty curtains part.
All is ended, all is done.
What has been, now must be gone.
What is done by Ancient Art,
Must Merry Meet and Merry Part,
    And Merry Meet again!

---

[63] *Mo Ghile Mear* ("My Gallant Darling") is an 18th century Irish song, written in Gaelic by Seán Clárach MacDomhnaill. It is a lament by the Goddess Éire for Bonnie Prince Charlie, who was then in exile. The poet personifies the country of Éire/Ireland as a woman who once was a fair maiden but is now a widow. Her husband, the "Gallant Boy," is not dead but far away. Consequently, the land is failing and Nature herself is in decline.

## May the Circle be Open
*Starhawk/Spiral Dance*

May the Circle be open,
But unbroken;
May the peace (love; joy) of the Goddess
Be ever in your heart!
Merry meet, and merry part,
And merry meet again!

From Earth and from Water
From Fire and from Wind
In the Circle of Life,
The dance never ends,
So merry meet, and merry part,
And merry meet again!

\*\*\*

## Recorded Elegies

Here are some beautiful musical elegies by various poets and recording artists. Most of these may be found on YouTube and played for funerals and memorial services:

*And When I Die* (1966) (Laura Nyro, Blood, Sweat and Tears)
*Angel of Bells* (JoEllen Lapidus)
*Anthem* (Leonard Cohen)
*Breaths* (1988) (Sweet Honey in the Rock)
*Closer to the Light* (Bruce Cockburn)
A *Daisy a Day* (Jud Strunk)
*Dance in the Graveyards* (Delta Rae)
*Dance Me to the End of Love* (Leonard Cohen)
*(Don't Fear) The Reaper* (Blue Oyster Cult)
*Eternal Child* (Lady Isadora)
*Hallelujah* (Leonard Cohen)
*Into the West* (Fran Walsh, Howard Shore & Annie Lennox)
*May It Be (*Enya)
*My Name Is Death* (The Incredible String Band)
*The Tree and Me* (Oscar Brown, Jr., 1926-2005)
*The Rainbow Bridge* (Gypsy)
*Return Again* (Rabbi Schlomo Carlebach, 1925-1994)
*Returning* (Jennifer Berezan) w/*Chant to Yemaya*
*Ritual of my Death* (Frank Cordeiro)
*She Carries Me* (Jennifer Berezan & friends)
*To Those I Love* (Isla Paschal Richardson)
*I'll be Reborn* (Gwydion Pendderwen, 1946-1982)
*We Do Not Die* (Velvet Hammer)

## Appendix D.
# In Memoriam:
## What is Remembered, Lives...
## Departed Pagan Pioneers, Founders and Elders

Since records began Samhain has been a night when the veil between the unseen world and ours is at its thinnest, a night when the spirits of our departed are free to roam the realms. As such, Samhain has always been considered the best time to honour our ancestors and other departed souls. Oberon Zell, George Knowles, Angie Buchanan, and others in the Pagan community have compiled this list of departed "Pagan Founders, Pioneers and Elders" who have died over the past century. It is currently being maintained by CAW's Rebecca Crystal. These are the people whose dedication and inspiration has helped shape the foundations of our religion.

### Died 1900-1939:
**Charles Godfrey Leland** (*Aradia*, 1899) (8/15/1824-3/20/1903)
**"Old George" Pickingill** (Cunning Man) (5/26/1816-1909)
**S.L. MacGregor-Mathers** (co-founder Golden Dawn) (1/8/1854-11/20/1918)
**William Wynn Westcott** (co-founder Golden Dawn, 1887) (12/17/1848-7/30/1925)
**Kenneth Graham** (*The Pagan Papers*; *Wind in the Willows*) (3/8/1859-7/6/1932)
**Rudyard Kipling** (*The Jungle Book*; *Puck of Pook's Hill*) (12/30/1865-1/18/1936)
**William Butler Yeats** (Golden Dawn; poet) (6/13/1865-1/28/1939)

### Died in 1940s:
**Sir James George Frazer** (*The Golden Bough*, 1890-1936) (1/1/1854-5/7/1941)
**Arthur Edward Waite** (*Rider-Waite Tarot*) (10/2/1857-5/19/1942)
**Dion Fortune (Violet Mary Firth Evans)** (Golden Dawn) (12/6/1890-1/8/1946)
**Ernest Thompson Seton** (Founder, Order of Woodcraft Chivalry; Boy Scouts) (8/14/1860-10/23/1946)
**Aleister Crowley** ("The Great Beast") (Magician; OTO) (10/12/1875-12/1/1947)

### Died in 1950s:
**Pamela Coleman-Smith (Pixie)** (Artist of the Waite Tarot Deck) 2/16/1878-9/18/1951)

### Died in 1960s:
**Eric Neumann** (*The Great Mother,* 1955) (1/23/1905-11/5/1960)
**Margaret Alice Murray** (*The Witch Cult in Western Europe,* 1921; *God of the Witches*) (7/13/1863-11/13/1963)
**Gerald Brousseau Gardner** (founder, Gardnerian Wicca) (6/13/1884-2/12/1964)
**Robert Cochrane/Roy Bowers** (Clan of Tubal Cain, 1734 Tradition) (1/26/1931-7/3/1966)
**Norman Lindsay** (Australian Pagan artist & author) (2/22/1879-11/21/1969)
**Gleb Evgenievich Botkin** (Church of Aphrodite, founded 1938) (7/29/1900-12/27/1969)

### Died in 1970s:
**Arnold Crowther** (10/7/1909-5/1/1974)
**Edith Woodford-Grimes (Dafo)** (Priestess of Gerald Gardner's initiating coven) (12/18/1887-10/28/1975)

### Died in 1980s:
**Jack Bracelin** (member of Bricket Wood coven, ran Five Acres naturist club, co-author of biography *Gerald Gardner Witch*) (6/2/1926-7/28/1981)
**Sybil Leek** (*Diary of a Witch*) (2/22/1917-10/26/1982)
**Gwydion Pendderwen** (the Faerie Shaman; CAW; Greenfield Ranch pioneer) (5/21/1946-11/9/1982)
**Francis Israel Regardie** (occultist, author, and Aleister Crowley's personal secretary) (11/17/1907-3/10/1985)
**Theodore Sturgeon** (Pagan sci-fi author, *More Than Human, Venus Plus X*) (2/26/1918-5/8/1985)
**Grady Louis McMurtry** (OTO, San Francisco) (10/18/1918-7/12/1985)
**Robert Graves** (*The White Goddess,* 1948) 7/24/1895-12/7/1985)
**Lady Gwen Thomson** (NECTW) (9/16/1928-5/22/1986)
**Joseph John Campbell** (*The Power of Myth*) (3/26/1904-10/30/1987)
**Alex Sanders (Orrell Alexander Carter)** (King of the Alexandrian Witches) (6/6/1926-4/30/1988)
**Edmund "Eddie" Buczynski (Lord Hermes)** (Minoan Brotherhood, NYC) (1/28/1947-3/16/1989)

### Died in 1990s:
**Manly Palmer Hall** (*Secret Teachings of All Ages*) (3/18/1901-8/29/1990)
**Herman Slater (Govannon)** (The Magickal Childe, NYC) (2/1/1938-7/9/1992)
**Scott Cunningham** (Solitary Wicca; herbalist) (6/27/1956-3/28/1993)

**Marija Gimbutas** (Goddess archaeologist; *Goddesses and Gods of old Europe*) (1/23/1921-2/2/1994)

**Lawrence Durdin-Robertson** (co-founder of Fellowship of Isis, Ireland) (5/6/1920-8/4/1994)

**Margaret St Clair** (Witch and author of *Sign of the Labrys*) (2/17/1911-11/22/1995)

**W. Holman Keith** (Church of Aphrodite; Neo-Dianic Faith) (6/11/1900-1996)

**Idries Shah** (author) (6/16/1924-11/23/1996)

**Vivian Godfrey (Melita Denning)** (Grand Master of the Order of Aurum Solis for 20 years) (6/16/1905-3/23/1997)

**Kerry Wendell Thornley (Omar Khayyam Ravenhurst)** (Discordian co-founder. *Principia Discordia*) (4/17/1938-11/28/1998)

**Doreen Edith Dominy Valiente (Ameth)** (Gardnerian Priestess, poet, author *ABC of Witchcraft*, 1973) (1/4/1922-9/1/1999)

**Marion Zimmer Bradley** (*The Mists of Avalon; Darkover*) (6/3/1930-9/25/1999)

## Died in 2000s:

**Stewart Farrar** (Alexandrian Wicca, Ireland) (author of several books on The Craft) (6/28/1916-2/7/2000)

**Leo Louis Martello** (Sicilian Strega, NYC. Founder of Witches Anti-Defamation League) (9/26/1030-6/29/2000)

**Gregory Hill (Malaclypse the Younger)** (Discordian co-founder, *Principia Discordia*) (5/21/1941-7/20/2000)

**Victor Henry Anderson** (Founder of Feri Trad) (5/21/1917-9/20/2001)

**Pauline Campanelli** (1/251943-11/29/2001)

**Baba Raul Canizares** (Oba, Santerían priest, artist, musician, professor of religion; founded Orisha Consciousness Movement) (9/24/1955-12/28/2002)

**Nelson White** (*The White Light; Knights Templar*) (10/29/1938-8/23/2003)

**Ellen Cannon Reed** (Priestess of Isian Tradition of Witchcraft; Author of *The Witches' Qabalah*) (3/21/1943-10/7/2003)

**Donald D. Harrison** (Church of Eternal Source) (5/31/1931-1/7/2004)

**Donna Cole Schultz** (Pagan Way, Chicago, IL) (5/15/1937-3/31/2004)

**Lady Circe** (Alliance of the Old Religion) (9/8/1921-5/29/2004)

**Alison Harlow** (co-founder Nemeton, Covenant of the Goddess) (8/29/1934-6/13/2004)

**Joseph "Bearwalker" Wilson** (brought 1734 Tradition to U.S.) (12/11/1942-8/4/2004)

**Elizabeth Pepper Da Costa** (*The Witch's Almanac*) (12/7/1923-7/14/2005)

**Monica Sjöö** (Swedish artist, Dianic Witch, author, *The Great Cosmic Mother*) (12/31/1938-8/8/2005)

**Rosemary Kooiman** (Pioneered effort to get the VA to allow the pentagram on tombstones in Arlington Cemetery.2002) (1929-3/5/2006)
**Robert Anton Wilson** (*Illuminatus!* trilogy & other books*)* (1/18/1932-1/11/2007)
**Frederick MacLaren Adams** (Founder of Feraferia) (2/4/1928-8/9/2008)
**John Lyon Burnside III** (Founder of Radical Faeries) (11/2/1916 to 9/14/2008)
**Marion Weinstein** (author *Positive Magic* and *Earth Magic*) (5/19/1939-7/1/2009)

## Died in 2010:

**Jean Dubois** (noted French alchemist, esotericist, and nuclear physicist. Founder of "Les Philosopes de le Nature") (1919-4/6/2010)
**Harold Moss** (Church of Eternal Source) (1/30/1937-7/15/2010)
**Phillip Emmons Isaac Bonewits** (Druid; ADF, AADL) (10/1/1949-8/12/2010)
**Richard Lance Christie** (co-founder: Association for the Tree of Life, Church of All Worlds, Earth First!) (4/7/1944-10/28/2010)

## Died in 2011:

**Ardath Elizabeth "Beth" Saunders Stanford (Bone Blossom)** (co-founder of Reclaiming Tradition) (12/21/1948-2/10/2011)
**Kenneth Grant** (Head of Typhonian Order, Isis Lodge in 1950's; spiritual heir to Aleister Crowley) (5/23/1924-1/15/2011)
**Merlin Stone** (author, *When God was a Woman*) (9/27/1931-2/23/2011)
**Lady Amythyst Avalon (Bobbie Osley)** (Avalon Isle, Highlands of Tennessee Samhain Gathering) (2/2/1932-7/2/2011)

## Died in 2012:

**Richard Joel Ravish** (Magister Azaradel, Temple of 9 Wells-ATC, Founder White Light Pentacles/Nu Aeon, Salem, MA) (12/26/1952-9/15/2012)
**Patricia Monaghan** (*Book of Goddesses & Heroines*) (2/15/1946-11/11/2012)

## Died in 2013:

**Stuart Wilde** (Metaphysician; founder of Taos metaphysical tradition; author of over 20 books) (9/24/1946-5/1/2013)
**Nevill Drury** (Australian author of books on Shamanism) (10/1/1947-10/15/2013)
**Deborah Bourbon** (Pathways New Age Books Music & Gifts, St Louis; OZ's first Craft teacher) (8/26/1949-10/20/2013)
**Lady Olivia Robertson** (Co-Founder Fellowship of Isis) (4/13/1917-11/14/2013)

## Died in 2014:

**Jonas Jaunius Trinkūnas (Krivis)** (founder of Lithuania's Pagan revival Romuva; ethnologist and folklorist; Vilnius, Lithuania) (2/28/1939-1/20/2014)

**Stanley Modryzk** (Founder of Pan Pagan Festival, Chicago, & Witches International Craft Association [WICA]) (8/15/1945-1/28/2014)

**Donald Michael Kraig** (Grey Council; author, *Modern Magick* & *Modern Sex Magick*) (8/17/1951-3/17/2014)

**Judy Harrow (Lady Cleindori)** (Gardnerian Elder; Proteus Coven; Cherry Hill Seminary) (4/3/1945-3/20/2014)

**Morning Glory Zell** (CAW Elder Priestess, poet, singer, writer, Goddess historian, lifemate of Oberon) (5/27/1948-5/13/2014)

**Loreon Vigne** (Isis Oasis, Geyserville, CA; Fellowship of Isis) (6/8/1932-7/15/2014)

**Margot Adler** (NPR New York; author *Drawing Down the Moon*) (4/16/1946-7/28/2014)

**Jeff Rosenbaum** (CEO Association for Consciousness Exploration; Starwood) (8/29/1955-8/31/2014)

**Pete "Pathfinder" Davis** (founder Aquarian Tabernacle Church) (3/22/1937-10/31/2014)

### Died in 2015:

**Sir Terence David John "Terry" Pratchett** (*Discworld* novels) (4/28/1948-3/12/2015)

**Deborah Ann Light** (Wiccan Elder, Interfaith worker, philanthropist; Earthspirit, Circle, COG, & CUUPS) (6/5/1935-7/21/2015)

**Michael Howard** (England; publisher of *The Cauldron* since 1976) (1948-9/24/2015)

**Carl Llewellyn Weschcke** (president/owner of Llewellyn Publications in Minneapolis since 1961) (9/10/1930-11/7/2015)

### Died in 2016:

**Charlie Murphy** (songwriter and musician; co-founder Partners for Youth Empowerment) (1943-8/6/2016)

**Gavin Frost** (Founded Church and School of Wicca with wife Yvonne in 1968) (11/20/1930-9/11/2016)

**Sara Cunningham Carter** (co-founding VP Church of the Eternal Source (1967); founder First Temple of Tiphareth (1957-1980), in Pasadena, CA) (10/6/1935-12/18/2016)

### Died in 2017:

**Dana Eilers** (Lawyer, Witch, Pagan civil rights advocate; member of AREN (Alternative Religion Educational Network), Lady Liberty League, Circle Sanctuary)

**Raymond Buckland ("Robat")** (Initiated under Gerald Gardner in 1963, brought British Witchcraft to America. Long Island Museum of Witchcraft & Magic, 1968. Founder Seax-Wicca Trad.) (8/31/1934-9/28/2017)

### Died in 2018:

**Morwen Two Feathers** (Sacred Drummer and Elder of Earthspirit Community, Concord, MA; wife of Jimi Two Feathers and co-founder of Earth Drum Council) (8/1/1956-7/17/2018)

**Abby Willowroot** (Willowroot Wands; artist) (9/23/1945-8/3/2018)

**Greg Stafford** (founder of Chaosium Games in 1975; founder of *Shaman's Drum* magazine) (2/9/1948-10/11/2018)

## Died in 2019:

**Deanna "D.J." Conway** (author of many books on magic, Wicca, Druidry, Shamanism, metaphysics and occult. Also designed Tarot cards.) (1939-2/1/2019)

**Raven Grimassi** (Strega, author of 20+ books on Stregheria, Witchcraft, Neo-Paganism. Co-director Ash, Birch and Willow trad.) (1/12/1951-3/10/2019)

**David Palladini** (author/artist of the *Aquarian Tarot* and the *New Palladini Tarot*. He also illustrated several children's books as well as other projects.) (4/1/1946-3/13/2019)

**Ralph Metzner** (Psychologist, participated in psychedelic research at Harvard University in early 1960s with Tim Leary and Richard Alpert. Professor emeritus of psychology at CIIS.) (5/18/1936-3/14/2019)

**Edain McCoy (Carol Taylor)** (Ghostbuster and author of more than 20 books, Edain was active in the Pagan community since her initiation in 1983.) (8/11/1957-3/21/2019)

**Sue Curewitz Arthen** (EarthSpirit Community Elder, Pagan Teacher, International Interfaith Networker, Passage Rites Officiant) (10/1/1951-7/26/2019)

## Died in 2020:

**Phyllis Serene Rawley** (The Oracle of Vilcabamba, Ecuador.) (12/17/1959-4/24/2020)

**Frederick Lamond (Robert)** Initiate of Gerald Gardner, from 1957; member of CAW and Fellowship of Isis; attended the 1993, 1999, and 2004 Parliaments of World Religions; author.) (7/5/1931-5/24/2020)

**Zanoni Silverknife/Jilaine Callison** (founding Priestess of the Georgian Tradition) (6/13/1946-6/4/2020)

**Cairril "Adair" Lee Mills** (Founder of Our Freedom Coalition. Co-founder of Pagan Educational Network (PEN)—the dictionary project.) (12/3/967-7/8/2020)

**Liz Fisher** (Author UU religious curriculum "Rise Up and Call Her Name") (10/15/1957-9/25/2020)

## Appendix F.
# Movies and TV series depicting the Afterlife

Graphic visions of Heaven and Hell dominated Christian art throughout the Middle Ages—primarily serving as warnings against heresy. But depictions of the Afterlife and the realms of the Gods were also major themes in paintings and sculpture of ancient Egypt, Greece, India, and elsewhere. When cinematography was invented in the 1890s, the early experimental films of inventive French illusionist Marie-Georges-Jean Méliès (1861-1938) included fantastic visions of Hell, replete with dancing devils. Since then, a number of films and a few TV series and documentaries have portrayed visions of the Afterlife—usually focusing on ghosts and reincarnation, however, and rarely attempting to depict the landscape of the nether regions.

**90 Minutes in Heaven.*** (2015) Based on a true account and *The New York Times* best-selling book. During the 90 minutes he is declared dead after a traffic accident, Don Piper experiences love, joy and life like he's never known. But when he finally wakes in the hospital, Heaven's bliss is replaced by excruciating pain and emotional turmoil.

**Afterlife.**\*\*\* (1978) An animated short by Ishu Patel that takes an impressionistic look at life after death, based on recent studies, case histories and myths. A film without words, *Afterlife* received numerous awards including a Golden Sheaf Award, a Genie Award for Best Animated Film and the award for Best Short Film from the Montreal World Film Festival.

**Afterlife Experiments.**\*\*\* (2011) By the Dreamscape studio, based on the book by Gary E. Schwartz. This award-winning documentary provides the most spectacular scientific evidence for life after death ever presented in any documentary.

**A Guy Named Joe.** (1943) Pete Sandidge (Spencer Tracy) is a reckless bomber pilot during World War II. Killed in an attack by an enemy fighter, Pete gets sent back to Earth to mentor dilettante Ted Randall (Van Johnson). The film was remade by Steven Spielberg in 1989 as *Always*, updating it to 1989.

**All Dogs Go to Heaven.** (animated musical comedy, 1989) Charlie B. Barkin (Burt Reynolds), a German Shepherd who is murdered by his friend, Carface (Vic Tayback), forsakes his place in Heaven to return to Earth where he learns an important lesson about honesty, loyalty and love.

**Always.** (1989) Romantic drama directed by Steven Spielberg, and starring Richard Dreyfuss, Holly Hunter, John Goodman, and featuring Audrey Hepburn in her final film appearance. *Always* is a remake of the 1943 romantic drama *A Guy Named Joe*. The film follows the same basic plot: the spirit of a recently dead pilot mentors a newer pilot, while watching him fall in love with his surviving girlfriend.

**Angel on My Shoulder.** (1946) American fantasy film about a deal between the Devil and a dead man. After his release from prison, gangster Eddie Kagle (Paul Muni) is killed by his partner in crime. Kagle ends up in Hell, where "Nick" (Claude Rains) offers him a chance to escape Hell and avenge his own death in exchange for help in destroying the reputation of an honest judge, Frederick Parker.

**Beetlejuice.**\*\*\* (1988) One of Tim Burton's first hits, *Beetlejuice* provided a comedic showpiece for the manic talents of Michael Keaton as the title character. Recently-deceased couple Barbara and Adam (Geena Davis and Alec Baldwin) find that the afterlife is a bureaucratic nightmare.

**Bill & Ted's Bogus Journey.**\*\*\* (1991) In this hilarious sequel to *Bill & Ted's Excellent Adventure,* Keanu Reeves and Alex Winter play two dimwitted musicians who are killed. On the other side they are met by Death (William Sadler) who challenges them to a game for their souls. They cleverly defeat Death, who thus becomes their unwilling servant, escorting the duo to Heaven, and a triumphal return to the mortal world.

**The Book of Life.**\*\*\* (animated musical, 2014) Manolo, a young man who is torn between fulfilling the expectations of his family and following his heart, embarks on a *"Dia de los Muertos"* adventure that spans three fantastic afterlife worlds where he must face his greatest fears. Directed by Jorge R. Gutierrez, and starring Diego Luna, Zoe Saldana, Channing Tatum.

**Brainstorm.**\*\* (1983) Brilliant researchers Lillian Reynolds (Natalie Wood) and Michael Brace (Christopher Walken) have developed a system of recording and playing back actual experiences of people. Then one of the researchers dies and tapes the experience. Directed by Douglas Trumbull.

**Circulation.** (2008) Fantasy-psychological thriller film written and directed by Ryan Harper. Gene (Sherman Koltz) dies and enters purgatory, where people slowly take on the characteristics of animals, and Gene's nature is a spider.

**Clean Pastures.**\* (1937) is a *Merrie Melodies* animated cartoon directed by I. Freleng, produced by Leon Schlesinger, and released by Warner Bros. The cartoon is a parody of Warner Bros.' 1936 film, *The Green Pastures*. It tells of an ersatz Heaven called "Pair-O-Dice" and its angels' efforts to win souls from "Hades Inc."

**Coco.**\*\*\* (computer-animated musical, 2017) Despite his family's generations-old ban on music, 12-year-old Miguel dreams of becoming a great musician. Desperate to prove his talent, Miguel finds himself in the colorful Mexican Land of the Dead. After meeting a charming skeletal trickster named Héctor, the two new friends embark on an extraordinary journey to discover the truth behind Miguel's family history. (Pixar/Disney)

**Corpse Bride.**\*\*\* (animated musical, 2005) When a shy groom inadvertently practices his wedding vows over the remains of a murdered young bride, she rises from the grave convinced he has married her. Colorful scenes of the Underworld in a "Dia de los Muertos" style contrast with the dreary Edward Gorey-esque Victorian "real world" above. Claymation by Tim Burton, starring Johnny Depp, Helena Bonham Carter, Emily Watson.

**The Discovery.**\* (2017) In the near future, a breakthrough scientific discovery by Dr. Thomas Harbor (Robert Redford), provides definitive proof of an "afterlife," and millions of people commit suicide in order to get there. The question is, where do they go? Very much in line with the paradigm of Biocentrism.

**Down to Earth.** (1947) A musical comedy sequel to the 1941 film *Here Comes Mr. Jordan*, also directed by Alexander Hall. Rita Hayworth stars as the Muse Terpsichore who is annoyed that popular Broadway producer Danny Miller (Larry Parks) is putting on a play which portrays the Muses as man-crazy tarts.

**Dragonfly.*** (2002) When his wife Emily dies, Joe (Kevin Costner) keeps getting signs that she somehow lives on, including via a near-death experience shared by a child (an interesting aspect of NDE research covered by Dr Melvin Morse). Though most of those in Joe's life reject his claims, he goes in search of answers to the mystery...with a surprising result.

**Enter the Void.**\*\* (2009) In Gaspar Noé's provocative film, Oscar, a small-time US drug dealer living in Tokyo, is killed in a drug deal, inducing a psychedelic "astral journey" as his soul seeks resurrection. Taking inspiration from mushroom trips, the *Tibetan Book of the Dead,* and Raymond Moody's NDE bestseller *Life After Life*, Noé hits the viewer with sensory overload to portray the altered states of consciousness that Oscar encounters.

**Flatliners.**\*\* (1990) Raymond Moody's seminal 1975 book *Life After Life* brought the near-death experience into the public consciousness. This movie starring Kiefer Sutherland and Julia Roberts takes it one step further, and wonders what might happen if people actively explore the near-death experience (NDE) through induced death and resuscitation.

**Ghost.**\*\*\* (1990) Written by Bruce Joel Rubin and directed by Jerry Zucker, this is a sentimental story of eternal love between a young woman (Demi Moore) and the ghost of her murdered lover (Patrick Swayze), who tries to save her with the help of a reluctant fake psychic (Whoopi Goldberg). The film received several Academy Awards nominations.

**A Ghost Story.**\*\* (2017) Director David Lowery's singular indie casts its own melancholy, meditative shadow across the haunting genre, reinventing it from the ground up. Starring Rooney Mara and Casey Affleck, the film boldly breaks with convention to contemplate what such isolation truly means, later moving unshackled through time and space to even more unsettling effect.

**Ghost Whisperer.** An American TV supernatural drama series, which ran on CBS from 2005-2010. Melinda Gordon (Jennifer Love Hewitt) can see and communicate with ghosts. She helps earthbound spirits resolve their problems and cross over into the spirit world.

**The Green Pastures.\*\*** (1936) An American film depicting stories from the Bible as visualized by African American characters. Starring Rex Ingram (in several roles, including "De Lawd"), Oscar Polk, and Eddie "Rochester" Anderson, it was based on the novel *Ol' Man Adam an' His Chillun* by Roark Bradford and the subsequent Pulitzer Prize-winning play of the same name by Marc Connelly. It is one of only six feature films in the Hollywood Studio era to feature an all-African-American cast.

**Haunts of the Very Rich.\*\*** (1972) Great hard-to-find made-for-television movie. A group of very rich people fly to an island resort where they are greeted by a mysterious black man (Seacrist), and the plot thickens. Just before setting off on their journey, each of the "guests" had narrowly escaped death—or had they?

**Heaven Can Wait.** (1943) American comedy film produced and directed by Ernst Lubitsch. The screenplay was by Samson Raphaelson based on the play *Birthday* by Leslie Bush-Fekete. An aged Henry van Cleve (Don Ameche) enters the opulent reception area of Hell, to be personally greeted by "His Excellency" (Laird Cregar). Henry petitions to be admitted. To prove his unworthiness, he tells the story of his dissolute life.

**Heaven Can Wait.** (1978) A remake of *Here Comes Mr. Jordan* (1941), directed by Warren Beatty and Buck Henry, and starring Warren Beatty, James Mason and Julie Christie. A Los Angeles Rams quarterback, accidentally taken away from his body by an overanxious angel before he was meant to die, returns to life in the body of a recently murdered millionaire.

**Heaven is for Real.** (2014) Based on Pastor Todd Burpo and Lynn Vincent's 2010 book of the same name. After their young son, Colton (Connor Corum), undergoes emergency surgery, Todd Burpo (Greg Kinnear) and his wife, Sonja (Kelly Reilly), are overjoyed at the child's miraculous recovery. Then Colton says that he went to heaven, and tells his parents things that he couldn't possibly know.

**Hercules.** (1997) An animated comedic film by Disney, *very* loosely inspired by the legendary exploits of the Greek hero Heracles. Several major scenes take place in the Underworld realms of *Erebos* (ruled by a bizarre and rather Satanic Hades with flaming hair, voiced by James Woods; no mention of Persephone). If you're into Greek mythology, you'll hate this for its countless inaccuracies.

**Hereafter.** (2010) Three individuals are touched by death in different ways, and each of them deals with their encounter with "the other side." Starring Matt Damon, directed by Clint Eastwood, co-produced by Steven Spielberg.

**Here Comes Mr. Jordan.** (1941) A romantic comedy-fantasy film in which a boxer, mistakenly taken to Heaven before his time, is given a second chance back on Earth. It stars Robert Montgomery, Claude Rains and Evelyn Keyes. The film was adapted by Sidney Buchman and Seton I. Miller from the play *Heaven Can Wait* by Harry Segall. *Here Comes Mr. Jordan* was followed by *Down to Earth* (1947). Remade as *Heaven Can Wait* (1978), and *Down to Earth* (2001) (sharing the title with the sequel to *Here Comes Mr. Jordan*).

**Jacob's Ladder.*** (1990) Mourning his dead child, a haunted Vietnam war veteran attempts to discover his past while suffering from a severe case of dissociation. To do so, he must decipher reality and life from his own dreams, delusion, and perception of death.

**Jhuk Gaya Aasman.** *(English: The Skies Have Bowed)* (1968) Indian film directed by Lekh Tandon. A remake of the Hollywood film *Here Comes Mr. Jordan* (1941). Sanjay (Rajendra Kumar) and Priya (Saira Banu) are planning their marriage when Sanjay dies in a car crash. Escorted by an angel to heaven, he learns that his death was a mistake.

**The Lovely Bones.*** (2009) A young girl who has been murdered watches over her family—and her killer—from purgatory. She must weigh her desire for vengeance against her desire for her family to heal. Peter Jackson's film adaptation of Alice Sebold's

*The Lovely Bones* features over-the-top CG rendering of the scenes where young Susie Salmon is stuck in the "In-Between."

**Made in Heaven.**\*\* (1987) Mike Shea (Timothy Hutton) drowns while rescuing a woman and her children from a river. He finds himself in Heaven, where he falls in love with a heavenly guide named Annie (Kelly McGillis). But Annie has not yet earned her wings, so she must put in time on Earth in a human body. Mike is also allowed to return to Earth, but neither he nor Annie will remember each other.

**Monty Python's The Meaning of Life.**\*\*\* (1997) The British comedy troupe's hilarious sketches include themes of gluttony, birth control, total insignificance and, of course, the meaning of life. What better Afterlife could there be? After all, it's Christmas every day in Heaven. Plus you get dinner and a show!

**Orphée.** (1950) Poet and filmmaker Jean Cocteau recasts the Greek myth about the poet who descends into hell to rescue his deceased wife as a unique cinematic spell about the price of an artist's immortality. Cocteau's inventive, practical visual effects use mirrors, water and reversed film to enter the underworld, where Orpheus – played by Cocteau's *La Belle et la Bête* star Jean Marais – makes his stand.

**Outward Bound.** (1930) A film based on the hit 1923 play Sutton Vane. Passengers on an ocean liner slowly realize they are all dead. Arriving at their destination, they await judgment by the "Examiner." Remade in 1944 as *Between Two Worlds*.

**Proof.** An American drama TV series that aired on TNT from June 16 through Aug. 18, 2015. Following the death of her son, Dr. Carolyn Tyler (Jennifer Beals) investigates supernatural cases of reincarnation, near-death experiences, and hauntings, in hopes of finding evidence that death is not final.

**The Restless.** (2006) South Korean fantasy film directed by Jo Dong-oh. The film's Korean title, *Joong-cheon*, is literally translated as "Midheaven." *Demon Empire* is an alternative English name for the film. In fictional ancient Korea, Yi-gwak is a demon hunter. He enters the Midheaven, a transitory place for spirits, only to find that the his lover has forgotten him.

**Romantic Heaven.** (2011) South Korean melodrama in four parts about fate, love, loss, and redemption. Three seemingly disconnected people cross paths at a hospital. It is in part four, "Romantic Heaven," that the various threads are brought together and ultimately resolved. As fate would have it, their counterparts are gazing down upon their loved ones from heaven, dealing with their own version of remorse and regret.

**The Sixth Sense.*** (1999) A boy who communicates with spirits who don't know they're dead seeks the help of a disheartened child psychologist. There are not a lot of afterlife visions, but a whole legion of Earth-bound ghosts that need poor little Cole Sear (Haley Joel Osment) to help them move on to the Summerlands. Warning: you'll see dead people. All the time.

**Stairway to Heaven** (original title, *A Matter of Life and Death*). (1946). A British wartime aviator who cheats death must argue for his life before a celestial court. Directed by Michael Powell, starring David Niven, Kim Hunter, Robert Coote.

**Surviving Death:** (2021). Is there life after death? This Netflix documentary series claims to prove there is. "Surviving Death" is based on a book of the same name by journalist Leslie Kean. It explores near-death experiences, mediums and séances, ghost-hunting and supposed past-life memories.

**What Dreams May Come.*** (1998) Robin Williams and Cuba Gooding, Jr. star in this visual masterpiece about a man determined to find his damned wife in the Afterlife so they can share eternity together. Directed by Vincent Ward, the film is based on the 1978 novel by Richard Matheson. With stunningly beautiful depictions of the Afterlife, it received an Academy Award for visual effects.

# Appendix F.
# Resources

## Home funeral advocates

**Crossings: Caring for our Own at Death – A Home Funeral & Green Burial Resource Center**
7108 Holly Ave.
Takoma Park, MD 20912
http://crossings.net/index.html

**Final Passages Institute of Conscious Dying, Home Funerals, & Green Burial Education**
Jerrigrace Lyons, Founder, Dir.
PO Box 1721
Sebastopol, CA 95473
www.FinalPassages.org

**Harmonizing Sacred Pathways – Honoring Rituals of Passage**
Rev. Judith K. Fenley, Director
PO Box 23, Graton, CA 95444
jkfenley@gmail.com

**National Home Funeral Alliance**
11014 19th Ave, SE, Ste #8, PMB #155, Everett, WA 98208
http://homefuneralalliance.org/

**Natural Transitions – A Resource for Green and Holistic Approaches to End of Life**
780 Quince Circle
Boulder, CO 80304
www.NaturalTransitions.org
http://www.naturaltransitions.org/contact-nt-mag/

## Alternative funeral professionals

**Compassion and Choices**
PO Box 101810
Denver, CO 80250
www.compassionandchoices.org/
(The leading nonprofit organization committed to helping everyone have the best death possible. Free consultation, planning resources, referrals and guidance for end-of-life options.)

**Funeral and Memorial Societies of America (FAMSA)**
PO Box 10, Hinesburg, VT 05461
www.funerals.org/famsa.
(Has current listings of all Memorial Societies in USA, as well as many other resources.)

**Rev. Dr. She` D`Montford** is available to officiate at Pagan funeral services in Australia. She` has several services you can chose from, or she can write an individual one that includes a personal Pagan eulogy and chants.
PO Box 3541
Helensvale Town Centre, QLD
Australia 4212
+61(0) 402-793-604
shambhallah@y7mail.com

## Green burials

**Green Burial Council**
Kate Kalanick, Programs Officer
PO Box 851 Ojai, CA 93023
http://greenburialcouncil.org/
(*The* environmental certification organization for green burials in US. Issues environmental certificates for cemeteries, funeral homes and product manufacturers.)

## Other alternatives for disposition of remains

**Celestis Memorial Spaceflights**
PO Box 66784
Houston, TX 77266-6784
https://www.celestis.com/
(The only company to have successfully conducted memorial spaceflight missions.)

**Coeio**
PO Box 390901
Mountain View, CA
http://coeio.com/
(Mushroom decomposition)

**Cryonics Institute**
24355 Sorrentino Court
Clinton Township, MI 48035-3239
www.cryonics.org/cihq@aol.com
(Freezing for future resurrection)

**Eternal Reefs, Inc.**
PO Box 3811, Sarasota, FL 34230
info@eternalreefs.com
(Embed cremains into undersea concrete reef)

**New England Burials at Sea**
Captain Brad White
NewEnglandBurialsAtSea.com
(Offers affordable, individualized and personal ash scattering services and full body sea burials all along the East and West Coasts.)

**Neptune Memorial Reef**
http://www.nmreef.com/index.html
(Largest man-made reef, located off Key Biscayne, Miami, FL, embedding cremains into concrete.)

**Promessa**
P. Organic AB
Lyr-Bö 254
SE-474 96 Nösund, Sweden
promessa.se/info@promessa.se
(Freeze-drying)

**Resomation Ltd**
Beechwood St.
Pudsey, UK LS28 6PT
http://resomation.com/about/need-for-change/
(Alkaline Hydrolysis)

**Return Home**
4146 B Pl NW
Auburn, WA, 98001
www.returnhome.com/contact/
(30-day "Terramation" process gently composts human remains into rich, fertile soil.)

**Summum**
707 Genesee Avenue
Salt Lake City, UT 84104
http://www.summum.org/
(Mummification)

**Trident Society**
1620 Tice Valley Blvd., Ste. 100
Walnut Creek, CA 94595
888-307-6001
www.TridentSociety.com
(America's cremation specialists)

**Sea Burials**
Sydney, Australia
www.seaburialsaustralia.com.au

## Mortuary resources

**TheFuneralSite.com**
www.thefuneralsite.com/
(A free consumer information and education resource on funeral planning, financing funerals, funeral products and services.)

**Shine on Brightly**
www.ShineOnBrightly.com
(Cremation urns, pet memorials, jewelry, books, grave markers, memorial keepsakes.)

## Donating organs and bodies

**Anthropology Research**
Maxwell Museum of Anthro.
MSC01 1050
1 University of New Mexico
Albuquerque, NM 87131-0001
http://www.unm.edu/~maxwell/

**Forensic Anthropology Center**
Texas State University
601 University Dr. ELA 232
San Marcos, TX 78666
http://www.txstate.edu/anthropology/facts/donations.html

**MedCure**
18111 NE Sandy Blvd.
Portland, OR 97230
http://medcure.org/
(Leading non-transplant tissue bank devoted to compassionate, ethical services that connect donors to medical research and education.)

**Mütter Museum**
The College of Physicians of Philadelphia
19 S. 22nd St.
Philadelphia, PA 19103
http://muttermuseum.org
(Exhibits display the mysteries and beauty of the human body while documenting the history of diagnosis and treatment of disease.)

**Nat'l Founda. for Transplants**
5350 Poplar Ave, Ste 850
Memphis, TN 38119
http://www.transplants.org

**Organ Donor Registry**
organdonor.gov/register.html
(U.S. Government Info. on Organ Donation and Transplantation)

**School of Medicine**
Wayne State University
5D-6 University Health Center
4201 St. Antoine
Detroit, MI 48201
http://home.med.wayne.edu/

## Near-death studies

**International Association for Near-Death Studies (IANDS)**
2741 Campus Walk Ave. bldg 500
Durham, NC 27705
http://www.iands.org
(Scientific research and education on near-death experiences.)

# Appendix G.
# Bibliography

Many of these books could be in multiple or alternate categories. Hopefully these will be of some assistance in choosing more to read on various sub-categories of this broad topic.

## General Death & Dying

Ebenstein, Joanna (ed.), *Death: A Graveside Companion.* Thames & Hudson, 2017.

Iserson, Kenneth, *Death to Dust: What Happens to Dead Bodies?* Galen Press, Tucson, AZ, 1987.

Jones, Constance, R.I.P., *The Complete Book of Death and Dying.* HarperCollins/Stonesong Press, 1997.

Rasberry, Sally, & Watanabe, Carole Rae, *The Art of Dying.* Celestial Arts, 2001.

Regardie, Israel, *A Garden of Pomegranates.* Llewellyn, Woodbury, MN, 1970.

## Natural Death Care & Home Funerals

Fenley, Judith, with Zell, Oberon, *Death Rights and Rites—a Practical Guide to a Meaningful Death.* Llewellyn, Woodbury, MN 2020.

Morgan, Ernest, *Dealing Creatively with Death: A Manual of Death Education and Simple Burial.* Barclay House, Bayside, NY, 1990.

Simpson, Michael, *The Facts of Death: A Complete Guide for Being Prepared.* Prentice-Hall, NJ, 1979.

Starhawk, with M. Macha Nightmare & the Reclaiming Community, *The Pagan Book of Living and Dying,* HarperSanFrancisco, CA, 1997.

## Spiritual Focus, Readings & Rituals

Anderson, Megory, *Sacred Dying––Creating Rituals for Embracing the End of Life,* Marlow & Co, An Imprint of Avalon Publishing Group Inc., New York, 2001; 2003.

Belk, Donna, & Unullisi, Kateyanne, *Home Funeral Ceremonies / Las Ceremonias Bonitas.* Sugar Skull Publishing, 2015.

Vest, Joe, Ed, *The Open Road—Walt Whitman on Death & Dying,* Four Corners Editions, AZ, 85215, 1996.

York, Sarah, *Remembering Well—Rituals for Celebrating Life & Mourning Death,* Jossey-Bass Inc., A Wiley Company, San Francisco, CA, 2000.

Zell-Ravenheart, Oberon & Morning Glory, *Creating Circles & Ceremonies: Rites & Rituals for All Seasons & Reasons.* New Page Books, Franklin Lakes, NJ, 2006.

## Religious Traditions, Doctrines & Philosophy

Ashcroft-Nowicki, Dolores, *The New Book of the Dead.* Aquarian Press, 1992.

Belanger, Michelle, *Walking the Twilight Path: A Gothic Book of the Dead.* Llewellyn Publications, Woodbury, MN, 2008.

Budge, Wallace (trans.), *The Egyptian Book of the Dead.* Penguin Classics, 2008.

Day, Christian, *The Witches' Book of the Dead.* Red Wheel/Weiser, 2011.

Fortune, Dion, *Dion Fortune's Book of the Dead.* Red Wheel/Weiser, 2005.

_____, *Through the Gates of Death.* Aquarian Press, 1968.

Gold, E.J. & Lilly, John, *American Book of the Dead.* Gateways Books & Tapes, 10th ed. 2005.

Kubler-Ross, Elizabeth, *Death: The Final Stage of Growth.* Simon & Schuster, 1986.

_____, *On Death and Dying.* Tavistock Publications, 1970.

_____, *Wheel of Life: A Memoir of Living & Dying.* Bantam Books, 1998.

Madden, Kristin, *Shamanic Guide to Death & Dying.* Spilled Candy Publications, 2005.

Rinpoche, Sogyal, *Tibetan Book of Living & Dying.* HarperSanFrancisco, CA, Revised edition 2012.

Wright, Philip & West, Carrie, *Death and the Pagan.* BCM, 2004.

## Multicultural Traditions

Ebenstein, Joanna, *Death: A Graveside Companion.* Thames & Hudson, 2017.

Habenstein, Robert W. & William H. Lamers, *Funeral Customs the World Over.* Bulfin Printers, Milwaukee, WI, 1960.

Kramer, Kenneth, *The Sacred Art of Dying: How the World Religions Understand Death.* Paulist Press, New York, 1998

Matsunami, Kodo, *International Handbook of Funeral Customs.* Greenwood Press, Westport, CT, 1998.

Obayashi, Hiroshi, ed. *Death and Afterlife: Perspectives of World Religions.* Praeger, 1991.

O'Gaea, Ashleen, *In the Service of Life: A Wiccan Perspective on Death.* Citadel Press, New York, 2003.

Parkes, Colin Murray, *Death and Bereavement Across Cultures.* Routledge, London, 1997.

Puckle, Bertram S., *Funeral Customs: Their Origin and Development.* Omnigraphics, Detroit, MI, 1990.

Rogak, Lisa, *Death Warmed Over: Funeral Food, Rituals, and*

Customs from Around the World. Tenspeed Press, Berkeley, 2004.

Segal, Alan F., *Life After Death: A History of the Afterlife in Western Religion*. Doubleday, 2004.

Turner, Ann Warren, *Houses for the Dead: Burial Customs Through the Ages*. David McKay Co., New York, 1976.

# Afterlife, Reincarnation & Near-Death Experiences

Alexander, Eben, *Proof of Heaven: A Neurosurgeon's Journey into the Afterlife*. Simon & Schuster, 2012.

Almond, Philip C., *Afterlife: A History of Life after Death*. London and Ithaca, NY, 2015.

Blackmore, Susan, *Dying to Live: Near-Death Experiences*. Prometheus Books, 1993.

Brown, Sylvia, *Life on the Other Side: A Psychic's Tour of the Afterlife*. Berkley, 2001

Chopra, Deepak, *Life After Death*. Rider-Random House, 2008.

Coddington, Robert H., *Death Brings Many Surprises: A Psychic Handbook*. Ivy/Ballantine Books, New York, 1987.

Cohn-Sherbok, Dan & Lewis, Christopher, eds., *Beyond Death: Theological and Philosophical Reflections on Life after Death*. Pelgrave-MacMillan, 1995.

Fontana, David, *Is There an Afterlife? A Comprehensive Overview of the Evidence*. O Books, 2005.

Grof, Stanislaw & Christine, *Beyond Death: Gates of Consciousness*. Thames & Hudson, 1980.

Holden JM, Greyson B, James D, editors. *The Handbook of Near-Death Experiences: 30 Years of Investigation*. Praeger/ABC-CLIO, Santa Barbara, CA, 2009.

Hugenot, Alan Ross, *The Death Experience: What it is like when you die,* Dog Ear Publishing, Indianapolis, IN 46268, 2012.

Hughes, Kristoffer, *The Journey Into Spirit: A Pagan's Perspective on Death, Dying & Bereavement*. Llewellyn Publications, Woodbury, MN, 2014.

Lanza, Robert, *Biocentrism: How Life and Consciousness are the Keys to Understanding the True Nature of the Universe*. BenBella Books, 2010.

Leek, Sybil, *Reincarnation: The Second Chance*. Scarborough House, NY, 1974.

Miller, Sukie, *After Death: Mapping the Journey*. Simon & Schuster, 1997.

Mirabello, Mark, *A Traveler's Guide to the Afterlife: Traditions and Beliefs on Death, Dying, and What Lies Beyond*. Inner Traditions, 2016.

Moody, Raymond, *Life After Life: The Investigation of a Phenomenon – Survival of Bodily

Death. HarperSanFrancisco, CA, 1975.

Moorjani, Anita, *Dying to Be Me.* Hay House, Inc. 2012.

Moreman, Christopher M., *Beyond the Threshold: Afterlife Beliefs and Experiences in World Religions.* Rowman & Littlefield, 2008.

Morey, Robert A., *Death and the Afterlife.* Bethany House Pubs, Minneapolis, MN, 1984.

Newton, Michael, *Journey of Souls: Case Studies of Life Between Lives.* Llewellyn Publications, Woodbury, MN, 1994.

Roach, Mary, *Six Feet Over: Adventures in the Afterlife.* Canongate, 2007.

Ring, Kenneth, *Life at Death: A Scientific Investigation of the Near-Death Experience.* Coward, McCann, & Geoghegan, New York, 1980.

Schwartz, Gary E., forward by Deepak Chopra, *The Afterlife Experiments: Breakthrough Scientific Evidence of Life After Death.* Atria Books, 2003.

Steiger, Brad, *You Will Live Again: Dramatic Case Histories of Reincarnation.* Blue Dolphin Press, Grass Valley, CA, 1996.

Stevenson, Ian, *Twenty Cases Suggestive of Reincarnation: $2^{nd}$ Edition.* University of Virginia Press, Revised edition, 1980.

Tucker, Jim. B., *Return to Life: Extraordinary Cases of Children Who Remember Past Lives.* St. Martin's Griffin, 2008.

_____, *Life Before Life: Children's Memories of Previous Lives.* St. Martin's Press, 2013.

Underwood, Peter, *Ghosts and How to See Them.* Anaya, 1993.

van Lommel, Pim, *Consciousness Beyond Life: The Science of the Near-Death Experience.* HarperOne, 2010.

Zaleski, Carol, *Otherworld Journeys: Accounts of Near-Death Experience in Medieval and Modern Times.* Oxford Univ. Press, 1988.

## Netherworlds: Realms of the Dead

Amjad, Moiz. "Will Christians enter Paradise or go to Hell?" *Renaissance - Monthly Islamic journal* 11(6), June, 2001.

Black, J.; Green, A.; Rickards, T., *Gods, Demons, and Symbols of Ancient Mesopotamia: an illustrated dictionary.* University of Texas Press, 1992.

Bottéro, Jean, *Religion in Ancient Mesopotamia.* University of Chicago Press, 2001.

Budge, Sir Wallis, *Egyptian Religion,* Bell Publishing, 1900.

Horowitz, W., *Mesopotamian Cosmic Geography*, Eisenbrauns. 1998.

Ions, Veronica, *Egyptian Mythology,* Hamlyn Publishing, 1965.

Leary, Timothy; Metzner, Ralph; Alpert, Richard, *The Psychedelic Experience: A Manual Based on the Tibetan Book of* the Dead. Citadel Press, Secaucus, NJ, 1967.

Lodo, Ven. Lama, *Bardo Teachings*. Snow Lion Pubs, 1987.

MacCana, Proinsias, *Celtic Mythology,* Hamlyn Pubs, 1970.

Nemet-Nejat, Karen Rhea, *Daily Life in Ancient Mesopotamia.* Greenwood Pub. Group. 1998.

Padmasambhava (Author), Chögyal Namkhai Norbu (Commentary), Karma Lingpa (Author), Elio Guarisco (Translator). *The Tibetan Book of the Dead: Awakening Upon Dying.* Shang Shung Pubs & North Atlantic Books, 2013.

Pincent, John, *Greek Mythology,* Hamlyn Publishing, 1969.

Rinpoche, Lati, *Death, Intermediate State, and Rebirth.* Snow Lion Publications, 1981.

Rinpoche, Sogyal, *The Tibetan Book of Living and Dying.* HarperCollins Pubs, NY, 1993.

Robinson, Herbert Spencer, & Wilson, Knox, *Myths and Legends of All Nations,* Littlefield, Adams & Co. 1976.

Schimmel, Annemarie, *Islam and The Wonders of Creation: The Animal Kingdom.* Al-Furqan Islamic Heritage Found, 2003.

Tedlock, Dennis, *Popol Vuh: The Definitive Edition of the Mayan Book of the Dawn of Life and the Glories of Gods and Kings.* Touchstone. 1996.

Temple, Robert, *Netherworld: Discovering the Oracle of the Dead.* Century, London, 2002.

Vandenberg, Phillip (translated from German by George Unwin), *The Mystery of the Oracles.* MacMillan, NYC, 1979.

# Historical Perspectives on Death

Barley, Nigel, *Grave Matters: A Lively History of Death Around the World*, Henry Hoh, New York, 1997.

Coleman, Penny, *Corpses, Coffins & Crypts: A History of Burial.* Henry Holt & Co, 1997.

Kerrigan, Michael, *The History of Death.* Lions Press, 2007.

Laderman, Gary, *The Sacred Remains—American Attitudes Toward Death, 1799–1883.* Yale University, 1996.

_____, *Rest in Peace—A Cultural History of Death & the Funeral Home in 20th-Century America.* Oxford Univ. Press, New York, 2003.

Shushan, Gregory, *Conceptions of the Afterlife in Early Civilizations: Universalism, Constructivism and Near-Death Experience.* Continuum, New York & London, 2009.

Taylor, Timothy, *The Buried Soul: How Humans Invented Death.* Fourth Estate, 2002.

Wilkins, Robert, *Death: A History of Man's Obsessions and Fears.* Barnes & Noble, New York, 1996.

## Appendix H.
# Index

Aaru, 115
Abraham, 95, 109
Acheron, 116-18
Acherusian lake, 116, 118
Adapa, 112
Aeacus, 116
Aesir, 124
Aether, 100, 158
Akashic, 28, 29, 155
Akh, 113
Akkadian, 111, 112
Alexandria, 126
Alkaline hydrolysis, 60, 61
Al kawthar, 134
Allah, 132, 134, 135
All Souls' Day, 142
Altar, 15-17, 23, 40, 44, 74, 93, 138, 168
Amenti, 114
America, 58, 61, 84, 161
Ammut, 115
Amu darya, 134
Ancestor, 23, 44, 46, 53, 74, 79, 80, 90, 93-95, 105, 124, 150, 152, 168
Angels, 47, 48, 95, 100, 127, 130, 132, 134
Angrboda, 124
An-nar, 134
Annwfn, 17, 69, 120-22
Anpu-khent-amenta, 48
Anubis, 114, 115
Anunnaki, 112, 113
Aor, 123
Apocalypse, 172
Apotheosis/apotheasis, 100, 159, 160, 172
Apple, 22, 23, 55, 92, 151, 152, 164
Arabia, 132
Arallû, 110
Arawn, 122
Ariadne, 167
Arianrhod, 121
Arran, 120, 121
Ascend, 48, 95, 100, 120, 161
Asgard, 124
Ashes, 19, 22, 23, 30, 49, 50, 53, 55-57, 62, 69, 70, 77
Asphodel, 116
Astral, 101, 103, 114, 120, 144, 145, 149, 154, 155, 157, 158
Athamé, 30
Atheism, 102
Athens, 93
Atlantic, 61, 150
Aura, 144, 145, 149, 157
Autumn equinox, 112, 135
Avalon, 25, 172
Avatars, 102, 161, 162
Awareness, 29, 52, 91, 97, 104, 106, 107, 132, 143, 156

Ba, 113
Babylonian, 111, 113
Baia, Italy, 127, 129
Balance, 19, 28, 48, 110, 115, 169, 170
Balder, 124
Bali, 58
Balor, 123
Bardo, 59, 100, 105, 130-32
Bat house, 136
Beer, 44, 48, 85
Belenos, 92
Belize, 135
Beltaine/Beltane, 18, 92, 123
Biblical, 49, 127

Bilé, 123
Biocentrism, 147, 155, 156, 162
Biocremation, 60
Bíodh sé amhlaidh, 45
Bioenergetic, 144, 155
Bioplasma, 145, 158
Birth, 14, 16, 17, 25, 37, 41, 46, 52, 73, 102, 108, 130, 132, 143, 147
Black cat, 83
Blood, 7, 37, 51, 76, 83, 89, 103, 119, 136, 137, 163
Bodhisattvas, 107
Bodrum, 53
Body donation, 63-65
Bon, 58, 89
Bone, 22, 25, 41, 54, 56, 58, 61, 64, 138, 167, 169
Book of the Dead, 48, 105, 114, 130
Boreas, 28
Brahma, 56
Brains, 99, 150, 151, 154, 156, 160, 162
Bran, 123
Brazil, 84, 88
Bretons, 86
British, 61, 98
Buddha, 47, 56-58, 91, 107, 130-132
Burial at sea, 57
Burial chamber, 53, 110, 114
Burial customs, 54, 98
Burial mounds, 124
Butterflies, 84, 169

Caer Feddwid, 120, 121
Caer Rigor, 121
Caer Siddi, 121
Caer Wydyr, 120, 122
Calavera, 108, 142
California, 14, 25, 68
Candles, 27-29, 31, 39, 52, 74, 77, 92, 93, 97
Cannibalism, 151
Capela dos ossos, 54
Capsula Mundi, 55
Caria, 53
Casket, 19, 55, 85, 87
Castle of Glass, 122
Castle of Revelry, 121
Cave of Cruachan, 120
Celebrate, 24, 41, 43, 46, 50, 71, 93
Celt, 18, 22, 24, 43, 84, 92, 105, 120, 122
Cemetery, 53, 55, 85, 91, 168
Cenotaph, 53
Cenote, 135, 137-39
Cerberus, 116, 126
Cernunnos, 28, 29, 31, 122
Cerridwen, 28, 29, 31, 95
Cerveteri, 53
Charnel house, 54
Charon, 116, 126
Chicxulub, 138
Chikhai Bardo, 132

Children, 18, 25, 37, 41, 43-46, 58, 73, 74, 80, 89, 113, 127, 147, 156, 164, 169, 171, 172
Chinese, 54, 57, 87, 89, 90, 145
Chod, 58
Chönyi Bardo, 132
Christianity, 49, 53, 79, 92, 94, 95, 100, 103, 105, 112, 120, 122, 127, 128, 130, 132, 151, 163, 169
Church, 23, 24, 54, 94, 119, 127, 166
Church of All Worlds, 24, 166
Citipati, 91
Coalescence of consciousness, 160
Cocytus, 117, 118
Coeio, 60
Coffin, 18, 22, 23, 54, 84, 85, 88, 114, 152
Cold House, 136
Columbarium, 56
Communion, 79, 119, 140, 151
Community, 40, 41, 55, 64, 67, 103, 151, 152
Connaught, Ireland, 120
Consciousness, 28-30, 47, 59, 72, 79, 89, 97-99, 101-3, 110, 130, 147, 148, 153, 156, 159-62

Corpse, 22, 23, 55, 57, 58, 86-89, 114, 116, 124, 139
Country-Under-Wave, 123
COVID pandemic, 67
Cremains, 55, 61, 62
Cremation, 22, 55-58, 60, 61, 70
Cretan labyrinth, 167
Cro-magnon, 98, 155, 167
Crossroads, 136-38
Cruachan, 120
Cryonics, 59, 60
Crypts, 22, 53, 167
Cuchulain, 123
Cumae, 127, 129

Dakhmeh, 58
Dance, 28, 30, 41, 42, 91, 96, 168
Dante, 100, 105, 127, 128, 129
Darya, 134
Delphi, 168
Demons, 69, 106, 127, 129, 135, 136
Devil, 127
Dharmapala, 91
Día de los Muertos, 93
Dilmun, 110
Diodorus Siculus, 43
Discorporation, 22, 145
Divine, 32, 34, 38, 100, 101, 105, 109, 114, 121, 151, 159, 162
DNA, 25, 59, 72, 149, 150
Dodona, 168
Donn, 34, 44, 45, 122
Douaumont ossuary, 54
Dozakh, 134
Dragons, 139, 161
Dreams, 14, 20, 29, 31, 32, 37, 72, 81, 82, 100, 132, 142, 170
Druid, 31, 43
Duat, 105
Dumb Supper, 27, 92
Dying, 21, 70, 86, 89, 96, 132, 145, 146, 149, 156, 158
Dzibichin cenote, 137

Easaidh Ruadh, 123
Eden, 110, 111
Egypt, 48, 53, 54, 63, 87, 100, 112, 113, 114
Ek Balam, 139
Elysian Fields, 95, 105, 115, 116
Emain ablach, 45
Embalming, 22, 54, 55, 85
Entombed, 22, 53, 54, 114, 120, 169
Ephyra, Greece, 127
Epiphany, 86
Epirus, Greece, 117, 118
Epops, 93
Equinox, 18, 94, 112, 118, 120, 135
Erebos/erebus, 100, 105, 112, 115-18
Ereshkigal, 105, 111
Erin, 123
Eriu, 122
Erset la tari, 111
Ersetu, 111
Etain, 123
Eṭemmu, 112
Etruscan, 53, 84, 86, 169
Euphrates, 110, 134
Europe, 25, 53, 89, 97, 98, 108, 120, 151, 164, 167
Eurus, 28
Évora, Portugal, 54

Fairy, 18, 25, 67, 122, 162
Fate, 15, 23, 34, 78, 113, 115, 134, 152, 172
Feast, 30, 86, 90, 94, 105, 114, 124
Feddwid, 120, 121
Fenrir, 124
Feralia, 93
Ferryman, 86, 126
Festival, 89, 92, 93, 166
Finland, 53
Firdaws, 134
Flowers, 18, 19, 21, 56, 81, 82, 98, 123

Fomorii, 122, 123
France, 54, 90, 122, 133
Freyja, 124
Fruit, 22, 24, 39, 55, 82, 134, 152, 169
Funeral, 21-23, 43, 53, 56, 57, 63, 70, 77, 83, 85-87, 89, 98, 113
Furat, 134

## G

Gaea, 143, 148, 158-60, 168
Gaelic, 25, 92, 123
Ganges, 56, 57
Ganzer, 110
Garm, 126
Gate, 17, 19, 28, 29, 32, 34, 39, 44, 45, 106, 112, 113, 116, 120, 123, 126, 130, 134, 135
Gemini, 112, 135
Genesia, 93
German, 54, 83
Ghost, 52, 88-90, 93, 96, 100, 112, 113, 116, 118, 158
Gidim, 112, 113
Gioll, 124
Giza, 53
Gnipahellir, 126
God, 24, 27, 30, 37, 38, 41, 46-48, 52, 92, 95, 103, 109, 111, 113, 114, 122, 123, 126, 127, 129, 130, 132, 151, 161, 162, 168
Goddess, 16, 18, 19, 24, 25, 27, 30, 41, 42, 46-49, 67, 73, 95, 111, 114, 121, 122, 148, 160
Gorgons, 169
Grave, 19, 22, 38, 42, 44, 49-51, 53-57, 62, 85-87, 89, 90, 92, 110, 123, 127, 134, 142, 151, 168
Greek, 53, 54, 84, 86, 93, 100, 105, 111, 112, 115, 117, 118, 126, 127
Green burial, 17, 22, 55, 60
Guardians, 113, 168, 169
Guatemala, 135
Guide, 29, 31, 33, 34, 41, 47, 71, 101, 106, 107, 120
Gwynn, 122

## H

Haawiyah, 134
Hades, 105, 111, 112, 116-119, 126, 168
Halakha, 55
Halicarnassus, 53
Hatamah, 134
Hawaii, 84
Heaven, 18, 48, 49, 52, 58, 71, 79, 82, 95, 96, 100, 105, 110, 114, 117, 127, 128, 130, 132, 134, 141, 166, 168
Hebrew, 112, 126, 127
Hecate, 75
Hecatonchires, 117
Hel/Hella, 124, 126
Hell, 82, 100, 105, 110, 118, 120, 122, 127-30, 134, 135, 168, 170
Hereafter, 70, 81, 109
Hermodr, 126
Herne, 122
Hieroglyphs, 114
Himalayas, 91
Hindu, 52, 56, 57, 101, 103, 130, 145, 155
Hologram, 154, 158
Homo Sapiens, 97, 161
Hopi, 171
Horus, 48
House of Donn, 34, 122
House of Xibalba, 139
Hunefer, 115
Hypnosis, 105, 153

## I

Identity, 100, 103, 109, 143, 144, 146, 149, 158, 159
Imbolc, 18
Immortality, 59, 112, 115, 140, 143, 145, 152, 153, 159
Inanna's Descent, 105

Inca, 22, 54
Incarnation, 59, 71, 72, 101, 105, 107, 109, 130, 132, 163-165
Indic religions, 109
Indo-Buddhism, 58
Infinity Burial Suit, 60
Inhumation, 56
Inquisition, 137, 165
Ireland, 25, 26, 88, 120, 122, 123
Irkalia/Irkalla/Ir-kalla, 100, 105, 110-13
Isis, 48
Islam, 55, 112, 134, 135
Israel, 53, 127
Ithaca, 118
Ixion, 116

Jaguar Chamber, 138
Jaguar House, 136
Jahannam, 100, 134
Jaheem, 134
Jaihan, 134
Jannah, 100, 132, 134
Jerusalem, 54, 55
Jesus, 14, 71, 92, 96, 103, 162, 169
Jinn, 134
Jormungandr, 124
Judaism, 54, 55, 67, 126, 152
Judgement, 100, 114, 116, 130, 132

K'iche, 135
Ka, 113, 114
Kaingang, 88
Kalderash, 86
Key Biscayne, 62
Kildare, 25
King Mausolus, 53
King Tethra, 122
King Tutankamon, 22, 87
Kirlian photography, 144, 145
Knossos, 53
Kore, 120
Kundalini, 25, 26
Kur, 111
Kurnugia, 111
Kyenay Bardo, 132

Ladthaa, 134
Laertes, 118
Lake Avernus, 127
Lammas, 24
Lares, 93
Latin, 93
Legacy, 21, 33, 71
Leicestershire, 88
Lent, 94
Lethe, 100, 116
Limbo, 127
Lir, 44, 45, 122
Liver, 66, 151
Loa, 100
Loki, 124, 126
London, 53
Lote tree, 134
Lucifer, 127
Lughnasadh, 18
Lutheran, 35

Maati, 48
Mabinogion, 122
Macrocosmic, 149, 155
Magh Meal, 122
Magic, 27, 67, 123, 157, 172
Magick, 28, 49, 121, 172
Mag Mell, 122
Magnetic field, 145, 160
Malta, 53
Mammoth, 170
Manannan Mac Lir, 44, 45, 122
Manes, 93
Marigold, 93
Mastaba, 114
Matryoshka, 102, 161
Mausoleum, 22, 53
Maya, 135, 136, 137, 139
Ma'at, 114, 115
Meatfare week, 94
Mecca, 55
Medcure, 65
Meditation, 28, 29, 132
Megatherium, 170
Mela, 43
Memnosyne, 116
Memorials, 22, 31, 40,

61, 62, 94
Memory, 15, 29, 30, 32, 33, 36, 40-44, 48, 70, 72, 75, 90, 92, 94, 100, 105, 109, 113, 116, 130, 144, 146, 148-50, 153-55, 161, 170
Mendocino County, 167
Merida, 137
Mesopotamia, 110, 111, 135
Messiah, 55
Mexico, 53, 84, 93, 139, 142
Miami, 62
Michelangelo, 153
Michigan, 59
Microevolution, 65
Middle East, 57
Mider, 123
Midgard, 124
Midworld, 44
Mil, 44, 45
Milam bBardo, 132
Milky Way, 112, 135
Mínghūn, 90
Minos, 116
Minotaur, 167, 169
Mnemosyne, 100
Moa, 170
Modgudh, 126
Molecular memory, 150
Monasteries, 54, 119, 167
Mongolia, 57
Mormons, 102
Morrigan's shrine, 34

Mortality, 143, 148
Moscow, 153
Moslem Badaga, 86
Mourn, 42, 80
Muhammad, 134
Mulo, 86
Mummies, 22, 54, 62, 110, 113, 167
Mushrooms, 60, 162
Muslims, 55
Mütter Museum, 63
Mycelial network, 162
Mycenaeans, 54
Mystics, 58, 156

Naples, 129
Naprapathy, 66
Nār, 134
NASA, 62
Nastrond, 124, 126
Nazareth, 53
Neanderthal, 53, 97, 98, 155, 110
Near-death experience (NDE), 98, 102, 103, 105
Necromancy, 101
Necromanteion, 117, 118, 127
Necropoli, 53, 120, 168
Nemeseia, 93
Nennius, 122
Neo-Pagan, 14, 18
Neptune memorial reef, 61
Nergal, 111
Nervous system, 98,

144, 153, 155
Netherworld, 109, 113
New Testament, 126
Niflheim, 100, 124, 126
Nile, 134
Nirvana, 59
Nome, 48, 114
Noosphere, 160
North America, 22, 58, 61
Notus, 28

Oak, 141, 152
Ocean, 18, 56, 140, 161
Odin, 105, 124, 126
Odysseus, 118, 168
Offerings, 22, 31, 44, 45, 93, 113, 115, 119, 120, 124, 136, 168
Ofrendas, 93
Old testament, 126
Olympus, 116
Omega Point, 160
Omen, 83, 84, 87, 123
Oracles, 116-118, 127, 129, 168
Oregon, 65, 141
Organ donation, 65, 66
Orgone, 145, 157
Orthodox, 54, 55, 94, 152
Osiris, 48, 114, 115
Ossuary, 54, 58
Osteological research,

64
Otherworld, 17, 29, 109, 120, 122
Ouroboros, 25, 41
Owl, 75, 83, 84

Pagan, 17, 21, 31, 67, 79, 80, 94, 120, 152, 153, 166
Pandemonium, 129
Pantheon, 28, 43, 100
Paper lotus lanterns, 90
Paradise, 109, 122, 127, 130, 132, 134, 170
Parentalia, 93
Parga, Greece, 118
Paris, 53, 168
Parsis, 22
Parsi Zoroastrians, 57
Paterfamilias, 93
Pathology, 64, 65
Pearly Gates, 130
Pentecost, 94
Perla del Oriente Maya, 139
Persephone, 105, 116-18, 120, 168, 169
Peru, 53, 54, 58, 119
Phantom, 124, 141, 158
Pharaoh, 54, 87
Phenomena 71, 103, 132, 144, 146, 158
Pine, 27, 31, 152
Pithecanthropus, 155
Plastinated, 63
Platonism, 112
Poland, 86
Polyamorous, 15
Pomana, 86
Pontnewydd cave, 97
Popol vuh 135, 136, 138, 139
Portland, 65
Portugal, 54
Poseidon, 115
Prana, 59, 145
Priest, 38, 41, 43-45, 127, 165
Priestess, 14-16, 17, 19, 38, 40, 41
Promession, 62
Prophets, 100, 132
Protestants, 130
Proto-conscious, 99
Punishment, 100, 112, 117, 123, 126, 127
Punjab, 56
Purgatory, 89, 127, 128, 130, 134
Pwyll, 122
Pyriphlegethon, 117, 118

Qafzeh, 53
Qinghai, 57
Quantum, 98, 99, 101-3, 147, 148, 159, 161, 162
Queen, 24, 29, 116, 119, 168, 169
Qur'an, 132, 134, 135

Radonitsa, 94
Ragnarok, 124
Rahma, 134
Rainbow, 48, 75, 95, 171
Realms of the Dead, 53, 109
Rebirth, 25, 28, 31, 34, 41, 52, 58, 61, 108, 113, 130, 131, 153, 157, 164, 166
Red cataract, 123
Reform Judaism, 55
Reincarnation, 29, 31, 58, 101, 103, 107, 109, 112, 153, 154, 156, 158, 163
Reliquary, 54
Resomation, 60, 61
Resurrection, 41, 127, 134
Rhadamanthus, 116
River Styx, 105, 116, 127, 168
Roc, 170
Roma, 85, 86
Roman/Rome, 35, 53, 54, 56, 84, 93, 118, 119, 127, 142, 165, 169
Russia, 94, 102, 153, 161

Sabbats, 18, 50
Safety coffins, 88
Sagittarius, 112, 135

Saihan, 134
Saints, 54, 92, 94, 100, 128, 130
Salsabil, 134
Salvation, 127, 132
Samadhi, Baron, 156
Samhain, 18, 92, 122, 123
Samten Bardo, 132
Santa Muerte, 108
Sapling 22, 50, 151, 164
Saqar, 134
Saqqara, 53
Sarcophagi, 53, 54, 110, 114, 167
Satan, 122, 127
Satori, 156
Sa'eer, 134
Scandinavia, 124
Scilly, 120
Sekhet-Aaru, 100, 105, 114
Shades, 93, 112, 116, 120, 126
Shallow grave, 62, 151
Shamash, 113
Shanidar, 97, 98
Shannon River, 123
Sharia, 55
She'ol, 100, 112, 126, 127
Shroud, 55, 60, 140
Sichuan, 57
Sidpa bardo, 132
Sikhism, 56
Simultaneous consciousness, 159
Sins, 114, 115, 123, 127, 129, 135
Sisyphus, 116
Skeletal pathology, 64
Skeletal remains, 54, 58
Skeleton, 63, 66, 91, 93, 98, 167
Skhul cave, 53
Skulls, 54, 93, 137, 139, 142, 167
Sky burial, 57, 58
Sky Father, 30
Sky Gods, 124
Sleipnir, 124
Soul, 15, 31, 47, 48, 51, 71, 76, 78, 80-82, 88, 89, 94, 96, 98-103, 105-7, 109, 114, 115, 130, 132, 134, 143, 144, 146, 147, 151-53, 156-59, 163
Space burial, 62
Spain, 53
Spirit, 14, 15, 18, 21, 22, 24, 26, 29-33, 35- 37, 41, 43, 46-49, 52, 56, 59, 71, 72, 79, 80, 81, 85, 86, 89, 90, 93, 95, 97, 99-101, 105-7, 109, 110, 112, 117, 120, 122-124, 126, 140, 157, 159, 161, 162, 165, 171
Spiritualism,101
Spirit world, 71, 105-7
Spring, 24, 31, 33, 78, 80, 82, 94, 112, 116, 118, 134, 135, 142, 168, 169
Spring Equinox, 94, 112, 118, 135
St. Thomas Sunday, 94
Styx, River, 95, 105, 116, 127, 168
Subconscious, 154, 155
Sudan, 90
Sudden discontinuity, 146
Sudden immersion, 104
Sugar skulls, 93
Suggestology, 153
Suicide, 43, 68, 78, 89
Sumerian, 105, 111, 112
Summerland, 31, 41, 47, 68, 100, 121
Summum, 62, 63
Superconsciousness, 160
Switzerland, 102
Syr Darya, 134

# T

Tantalus, 116
Taphophobia, 88
Tartarus 89, 100, 115-17
Tech Duinn, 45, 122
Tethra, 122
TheaGenesis, 166
Theosophists, 121
Thessaloniki, 94
Third Saturday, 94
Thoth, 48, 114

Thylacine, 170
Tibet, 57, 58, 91, 105, 130, 131
Tigris and Euphrates Rivers, 110
Tiresias, 118
Tir-fo-Thonn, 92
Tir na Nog, 45
Titanomachia, 117
Titans, 117
Transmigration, 101, 132
Transmutation, 132
Trials, 100, 136, 162
Tribe, 22, 58, 86, 88, 127, 141, 164, 171
Tumulus, 53
Turkey, 53

Underground, 53, 116, 118, 127, 137
Underwater land, 123
USA, 61, 88, 161
Universal Anatomical Gift Act, 63
Universal consciousness, 162
Universe, 46, 47, 99, 103, 104, 147, 148, 156, 157, 162
Unquiet dead, 38, 39
Upperworld, 28

Vajrayana Buddhism, 57, 91
Valhalla, 95, 100, 105, 124
Valkyries, 105, 124
Vanaheim, 124
Vanir, 124
Venice, 53
Verapaz, 135
Verdun, 54
Vernal Equinox, 118, 120
Victorian England, 85, 88
Viking 54, 56, 87, 105, 124
Virgil, 53
Vucub-came, 135

Wake, 23, 42, 70, 71, 92
Waking dreams, 14
Wales, 97
Warrior, 17, 56, 105, 124, 165
Water, 24-28, 30-32, 40, 46, 47, 49, 52, 53, 56, 57, 60, 61, 76, 86, 90, 92, 95, 101, 127, 134, 135, 137, 139, 161, 168
Water-brother, 151
Water burial, 56, 57
Water cremation, 60
Weaver, 36
Web of Consciousness, 29
Weighing of the heart, 113
Welsh, 18, 122, 123
Whale, 169, 170, 171
Wiccan, 35, 121
Winter, 33, 92, 164, 168, 169
Witch, 47, 68, 84, 126, 165
Witch hunters and Inquisitors, 165
Witch of Endor, 126
Wizard, 68, 165
Womb, 46, 52, 154, 158, 165, 166, 168, 170
World War I, 54

Xibalba, 100, 135-39

Yahweh, 126
Yalu, 114
Yama, 103, 130
Yaqui, 145
Yawm al-Qiyāmah, 134
Yeheshuah, 47
Yggdrasil, 125
Yucatan, 135, 137, 138
Yulan, 89

Zaqqum, 135
Zephyrus, 28
Zeus, 115, 168
Zombies, 116, 120
Zoroastrians, 54, 57

# Web links for Oberon Zell

OZ's Website: www.OberonZell.com
OZ's Facebook page: www.facebook.com/oberon.zell
OZ's friends & fans FB page:
    www.facebook.com/pg/oberonzellwizard/community/
OZ's Patreon page: www.patreon.com/oberonzell
OZ's statues, jewelry, books: www.themillennialgaia.com/
Church of All Worlds: www.CAW.com
*Green Egg* magazine: greeneggmagazine.com/
Grey School of Wizardry: www.GreySchool.com
2020 Vision: The Awakening: http://2020visionawakening.com/
Apotheasis Project: https://apotheasis.com/
*Song of Gaea* (children's book): https://songofgaea.wordpress.com

*The Wizard OZ* (film documentary by Danny Yourd, 2017)
    Boston SciFi Film Festival – Best Documentary Short
    https://vimeo.com/215849774

OZ online TED talk on the Grey School of Wizardry at the American University in Bulgaria (TEDxAUBG):
    www.facebook.com/StartUPBlagoevgrad/videos/2458570241116224/

"The Great and Powerful OZ: Unicorn, an Unusual Tale." Featured Interview by Rick West, *Sideshow World* (2007).
    www.sideshowworld.com/9-ms-pi/interview-OZ.html

An Exclusive Interview of Oberon Zell on Gaia as TheaGenesis (Jan. 2, 2020). With the Millennial Gaia. This is a fundamental look at what is becoming the essential truth of the next age.
    www.youtube.com/watch?v=nhlNf8rl_KE&feature=share

www.ingramcontent.com/pod-product-compliance
Lightning Source LLC
Chambersburg PA
CBHW032151080426
42735CB00008B/661